Research Methodologies
in the 'South'

Research Methodologies
in the 'South'

Edited by
ANJUM HALAI
DYLAN WILIAM

OXFORD
UNIVERSITY PRESS

OXFORD
UNIVERSITY PRESS

No. 38, Sector 15, Korangi Industrial Area, PO Box 8214,
Karachi-74900, Pakistan

Oxford University Press is a department of the University of Oxford.
It furthers the University's objective of excellence in research, scholarship,
and education by publishing worldwide in

Oxford New York

Auckland Cape Town Dar es Salaam Hong Kong Karachi
Kuala Lumpur Madrid Melbourne Mexico City Nairobi
New Delhi Shanghai Taipei Toronto

With offices in

Argentina Austria Brazil Chile Czech Republic France Greece
Guatemala Hungary Italy Japan Poland Portugal Singapore
South Korea Switzerland Turkey Ukraine Vietnam

Oxford is a registered trademark of Oxford University Press
in the UK and in certain other countries

Published in Pakistan by Oxford University Press, Karachi

ISBN 978-0-19-906356-7

Typeset in Minion Pro
Printed in Pakistan by
Delta Dot (pvt) Ltd, Karachi.
Published by
Ameena Saiyid, Oxford University Press
No. 38, Sector 15, Korangi Industrial Area, PO Box 8214,
Karachi-74900, Pakistan.

Contents

Acknowledgements

This book is the result of collaborative effort between various institutions and individuals. While it is not possible to name all those involved, it is important to recognize some key individuals and institutions whose support made this significant work possible. The Aga Khan University Institute for Educational Development (AKU–IED) in Pakistan, and the Institute of Education, University of London UK (IOE), provided institutional support in the form of funds, logistics, and numerous other ways that made it possible to exemplify, in spirit, a North–South collaboration.

The Higher Education Commission Pakistan–British Council Link Award (2007–09) supported collaborative activities between IOE and AKU–IED, including a conference in Karachi in December 2007 on the issue of 'Research Methodologies in the South'. We are very appreciative of their generosity, which made it possible to undertake this significant work and which, in turn, formed the basis for this book.

Staff at the Research and Policy Studies Unit at AKU–IED were instrumental in providing sustained support throughout the process, enabling the idea to move from conception to fruition. We are indebted to them for being steadfast in corresponding with authors across the globe, painstakingly managing the process of submission and re-submission of papers, and supporting the editorial process.

Editors
June 2011

1

Researching Education Research Methodologies in the 'South': An Introductory Discussion

Anjum Halai

Partnerships in research have been around for a few decades and have varied tremendously in purpose, form, and process. In the 1960s, research cooperation consisted of technical assistance and consultancies from the North to the South. The late 1970s saw the emergence of strengthening research capacities in developing countries themselves, and of improving access to sources of scientific information in the North. However, donor policies regarding North–South research cooperation have changed considerably over the past thirty years. In the early 1990s, the policy emphasis shifted to fostering collaborative research networks in which Northern and Southern partners could participate on equal terms, including both concrete collaborative research projects and research capacity development. The research community now appreciates the need to comprehend the social, political, and international contexts in which new technologies and ideas are deployed to reduce poverty and promote development. Increasingly, there is funding being made available for these kinds of research partnerships. This shift to a balanced North–South research partnership, to include development, training, and capacity building of partners in the South, which recognizes the need for equality among participants, has led to several positive outcomes for all involved but has also raised certain issues which have remained problematic for several reasons. For example, much thinking about education and development in the South is dominated by the agendas of the donor agencies and other providers of foreign aid. Perhaps not unreasonably, many, if not most, funding agencies link aid to evidence of effective utilization of funds, but the criteria used in the evaluation of the use of aid too often rely on research methods derived from the physical sciences. This situation raises important questions, not least whether or not research methods in education are universal. Valero and Vithal (1999) and Vithal and Valero (2003) have argued that differences in context and culture require the development of different methods, and even definitions, of research. Others (e.g., Pring this volume and Khamis, this volume) argue that these differences can be accommodated within the standard approach. Until recently, there has been little research into methodological and theoretical issues when research is undertaken in diverse contexts with largely non-English speaking participants, with data in multiple languages and with different notions of epistemology and ontology. This situation is beginning to change, and a number of studies have been completed in different parts of the world, including the work of Vithal and colleagues in South Africa (Vithal 2008) or the work undertaken at the Aga Khan University Institute for Educational Development (AKU–IED) in Karachi, Pakistan (see also Shamim and Qureshi [2010] for a discussion of research issues in the South especially from the perspective of qualitative research).

The Aga Khan University has had a long history of successful and productive partnerships, mainly with universities in the more technologically advanced countries in the North or West. One such partnership is with the University of London, in particular with its Institute of Education (IOE). In late 2006, at a meeting of representatives of IOE and AKU–IED, including the two editors, the discussion was about making the partnership more equitable, so that the partners from the South could also contribute on the basis of the knowledge and insights that they have from field experiences and research in their context. At the meeting, it was agreed by the representatives of AKU–IED and IOE that debating these issues and bringing them into the public domain would be worthwhile. The approach that was agreed upon was to organize a symposium on this topic at the 2007 annual meeting of the British Educational Research Association (for details see, www.bera.ac.uk), to be followed by a conference in Karachi on 'Research Methodologies in the "South".' The label 'South' is employed broadly to include countries or settings that are technologically less developed—the so-called 'developing countries'. Mostly, though not exclusively, these countries are in the 'geographical south', hence the usage of this label. The main objective of the conference was to present and discuss examples of research methodologies and methods from a range of contexts, mainly from the South, and use these examples to draw out and discuss key issues for the research in education in diverse settings.

This book includes papers presented at the conference in Karachi, but goes beyond to include contributions from experts in the field who responded positively to a wider invitation to contribute. It consists primarily of a collection of descriptions and critical analyses of educational research settings in different parts of the world, and draws on recent emerging insights and understandings about the purpose, process, significance of, and approaches to, research undertaken in settings as described above. The first six chapters mainly discuss issues about theoretical positions and ethical aspects of research methodologies in the context of the South. The next six chapters draw on illustrative examples of research projects situated in the context of South and discuss methodological, political, and practical issues and questions that arose in the context of undertaking these research projects. The final two chapters provide a synthesis of issues arising from the range of perspectives and practice of research in the South.

Following this introductory chapter, Renuka Vithal provides a historical account of the development of interest in research methodologies from the perspective of the South. Building on her original work (Vithal 1998, reproduced as chapter 3 in this volume), she maintains that disruptions in data actually lead to significant influences on the methodology, at times leading the researcher to modify the research question and methods. She goes on to explain that earlier discussions on issues arising from disruptions in data collection were positioned more or less in 'oppositional terms', such as North–South; developed–developing; marginal–central. Moreover, initially, disruptions in the research process were usually seen with reference to conflict, whether social, political, cultural, or religious conflict. However, experience has shown that disruptions in the research process do not always occur because of conflict. She maintains that a major reason for disruption in research is the huge diversity within which education is enacted in the South.

In chapter 4, Anil Khamis reflects on the central questions of the present volume: what are the approaches to research in the South (and for what purposes), and are these approaches markedly different from those undertaken (and developed) in the North? In doing so, he considers research in contexts that arise from geo-political and cultural changes—in the light of demographic changes—both in Pakistan and the UK. His chapter provides lessons learnt in approaches adapted to the study of teachers, as well as developing teacher leaders in challenging and changing situations. His main premise is that the idea of multiple modernities provides a powerful theoretical 'lens' for analysis, which is all the more attractive in an era of globalization, hyper-communication, and dissemination of information. He also suggests that one route to development, with roots in post-enlightenment Europe, needs to be abandoned. One pervasive effect of mass public schooling has been to reproduce inequalities in society. If we wish to create more equity and harmony between, and within, countries—so that the world's population enhances one another's life chances rather than operating on a zero-sum gain (my loss is your gain)—then fundamental empirical realities of disadvantage and disenfranchisement must be highlighted, and addressed, as a matter of priority.

In chapter 5, Richard Pring contests the notion of 'Research Methodologies of the South'. He maintains that much research, even in the South, is either conducted by researchers from a very different culture or dominated by the research traditions of a different culture. How can people from one culture really understand the problems and the contexts of a very different society? He says that this is a serious question, highlighted by 'evidence-based' research, funded by international agencies, on the basis of which support is given to less advantaged countries on certain terms. The problem is of how researchers, from one tradition, can get inside the minds of people and societies from very different traditions. And furthermore, if they do, how can they communicate that understanding to people who inhabit very different traditions? The problems can be seen on different levels. At one level, there is the problem of researchers who quite uncritically assume that those researched think and act in much the same way as people do in their own societies. They simply have not tried to understand things from the others' point of view—the understandings, customs, and values that shape the ways in which the objects of research see the world. People operate within different social and moral traditions, which have to be entered into if sense is to be made of what they do. At another level, however, the accusation is that cultures are so different—in the conceptions of human nature, of the nature of society, of human flourishing—that understanding them is impossible and that the language will reflect these differences: hence the difficulty of getting on the inside of a very different culture, and then (if one does) of translating this insider understanding into terms and understanding shaped by a very different language and social customs. With this clear and lucid articulation of the problem, Pring explores some answers, illustrated through examples, and argues both for the logical possibility of such unity of understanding, while recognizing the practical difficulty.

In chapter 6, Rashida Qureshi takes the theoretical and philosophical discussion towards another dimension of research, i.e. the issue of 'vulnerability' in the ethics of research. Extending the work of Roberts and Roberts (1999), she employs the notions of 'extrinsic vulnerability' and 'relational vulnerability' to explain why vulnerability in educational research in developing world settings requires certain further safeguards in the formal standards and procedures of ethics. According to her, extrinsic vulnerability is concerned with the participants' right to information about the research study they are being asked to participate in. However, in a situation like Pakistan where the majority of people are illiterate and the research culture is weak, the meaning of research itself is hard to explain. Researchers face difficulties in sharing the purpose and procedures of the research with participants who may not be able to grasp the real meaning of the activity they are supposed to be part of. Not only does violation of the research participants' right to information increase their extrinsic vulnerability, but it also has deep implications for the enactment of other rights. For instance, their informed consent becomes a token activity. She goes on to develop the notion of 'relational vulnerability', which she maintains applies to the researchers as well. The nuances of researchers' relational vulnerability have not been discussed in literature on research ethics, and yet they have implications for the process of research in Pakistan and in similar contexts. In Pakistan, where the cultural codes governing human interactions are relational, researchers' relational vulnerability is equally (if not more) worth considering because the range of choices, and the degrees of freedom available to them, are determined by how they are introduced to community members and by the relational category/categories assigned to them. Put in the broader perspective of research, both the extrinsic vulnerability of research participants and the relational vulnerability of researchers impinge upon the quality of data gathered in such contexts. The chapter discusses the relationship between these vulnerabilities and cross cutting issues, like authenticity, trustworthiness, and transferability that can affect the quality of field research.

In the chapter that follows, Almina Pardhan draws on illustrative examples of ethnographic and biographical research to focus on issues related to negotiating entry, space, and mobility during the process of research related to women and education in Pakistan in the remote, mountainous village of Booni Valley, Chitral District, Pakistan. She problematizes the process of selecting research sites in Pakistan, and goes on to discuss the complexity of negotiating entry and sustaining ethically acceptable research relationships within prevailing cultural norms—where ethical and moral codes governing social relations and practices may hold different meanings than those in 'Northern' contexts. Notions of informed consent and voluntary participation are problematized in a context where contact with potential research participants and, at times, their consent to participate is mediated by various gatekeepers. Her negotiation of the issues of space and mobility are presented in relation to her position as a female researcher in the visibly patriarchal context of Pakistan, and the tensions for her as a researcher who is used to a relatively greater independence in the Canadian context. Her main premise is that ethnographic field methods require constant negotiations in cultural contexts, where current ethnocentric standards governing ethics in research cannot be imposed piecemeal. While crossing geographical borders has immense potential to develop educational insights, educational researchers have increasing responsibility to adopt ethical approaches which consider and respect social relations and practices within diverse cultural contexts to ensure the well-being of the research participants.

Drawing on self-study and narrative inquiry projects with teachers from different parts of Pakistan, Ayesha Bashiruddin considers issues related to the methodological aspects of auto/biographical research. She maintains that auto/biographical research requires in-depth interviews with the research participants as they engage in storytelling. A relationship of reciprocity and trust is a pre-requisite, to ensure that participants do not feel vulnerable in divulging personal and potentially sensitive information to the researcher. However, her research and experience demonstrated that, in the relatively traditional social and cultural context of Pakistan, traditional notions of respect for authority prevail, inhibiting an open and reciprocal relationship. Consequently, teachers are very reluctant to critique teaching practices and prevailing norms in teaching because they maintain that it would be 'disrespectful' of them to critique the teaching methods conveyed to them by their elders and teachers. Ayesha Bashiruddin holds that the rich oral culture, with a strong tradition of storytelling, provides a conducive context for this approach to research. However, a concern in this respect is that generating knowledge of teaching development through story telling requires participants to write iterative drafts of their stories; each draft would then be developed on the basis of critique and reflection. However, as writing, particularly in the language of academia—English in this case—was not easy for them, the potential for generating rich insights into teacher development were marred by this methodological glitch. Moreover, the local experts had fixed notions of knowledge. The notion of storytelling, as development of knowledge, was not acceptable to the teachers and other participants in the research. Considerable negotiation, with the teachers and other stake-holders, was required in order to gain their consent to participate in this form of research.

In chapter 9, Paola Valero and Alexandre Pais point out the significance of context in undertaking research in the developing world. They maintain that educational practices in schools and classrooms, in the so-called 'developing world', are always at the mercy of societal 'disruptions': strikes, budget shortages, teachers' rotation, school closures, and even school participants' disappearances. These realities strongly bring to the fore, for educational researchers, the need to address the way in which 'context' is a constitutive element of educational practices in schools and classrooms. They argue that (mathematics) education research needs to develop ways of conceptualizing and dealing with 'context', so that it is possible to understand the social and political complexity of these practices in developing societies. With an analysis of schools in South Africa and Colombia, they illustrate a conceptualization of context, and point to the elements of a research strategy that allows context to be addressed in research by linking micro-contexts and macro-contexts of practice.

In the next chapter, Rana Hussain and Anjum Halai raise several issues relating to the politics and practice of action research when undertaken in rural, disadvantaged, and the often conflict-ridden, contexts of the South. Action research, as a methodology for generating knowledge and as a paradigm of change, is gaining prominence in the context of social and educational development. This is evident, for example, from the shifting policy emphasis of donor funding towards fostering collaborative research in which partners, often Northern and Southern, aspire to participate on equal terms. Increasingly, action research projects in education aim to generate knowledge rooted in the reality of the schools and classrooms, to provide a nuanced understanding of local issues in education that also have a greater relevance. This knowledge is empowering because it provides insights that offer possibilities of social transformation; merging the world of the researcher and practitioner is also beneficial because it creates a critical mass within the community, to ensure that the process of change is sustained beyond the life of the project. However, participation in action research projects requires commitment on a long-term basis. Academics at universities are willing to make this commitment because it yields professional and career benefits for them, but practitioners in the field do not necessarily see any advantages in investing considerable time and effort. Furthermore, long-term commitment is built on the assumptions of social and political stability in the region, to allow for continuity of the process. However, the context of research in the South is usually characterized by political disturbance and conflict, thereby raising questions about the assumptions that underpin action research methodology. The chapter also highlights issues that arise when power dynamics are seriously skewed among the various participants of the research project. For example, in the largely unschooled community such as those described in this chapter, the academic knowledge residing in textbooks, the position of the teacher as a knowledgeable expert, and the prestige of a university academic, become 'powerful'; engaging community members to become active participants created social dynamics which conflicted with the ideals of action research as transformative in nature.

In the following chapter, Hasina Banu Ebrahim and Helen Penn take a dialogical and grounded approach, and recount from research commissioned by UNICEF on early childhood programmes as resources for poor and vulnerable young children (0–4) in rural KwaZulu-Natal in South Africa. It describes the UNICEF brief (for details see www.unicef.org) for exploring the practice of two projects that used a community-based approach to early childhood development (ECD) for poor and vulnerable young children who were not accessing centre-based provision. It also describes the way in which the research team chose to interpret the brief. Traditionally, UNICEF works from scientific understandings of early childhood. The evidence for effective ECD interventions are drawn from the North, and used to shape programming in the South. However, the complexity of ECD in poor and vulnerable communities in the South is creating the need for international agencies to recognize how local realities shape programming. This chapter describes a grounded research approach that was developed to be sensitive to the contextual realities and experiences of young children, their caregivers, and the leaders who acted on their behalf. The chapter then discusses the ways in which research findings may feed into national policy; it considers their possible international relevance, and the ways in which they confirm or challenge existing international discourses on early childhood.

In chapter 12, Roshni Kumari, Razia Fakir Mohammad, and Nilofar Vazir maintain that research training in academic institutions derives mainly from texts and paradigms developed in the North. Researchers tend to accept the concepts, practices, and approaches as standard without necessarily questioning them or taking into account the contextual relevance. They present, in painstaking detail, the methodological decision that they took during the course of a large-scale impact study of donor-funded in-service teacher education projects on teaching and learning in the province of Sindh. Through sharing their journey from conceptualization of a research methodology to its implementation, they emphasize the contextual realities *vis-à-vis* the methodological choices and approaches they had to make. Through examination of gaps in the data, and the limitations of the research methods employed, they agree with Vithal (this volume) that in settings where normative assumptions about contexts are not met, the methodological approach needs to be responsive to the emerging contextual realities and challenges.

In chapter 13, Dylan Wiliam uses the classification of inquiry systems developed by Churchman to attempt a synthesis of apparently conflicting perspectives on education research. Churchman (1971) proposed that inquiry systems could be categorized according to the evidential basis of claims to knowledge, and labelled each category with the name of the philosopher who he most strongly identified with that approach. Churchman described methods of inquiry, where reason and rationality are held to be the most important sources of evidence, as *Leibnizian* inquiry systems: the classic example is mathematics. In educational research, such forms of inquiry rarely take us very far, and it is necessary to collect empirical data. He maintained that we collect data to build coherent accounts of the data, or we might instead attempt to validate theoretical accounts by determining whether they accord with our observations. This interplay of observation and theory is the hallmark of *Lockean* inquiry systems. The major difficulty with Lockean approaches is that, because what we observe is based on the personal theories we hold, different people will observe different things. Thus, for less well-structured problems, a *Kantian* inquiry system is more appropriate. This involves the deliberate framing of multiple alternative perspectives on both theory and data (thus subsuming Leibnizian and Lockean systems). One way of doing this is by building different theories on the basis of the same set of data. Alternatively, we could build two theories related to the problem and then, for each theory, generate appropriate data—it might well be that different kinds of data were collected for the two theories. This idea of reconciling two or more rival theories is more fully developed in a *Hegelian* inquiry system, where antithetical and mutually inconsistent theories are developed. Not content with building plausible theories, the Hegelian inquirer takes the most plausible theory, and then investigates what would have to be different about the world for the *exact opposite* of the most plausible theory to be plausible. The tension produced by confrontation between conflicting theories forces the assumptions of each theory to be questioned, thus possibly creating a synthesis of the rival theories at a higher level of abstraction. Wiliam maintains that one can inquire about inquiry systems—which is itself an inquiry system—termed *Singerian* by Churchman. The important point about adopting a Singerian perspective is that with such an inquiry system one can never absolve oneself from the consequences of one's research. Educational research is a process of *modelling* educational processes, and the models are never right or wrong, merely more or less appropriate and more or less justifiable for a particular purpose. He employs Churchman's framework to analyse the central arguments about whether educational research can be universal, or whether methods, and even definitions, of research need to be different in the South and the North. By focusing on the central issue of what counts as evidence, he shows that a universal perspective on research is possible, but only by the explicit adoption of Singerian inquiry systems.

Finally, Michael Nettles provides a succinct afterword. He discusses the questions: What model of research would be suitable for the global South? Can we point to one different from the North—unique, site-specific, and yet universally acceptable? Drawing on his experience of the educational context of the North, he juxtaposes the issues in research in the South with similar issues in the USA (global North). Through a comparative analysis of these issues, he maintains that similar problems exist in the USA. For example, there are remote rural areas, urban ghettos, and isolated mountain and prairie areas. These regions share global northern values and standards, yet some students do not attend school; some schools lack sufficient texts, and some endure leaky roofs; some recall students killed by gangs, causing student body shifts. Can a US Northerner appreciate, relate to, or intelligently discuss the problems of the US South? Nettles' position is that a different paradigm or model of research would not address the issues of research in the South because each study is so different: the idea of one model or paradigm is untenable. He holds that researchers need to become more embedded in, and understanding of, the cultures being researched. He recommends researchers behave as co-inquirers and not data extractors. This perspective, he believes, would enable the researcher to engage with different cultural settings and induce the trust and participation of different cultures so that the research progresses with mutual trust.

With this range of chapters exemplifying complex theoretical and philosophical issues in a simple, easy to understand manner, the question arises: who will read this book? It should be of value to a broad range of academics and practitioners, and therefore its potential audience is wide and far-reaching. It can be seen as a complement to the textbooks and readers on research methodology which provide valuable guidance on research methods from a general perspective. The book makes a valuable and much needed contribution, providing significant insights into issues that could guide academics and policy makers—for example, in Ethics Review Boards, or those engaged in assessment and evaluation of research.

References

Churchman, C.W. (1971). *The design of inquiring systems: basic concepts of systems and organization.* New York, NY: Basic Books.

Roberts, L.W., and Roberts, B. (1999). 'Psychiatric research ethics: an overview of evolving guidelines and current ethical dilemmas in the study of mental illness.' *Biological Psychiatry*, 46(8), 1025–1038.

Shamim, F., and Qureshi, R. (Eds.). (2010). *Perils, pitfalls and reflexivity in qualitative research in education.* Karachi: Oxford University Press

Valero P., and, Vithal R. (1999). 'Research methods of the "North" revisited from the "South".' *Perspectives in Education*, 18(2), 5–12.

Vithal, R. (3–4 December 2008). Research Methodologies in the 'South'. Keynote address to a conference on 'Research Methodologies in the 'South'. Karachi, Pakistan.

Vithal, R., and Valero, P. (2003). 'Researching mathematics education in situations of social and political conflict.' In A. Bishop, M.A. Clements, C. Keitel, J. Kilpatrick and F.K.S. Leung (Eds.), *Second International*

Handbook of Mathematics Education (pp. 545–592). Dordrecht, Netherlands: Kluwer Academic Publishers.

Vithal, R. (1998). 'Disruptions and data: the politics of doing mathematics education research in South Africa.' In N.A. Ogude and C.A. Bohlmann (Eds.), *Proceedings of the sixth annual conference of the Southern African Association for Research in Science and Mathematics Education* (pp. 475–480). Pretoria, South Africa: Unisa.

2

Research, Researchers, and Researching in the South

Renuka Vithal

When I first penned the paper 'Data and Disruptions: The politics of doing mathematics education research in South Africa' more than a decade ago for the sixth annual meeting of the Southern African Association for Research in Mathematics and Science Education (Vithal, 1998), while completing my doctorate (Vithal, 2003), I could not have anticipated the extent to which it would resonate with researchers across different continents who were working in similar contexts.

I have become aware, over the years, of the number of research students from the South—or developing countries—who, while pursuing studies in the North—or Western countries—referred to the paper to help the promoters and supervisors of their doctoral studies understand the difficulties and challenges of undertaking research and, indeed, the very questions being engaged. It has sharply brought home the need for, and importance of, theorizing educational research methodologies that emerge from, and are relevant to, the South or developing world.

This initial paper, which follows in the next chapter, was the inspiration for two further papers with fellow colleague Paola Valero, who was researching mathematics education in Denmark,

South Africa, and Colombia (Valero, 2002). The paper, 'Research methods of the "North" revisited from the "South"', was presented in both the Psychology of Mathematics Education and the Mathematics Education and Society conferences in 1999, and published in the journal *Perspectives in Education* (Valero and Vithal 1999a; 1999b; 1999c). Later, we were invited to contribute a chapter on 'Researching mathematics education in situations of social and political conflict' to the *Second International Handbook of Mathematics Education* (Vithal andValero, 2003).

That paper, on 'Disruptions and Data', came vividly to mind on my first visit to Pakistan. As I·arrived in the city of Karachi, to speak about this very work at a conference on 'Research Methodologies in the South', I was informed that the conference might or might not take place because a conflict between various groups had led to a suspension of public transport and other services.

The issue of disruptions in research methodology arose from my doctoral studies, and the arguments made in the paper were mainly with reference to that study, which focused on student teachers who were trying to realize a social, cultural, and political approach to mathematics education in schools while engaged in their university teacher education curriculum. The paper was written with reference to research in mathematics education, and attempted to bring issues of context and politics to the forefront of methodology discussions because of the ongoing strike action within schools and universities—not an uncommon occurrence during fundamental societal transformation. It is re-presented here, and reflected upon, for a broader educational research terrain, and beyond mathematics education to contribute toward continuing to build scholarship in research methods and methodology for 'South-like' contexts which are found all over the world. In these reflections, I return to the questions I posed on disruptions in the first paper, to comment again on: why disruptions occur in educational research; how they occur; and what can be done with them.

Those publications, arguably in large measure, set up the discussion in oppositional terms—North–South; developed–developing world; Margin–Centre; wealthy–poor—in finding explanations for why and how mathematics education research and research methodologies seemed to be ignoring the educational contexts of the South, and were failing to capture an understanding of the educational phenomena and challenges commonly associated with the South. These debates have continued to be taken up, especially in mathematics and science education research (e.g. Setati, Vithal, Malcolm and Dhunpath, 2009), and particularly with respect to globalization and internationalization (e.g. Atweh, Calabrese Barton, Borba, Gough, Keitel, Vistro-Yu and Vithal, 2007).

A further observation is that the earlier papers characterize disruptions and instability in research and methodology in the South, with reference to conflicts—whether social, political, economic, religious, or cultural. However, a focus on the South must also mean focusing on educational challenges and topics arising not only from conflicts but also from a range of different contexts, such as a developmental context.

One of the reasons for disruptions in research in the South is the huge diversity of contexts characterizing education, and within which it is carried out. Rural contexts, for instance, are not necessarily fraught with conflict, but they are different in terms of values, systems of authority, and worldviews, and may require different methodologies and theorizing to generate knowledge about education. Situations of poverty, which may not be caught in the grip of overt conflicts, continue for decades or generations with inherent disruptions that need to be researched to enrich, broaden, and deepen our understanding about education.

Disruptions in data arise for a number of reasons, not least because assumptions about educational practices or values—which vary widely in different contexts—are ignored and not factored into research designs or are absent in theories used, or created, to explain educational phenomena. Schooling is typically organized and conducted according to the values, life conditions, rhythms, and culture of certain dominant groups in societies, such as the urban middle classes. Children may not go to school during periods of harvest or because they do not have money for school—fees, travel, materials—or they may go to school because they are assured of a meal or for other reasons unrelated to learning.

In South Africa, for example, significant variations are found among suburban, township, peri-urban, and rural schooling contexts. A focus on the South brings, into sharp relief, the understanding that *context* matters, and this is infused into the research questions, methods/methodologies, analyses, and theories that are produced. Whatever one might mean by context, research is not free of context—from the micro setting of researching a student or teacher or school to the macro settings of education systems and structures.

The South is not only a geographical South but increasingly a metaphor for a particular context—a context that symbolizes, variously, the under-resourced and constantly developing, the traditional within and against the growing modern, the margin or marginalized and the centre. It spans spaces within the regions of a country, within continents, and within the world, though differing in scale and character from place to place. But the South is also the majority context—there are more children who live in 'South-like' contexts. There are more children in South-like contexts who do not go to school, or do not attend school regularly, than all the children in the North who attend school, and yet very little is known about education in the majority context, or the education of the majority learners.

The 2006 World Development Report on *Equity and Development* starts with a narrative on the South which shows and recognizes these differences within and across contexts, and offers the following exemplar from the South African context:

> Consider two South African children born on the same day in 2000. Nthabiseng is black, born to a poor family in a rural area in the Eastern Cape Province, about 700 km from Cape Town. Her mother had no formal schooling. Pieter is white, born to a wealthy family in Cape Town. His mother completed a college education at the nearby prestigious Stellenbosch University.
>
> On the day of their birth, Nthabiseng and Pieter could hardly be held responsible for their family circumstances: their race, their parents' income and education, their urban or rural location, or indeed their sex. Yet, statistics suggest that those predetermined background variables will make a major difference in the lives they lead. Nthabiseng has a 7.2 per cent chance of dying in the first year of her life; more than twice Pieter's 3 per cent chance. Pieter can look forward to 68 years of life; Nthabiseng to 50. Pieter can expect to complete 12 years of formal schooling; Nthabiseng less than 1 year. Nthabiseng is

likely to be considerably poorer than Pieter throughout her life. Growing up, she is less likely to have access to clean water and sanitation, or to good schools. So, the opportunities these two children will face, to reach their full human potential, are vastly different from the outset—through no fault of their own.

Such disparities in opportunity translate into different abilities to contribute to South Africa's development. Nthabiseng's health at birth may have been poorer, owing to the poorer nutrition of her mother during her pregnancy. By virtue of their gender socialization, their geographic location, and their access to schools, Pieter is much more likely to acquire an education that will enable him to put his innate talents to full use. Even if, at age 25, and despite the odds, Nthabiseng manages to come up with a great business idea (such as an innovation to increase agricultural production), she would find it much harder to persuade a bank to lend her money at a reasonable interest rate. Pieter, having a similarly bright idea (say, on how to design an improved version of promising software), would likely find it easier to obtain credit, having both a college diploma and quite possibly some collateral. With the transition to democracy in South Africa, Nthabiseng is able to vote and so indirectly shape the policy of her government—something denied to blacks under apartheid. But, apartheid's legacy of unequal opportunities and political power will remain for some time to come. It is a long road from such a (fundamental) political change to changes in economic and social conditions.

As striking as the differences in life chances are for Pieter and Nthabiseng in South Africa, they are dwarfed by the disparities between average South Africans and the citizens of more developed countries. Consider the cards dealt to Sven—born on that same day, to an average Swedish household. His chances of dying in the first year of life are very small (0.3 per cent), and he can expect to live to the age of 80–12 years longer than Pieter and 30 years more than Nthabiseng. He is likely to complete 11.4 years of schooling—5 more years than the average South African. These differences in the amount of schooling are compounded by differences in quality: in the eighth grade, Sven can expect to obtain a score of 500 on an internationally comparable math test, while the average South African student will get a score of only 264—more than two standard deviations below the median of countries that are members of the Organisation for Economic Cooperation and Development (OECD). Nthabiseng, most likely, will never reach that grade and so will not take the test". (World Development Report 2006, pp. 1–2).

Although the majority of learners in the world are those whose context is similar to that of Nthabiseng, the dominant focus of much educational research, and the point of its departure that drives the generation of research questions, topics, methodologies, theories, and the scientific criteria by which this research is judged, are Pieter and Sven based on assumptions of particular regularity, stability, and continuity of context.

However, creating a single frame that holds Nthabiseng, Pieter, and Sven together requires the identification of research questions and methodologies that cut across these contexts. This may be easier said than done. Setting oppositional discussions— of North–South, developed–developing, wealthy–poor, as the earlier papers mentioned above did—have been useful for drawing attention to the South, but may be limited in growing 'South-specific' education research as the connectedness of our lives is emphasized more. Yet, an unfettered focus on the South, and greater South–South dialogue, are precisely what may be required to generate a different scholarship that does not always have to develop and legitimize itself with reference to the North. When notions of poverty, violence, illness, and social or cultural tradition and practices protrude into the research frame, the educational and learning aspects often appear to retreat, and vice versa. The refrain that the context needs to be corrected, before the focus can fall on how learners in such contexts do in fact learn, has resulted in a dearth of research and a deeper understanding about this largest cohort of learners across the world, since such contexts have endured over time and the inequalities deepened. Students who live and learn in such contexts (wherever and whatever it is they learn) do go to school when they can, even if it is without warm clothes, food, learning materials, or in fear of violence; often, they go to schools that might lack even the minimum resources of proper classrooms, water, sanitation, and electricity. The challenges of undertaking research in such contexts is often spoken about, but much less formally written about and theorized.

Privileging context in educational research means that researchers focus and attend to poverty and unemployment, instability and discontinuities, conflict and violence, rurality and indigenous contexts, even if they do so from different methodological, theoretical, and paradigmatic stances, and do so in different ways. One may distinguish between research *in* contexts and research *on* contexts. Research *in* such contexts keeps the context in the background while focusing on a specific topic or question. A researcher may be interested in learners' conceptual understanding of, or performance in, some content, but this cannot be fully understood without knowing the broader conditions in which that learner is responding, or their intentions and reasons for being in school and participating in the research. This implies that a researcher may continue to focus on such questions, but does so by recognizing the background context issues and their impact.

Researching *on* context brings the context to the foreground and makes the context itself, or elements thereof, the focus. In this, the researcher focuses on a contextual aspect, such as, why learners do not regularly attend school or why a school is 'dysfunctional'. In this case, the context is in the foreground and the focus of the research. However, its relation to learning and how this impacts what happens to teachers or learners in the school or classroom is also maintained, though in the background.

Disruptions may occur in research because of the kinds of questions posed or topic chosen. For example, Nomali Mncwabe (2009), in her study on the working lives of learners, focused on what students were doing when they were not at school, and particularly on those who were involved in economic activities to earn a living to survive and pay school fees to remain in school. Disruptions had to be confronted when students who had not paid their school fees were suspended by the school, just as focus group interviews were to proceed with those who had been identified as being involved in various income-generating activities through a survey. Further challenges arose from those learners who refused to allow interviews to be taped because of participation in illegal activities, and others who had agreed to participate in individual in-depth life history interviews but could not be located. Research questions that focus on discontinuities—such as what happens during strike action in education institutions or why students in poor or rural settings dropout of school—create disruptions in data production.

Depending on the educational research question, disruptions in the research can be anticipated and therefore factored into the research design. In this sense, research discontinuity, instability, or disruptions have a different quality because they may be actively managed and accommodated in the research before it begins. However, disruptions often occur unexpectedly. Usually, the approach is to discard such data. In such situations the researcher may need to consider moving the focus of the research question or topic to accommodate or incorporate the disruption. This decision may be informed by how the disruption manifests itself, or might itself enhance understanding of the phenomenon under investigation. Moving the question may mean moving the focus of the study away from the planned research, or it may mean broadening the scope of the study—zooming out, as it were—to examine the phenomenon more broadly.

Disruptions in data may be due to the research design, or the methods or methodologies deployed. Surveys, observations, and interviews assume continuity and reasonable availability of the participants and settings for research throughout the period of the fieldwork. Disruptions may be produced by the selection of a particular sample or a particular site for the research. In her study, originally intending to follow a group of 'street children' attending a 'shelter school' to their placement in public schools the following year, Rhughubar (2003) was unable to locate any of the learners (she had observed and interviewed) the following year. Instead, the research question and sample had to be adjusted so that, instead of following the group of learners from one school setting to another, a 'street child' was located from another shelter who was attending a public school and the (mathematics) teaching and learning at the two settings became the focus of the inquiry (Vithal, 2009).

Choosing samples and sites of deep poverty, or known conflict and violence, or those that are radically different culturally or politically, for instance, are more likely to yield disruptions in research—which, in turn, explains why these are often avoided and, when they emerge, leave researchers confounded in dealing with them. Methodologically, and in undertaking the fieldwork, the occurrence of disruptions may result in researchers re-considering the sample or sites in the study. The inclusion of sites or samples prone to disruption may mean greater risks in the research because participants may be difficult to locate and retain in the study or it may be more difficult to continue to access the places chosen for the research. Negotiations for interviews or observations, for example, often become more sensitive or politicized. The research methods used may yield data that present significant dilemmas for the researcher. In her survey on the work school children undertake, Mncwabe (2009) found over a dozen letters and notes attached to the questionnaire, or anonymously sent or placed, which included details on experiences of work abuse and exploitation.

Disruptions may also be produced as a result of the research approach or paradigm selected, and the ways in which a researcher might choose to adhere to its prescriptions. This may be because of what a particular research approach or paradigm allows to be admitted as data. Arguably critical and feminist research perspectives may, more readily, invite disruptions into the study than perhaps more positivist and some interpretivist approaches—in which disruptions may be conceived of as data having to be 'cleaned or sanitized'. Different research approaches and paradigms are also linked to different criteria of quality. Hence, while disruptions may be viewed from some research perspectives as reducing rigour—such as the potential for generalization—they may be viewed as providing generative potential in others, depending on the underpinning epistemologies and methodological theories. To confront and embrace disruptions, or become immersed in them, are very deliberate decisions on the part of researchers that imply choices have been made. Researchers may have to cross boundaries of research paradigms and approaches and manage the inherent epistemological or ontological contradictions and risks that might get thrown up.

Researchers are less likely to remain, or regard themselves as neutral objective observers, in situations of instability or discontinuity. No doubt, disruptions can also be produced by the identity of the researchers, their status as insider or outsider, their investment and commitment to the study, and their socio-political positioning. Researchers with strong activist orientations are more likely to choose questions or topics that are likely to yield disruptive data, or confront disruptions in their fieldwork and seek to admit the unstable or disruptive data. In a study on racism in the biology classroom, Patel (2005) sought out learners at risk of failure, those who were failing, and those who had dropped out, and included them in the study to deepen and widen understandings of discrimination in science classrooms—which led to the need to deal with their lack of attendance and availability in the study. Disruptions in research studies, by their nature, create fear and anxiety for the researcher because of the feeling of the imminent collapse of the study and uncertainty about how and what to do with the disruptions since research education and training programmes seldom deal with these issues. In the examples already cited, Mncwabe and Rughubar almost abandoned, and dropped out of, the study.

Issues of ethics are heightened in contexts of research where disruptive data are being generated. A researcher will need to confront directly, for instance, what it means to continue a study when a strike is underway; or consider how far a researcher can follow and intrude on a learner's life whose school attendance is erratic or who has dropped out of schooling; or have to decide on what to do when confronted with illegal activities on the part of participants. Difficulties also arise when what emerges from the data, in these kinds of ethically challenging situations, resonates with the researcher's own life and experiences. Depending on the kind of study being undertaken, one approach may be for researchers to declare, or include, their life histories or biographies (e.g. Mncwabe, 2009), or research relationships (Patel, 2005), as part of the data, or at least include it in the report. Documenting disruptions in methodological descriptions, or even as part of the analysis, are important to enable greater theorizations so that they are better understood and dealt with in research.

A main assumption, challenged in the early papers, was of the stability and continuity of context in research methodologies investigating educational phenomena; this was implicitly fused into the research approaches and their knowledge productions. A decade later, instability and inequities in contexts have not only continued, they have increased and intensified. It is appropriate and necessary, if not overdue, that a focus on methodologies of and for the South—which is discussed in the main with reference to the South itself—is grown and extended to broader educational research. The kinds of research questions, the methodologies for investigating them, and the theories underpinning educational practices and research need to be generated from the ground in, and for, the South.

References

Atweh, B., Calabrese Barton, A., Borba, M.C., Gough, N., Keitel, C., Vistro-Yu, C., and Vithal, R. (Eds.). (2008). *Internationalisation and globalisation in mathematics and science education.* Dordrecht, Netherlands: Springer.

Mncwabe, T.C.N. (2009). *Inside the lives of township high school learners.* Unpublished PhD thesis, Durban, South Africa: University of KwaZulu-Natal.

Patel, F. (2005). *Racism and the science classroom: towards a critical biology education.* Unpublished PhD thesis. Durban, South Africa: University of KwaZulu-Natal.

Rughubar, S. (2003). *The mathematics education of youth-at-risk: Nellie and Wiseman.* Unpublished MEd thesis. Durban, South Africa: University of Durban-Westville.

Setati, M., Vithal, R., Malcolm, C., and Dhunpath, R. (2009). *Researching possibilities in mathematics, science and technology education.* Hauppauge, NY: Nova Science Publishers.

Valero, P. (2002). *Reform democracy and mathematics education. Towards a socio-political frame for understanding change in the organization of secondary school mathematics.* Unpublished PhD thesis. Copenhagen, Denmark: Danish University of Education.

Valero, P., and Vithal, R. (1999a). 'Research methods of the "North" revisited from the "South".' In A. Olivier and K. Newstead (Eds.), *Proceedings of the 22nd Conference of the International Group for the Psychology of Mathematics Education* (Vol. 4, pp. 153–160). Stellenbosch, South Africa: University of Stellenbosch.

Valero, P., and Vithal, R. (1999b). 'Research methods of the "North" revisited from the "South".' In P. Gates (Ed.), *Proceedings of the First International*

Mathematics Education and Society Conference (pp. 401–407). Nottingham, UK: University of Nottingham.

Valero, P., and Vithal, R. (1999c). 'Research methods of the "North" revisited from the "South".' *Perspectives in Education,* 18(2), 5–12.

Vithal, R., and Valero, P. (2003). 'Researching mathematics education in situations of social and political conflict.' In A. Bishop, M.A. Clements, C. Keitel, J. Kilpatrick and F.K.S. Leung (Eds.), *Second International Handbook of Mathematics Education* (pp. 545–592). Dordrecht, Netherlands: Kluwer Academic Publishers.

Vithal, R. (1998). 'Disruptions and data: the politics of doing mathematics education research in South Africa.' In N.A. Ogude and C.A. Bohlmann (Eds.), *Proceedings of the sixth annual conference of the Southern African Association for Research in Science and Mathematics Education* (pp. 475–480). Pretoria, South Africa: Unisa.

Vithal, R. (2003). *In search of a pedagogy of conflict and dialogue for mathematics education.* Dordrecht, Netherlands: Kluwer Academic Publishers.

Vithal, R. (2009). 'Researching, and learning mathematics at the margin: from "shelter" to margin.' In P. Ernest, B. Greer and B. Sriraman (Eds.), *Critical issues in mathematics education* (pp. 475–484). Charlotte, NC: Information Age Publishing.

World Development Report (2006). *Equity and development.* World Bank and Oxford University Press. ISBN–10: 0–8213–6249–6. DOI: 10.1596/978–0–8213–6249–5.

3

Disruptions and Data: The Politics of Doing Mathematics Education Research in South Africa[1]

Renuka Vithal

Introduction

If you talk to any education researcher in South Africa who is collecting data, you will find that he or she has consistent stories about arriving at a school after careful and extensive discussion only to find the school completely empty or under new management, disrupted by protests, or some other unanticipated situation. Disruptions to carefully conceived plans are the norm rather than the exception. Thus, *disruptions experienced in research designs produce disruptions in the data.* Such disruptions may or may not be severe, but their impact on a researcher's intent to continue with the same research focus or question may indeed be crucial.

The concerns that are dealt with here arose directly from my research into how and why student teachers implement what I refer to as a social, cultural, and political approach to a mathematics curriculum. In adopting this critical perspective, I hoped to understand and advance both the theory and the practice related to such an approach within the South African context.

Like most researchers, I developed a comprehensive research plan through which I could engage this research focus. The research dilemmas that emerged stemmed from the significant changes that had to be made in the research design in response to a constantly changing context, as well as to my reluctance to 'sanitize' the data to meet conventional methodological criteria and rigour in the research process. I wished to consider the implications for the research question, for data production and analysis, and for the findings that would eventually emerge. How would bringing in, or throwing out, disruptions in the research and the data produced impact on the knowledge that is produced through the research process? In this chapter, I focus on *why* disruptions occur in research, *how* disruptions come to be produced, *what could be done* with disruptive data, and finally rethink what may be considered *appropriate criteria* for judging research in such contexts.

Why are Disruptions Produced in Research?

To answer this question, requires problematizing the context in which the research(er) is located. One way to address this is to create a dialogue around the dilemmas that currently face (mathematics) education researchers in the South African context, and to examine the political nature of that context. The question then becomes, 'What does it mean to make context a central consideration in research methodology, and to interpret that as political?' I use my own research methodology to illustrate and develop this discussion. It is quite possible to provide a description of the research methodology in my study as a relatively normal, smooth, clear process. I need not provide any indications of the history of the research process, the material conditions in which it was located, or the transformations that were taking place in the context in which the research was happening. Yet, doing research in South Africa is an intensely political affair.

In what sense can one speak of research methodology as being political? We can talk about all research being political activity, in the same way as we can talk about all education being political activity. Researchers bring particular interests, identities, histories, and goals to the research endeavour; these influence the selection of the topic, the construction of research questions, the design, and the resultant findings (Sjöberg, 1971). We can also talk about research as being political in the sense that critical researchers and critical educators use the term. Here, a deliberate political position is taken in research by relating their work to, for instance, critical theory, issues of equity, or a feminist standpoint. But we can also talk about research as being political in the sense that there are overt, explicit, and unavoidable conflicts and contestations that impact on, and become a part of, the research process. In the same way, education can be seen as being political when it is characterized by actual student or teacher protests.

In education, South Africa provides a direct challenge to theories presented elsewhere, usually as universal explanations. For example, at the time when the early 'reproduction' theories of education were being advanced in parts of the Western world, students in South Africa were protesting on the streets against apartheid and the inferior education they were receiving. A similar situation can also be observed in research where methodologies and their corresponding criteria for rigour and scholarship in research, developed in particular contexts and in response to particular situations and questions, then become the methodologies and criteria to judge in for all other contexts. The question that can be considered here is: to what extent, and in what ways (if at all), is it possible to consider issues about the 'Westernization' or 'Eurocentrism' of research methodology? Countries like South Africa import not only knowledge about (mathematics) education from other countries, especially from the English-speaking world dominated by the USA and UK, but also the means and techniques for producing that knowledge. Research methodologies are copied, and sometimes adapted, and continue to inherently carry with them the criteria for rigour, quality, and relevance developed elsewhere. The critique thus responds to this importation of methodology and its application to very different contexts. The double bind for researchers in countries like South Africa is that if the criteria for rigour are preserved in the research design, the knowledge produced runs the risk of lacking relevance to the context; and, if the methodology is made relevant to the context, it runs the risk of being considered a poor research design. For example, I could do my research in the context of relatively disruption-free former white suburban schools or choose African township schools—which are the majority context—in which my research methodology and design could face several problems or resourcing, become destabilized, or even have to be abandoned.

The debate about theories and methodologies, that have led to the different research paradigms (e.g., positivist, interpretivist, and critical), also need to take into account what those debates could come to mean in radically different contexts. In Kincheloe and McLaren (1994), we can see some attempts to grapple with this sort of problem; they write:

What we have described as resistance to postmodernism can help qualitative researchers challenge dominant Western research practices that are underwritten by a foundational epistemology and a claim to universally valid knowledge at the expense of local, subjugated knowledges (Peters, 1993). The choice is ... one of whether or not to challenge the presuppositions that inform the normalizing judgements that one makes as a researcher. (p. 153)

More recently, the question of whether the epistemologies themselves—on which education research is based—may be racially biased has been opened for debate (Scheurich and Young, 1996).

The shifts in the research paradigms can be seen as shifts resulting from the challenging of what is considered 'normal' and taken for granted. Bringing the differing contexts into the centre of the discussion provides new challenges for methodologies in countries with very different situations. What exactly is different about the South African context? Critical researchers such as Roman and Apple (1990), Lather (1991), Kincheloe and McLaren (1994), and others refer to, and draw attention to, the political nature of research and the act of research. They relate the research process to broader power relations within society, and focus on the history and material conditions of the people in their studies. The context in which their research is located is often with marginalized groups who are also minority groups. Much of this research usually occurs in the context of relatively stable societies—where there is some reform in their economic, political, educational, or other institutions. This is markedly different from a country like South Africa where the marginalization is of the majority, and these major institutions are undergoing fundamental, radical, and rapid change virtually simultaneously. In this context, research is obviously and overtly political as new policies and practices are debated, implemented, and begin to take effect on the ground. A consequence is that a researcher can never be certain about what will happen in the field.

It is possible, therefore, to posit that disruptions in data are in fact normal during research in situations like South Africa. Skovsmose (1994) argues that societies today are characterized by crises and critical situations. Just as we may speak of 'politics' or 'politics of research' and education, in societies like South Africa we could refer to deep and constant crisis and critical situations. In societies in which there are fundamental and rapid changes and uncertainty and instability in virtually all the major institutions, conflicts and contestations abound around the researcher and at many levels. It is these situations that lead to disruptions in the research process. The researcher has to deal with not only several political issues but also ethical issues that must be confronted, especially in research that claims to reflect a critical stance. Critical situations marked by multiple 'crises' engender disruptive kinds of data. This means that it is imperative to consider them seriously and not discard or 'clean' them—especially in a critical inquiry, and in any study of critical education, because they may be generative of knowledge and insights that might not have otherwise become available.

How are Disruptions Produced in Research?

Although it is quite common for research plans, in practice, to not work out quite as envisaged on paper, the extent of adjustments can be significant in the South African context. Often, they cannot be anticipated and are beyond the control of the researcher.[2] My research could be described as researching the possibilities for change in a changing context. An analogy may be that of trying to study the building of a ship in the middle of an ocean while the ship's design has to be constantly adapted as it is at the mercy of the ever-changing elements.

In my research, I worked with student teachers at a primary school during their teaching practice sessions, as they developed and implemented project work in their mathematics classrooms. This was during a time when the curriculum, and the very notion of teaching practice, was constantly undergoing change in the faculty in its conceptualization of more progressive pedagogy—such as creating new partnerships with schools, and changing practices within the context of an unfolding general faculty review. At the same time, new national norms and standards for teaching practice were also being planned and debated.

But, there was also change in response to other pressures within the broader university. One significant factor, that forced the faculty to reconsider teaching practice per se, was that students had pressured the faculty through protest action to take in 50 more students than it had planned for and anticipated. The means to solve this problem were discussed in different ways. At one level, the debate was about the technical administration of the six weeks of teaching practice that student teachers were obliged to undertake to graduate: where they should be placed (in schools in which they were educated or across previously racially segregated schools: students could choose); how the time should be organized for teaching practice across the two semesters (all 6 weeks together; 3–3 split; or a 2–4 split: the last option was agreed upon); how should they be attached to the resident teachers in school (individually or in groups: groups would be encouraged where possible); how would supervision and assessments be managed (by discipline-specific or generalists: both forms were used). At another level, but related to the first, there was also a concern about the philosophical and pedagogical assumptions that underpinned whatever decisions were being taken. These decisions were simultaneously affecting the research plans I was developing, to investigate the research question I had chosen.

There are inescapable political and ethical issues here, for researchers, as they participate in both development and research simultaneously. I was a member of the teaching practice committee that deliberated on these issues at great length. The possible conflict of interest here was my dual role as a teacher educator and as a researcher—for example, I participated in the decision to go for a 2–4 week split in teaching practice. This decision was supported because of the way in which the action research projects that the student teachers were expected to undertake during their teaching practice sessions were organized. However, this also harmonized with a research decision that I was making, and contributed positively to student teachers seeing themselves as researchers, in my research. My research was planned so that the first two weeks were used to negotiate, jointly with the school's teachers, an innovation to the curriculum. A triad of teacher, student teacher, and teacher educator/researcher was envisaged. This was crucial, not only theoretically as a condition of a critical perspective, but also because the nature of the intervention was closely linked to the context. The two weeks, and the period thereafter, would give me time to work with the teachers and student teachers, and to collect data to see how and why these implementation ideas had developed. The time, when the student teachers would return to campus, was to be used to plan, develop, share, and reflect more critically on their ideas for the particular class, school, and context in which they were placed for their teaching practice. When they went back in the second semester, they would be ready to implement their ideas.

None of this happened; instead, it was all replaced by five preparation sessions. Even the five preparation sessions held prior to the teaching practice, to help the student teachers prepare for their teaching practice, were disrupted by the way in which general university student meetings were called spontaneously and without warning. One session had to be cancelled as the university's political climate affected student attendance at these sessions. As it turned out, a great deal of the organization fell by the wayside. The university closed down as a result of student and staff disruptions on the wider campus, just prior to the students going on the two weeks' preparation-phase teaching practice session in the first semester. The effect of this was that the negotiation process with the schools and teachers was left to the students to manage on their own. Some of them went to the schools independently, to begin to establish some contact, where they met with varying receptions. I became a resource that the student teachers came to as a last resort, when there was complete resistance to their ideas. This happened at one school, where a special meeting was called in the afternoon, so that I could address the principal and teachers about what was being planned by the student teachers.

What is observed is how the research process is battered by fundamental and multiple changes in the context as it copes with the question that it sets out to investigate. On the one hand, there are the broader university transformations which were manifested in disagreements about admissions, fees, salaries, and other issues and, on the other hand, faculty transformations which include curriculum concerns, contestations, and changes. I am implicated, through my involvement and commitment to the very necessary broader faculty review and restructuring processes as a teacher educator, while at the same time seeking to preserve the integrity and rigour of the research that I am trying to conduct and to act in ethically appropriate ways.

The disruptions did not end there. Once at the schools, the student teachers enjoyed (or suffered) different relationships with the teachers to whom they were assigned. As a consequence, the plan to use the first two weeks for preparation did not work out because some students began implementing their ideas almost immediately—especially in those cases where they had done some groundwork on their own—while others were not allowed to begin at all until well into the teaching practice session. Any hope that I might have had of having a sustained presence in at least some of the student teachers' projects were further dashed when the issue of violence, which was a chronic problem in some of the township schools, came to a head with the shooting of a school principal in KwaMashu. Violence in schools is a significant factor that also affects students' selection of schools for teaching practice. All the teachers went on an immediate 'chalk down' in the township and demanded better security and protection. One of the student teachers—who had been placed in the same area and had done considerable preparatory work in developing an electricity project, and in working with the teachers at the school—was transferred to another school as all the schools had closed down and it was unclear, at the time, how long this would continue. Thus, he was unable to implement any of his ideas. It was this event, in particular, that focused my attention on the notion of disruptions in data—which emerge through disruptions in the research process arising from the context. I was reluctant to allow his participation in the research to disappear in the analysis and from my writing. Several reasons began to emerge: the disruptions were constant and chronic, and examining them should tell us something about what it means to do research in South Africa at the present time; also, about the research question that would not otherwise be revealed. As I began to focus on the discontinuities, it was beginning to become more apparent that they had something to offer about the implementation of these projects and critical mathematics-related ideas—about the process of their development and evaluating how context-bound they were—and also for the need to re-examine methodological issues.

Gradually, the teachers' strike spread and all the former 'Indian' and 'African' schools went on strike. (Strikes related to education seldom affect the former white schools.) Neither school strikes nor university boycotts during teacher practice are uncommon features, and they have raised important and difficult dilemmas for student teachers about their position both in relation to the schools in which they are placed and in relation to the university. Are they students or are they teachers? Where does their allegiance lie at any one time? In the context of this research, their role played out in different ways at different schools. The impact of the strikes, on the projects they were attempting to implement within the schools and on the research process itself, can be interpreted both positively and negatively.

What I am portraying here is how research involving student teachers, as carriers of change within a rapidly and constantly changing and constantly contested context, created dilemmas for the research methodology.

Another source of disruptions in research design comes from the relationship of the researcher to the participants in the research process, and in particular from the attitudes of the participants to the researcher and the research. How research, in general, is viewed and has been experienced by student teachers and teachers is important. Here, one needs to consider the role and function of research and researchers during apartheid, in particular the way in which research was 'done on people', especially Black people. This also coincides with positivist approaches to research. One response often articulated by those participating in the research, but usually not directly to the researcher, is the question, 'What's in it for me?' Within the context of disruptions, the researcher and the participants often become co-dependent, with each having something the other might want. I wanted the student teachers to assist in data collection and production that I was unable to facilitate, and they wanted to develop a joint paper and attend a mathematics teachers' education conference.

What Can We Do With Disruptions in Data?

The 'outliers' in statistical data are dealt with clearly in statistical research—usually they are discarded. Recently, for example, it was while considering such discarded data that researchers gained knowledge about the hole in the ozone layer. What happens in a parallel situation of qualitative studies? Could new ideas emerge from focusing on the disruptions, rather than the continuities, in the research process? Within qualitative data, it is possible to discern at least two attitudes toward data that is characterized by disruptions. The first is to eliminate the data containing the disruption: for example, to drop the case containing the disruption. The second is to work around disruptions in the data: for example, acknowledge the disruptions and use the data before and after the disruption. This is underpinned by an approach to disruptions in the data that seeks to include a 'corrective function', when in fact the disruptive data are the 'accurate' or 'authentic' data.

A third approach that may be suggested is to face the disruptions. What does this mean? Here, the researcher may be forced into observing something else that may or may not be the focus of the study but may nevertheless be relevant to it. The underlying assumption is that disruptions in data are seen as being constructive and providing the possibility to generate new ideas that would otherwise remain unseen, rather than something that must be confessed to and is problematic. Thus, an understanding of data having a *generative* function is built into the analysis rather than, say, a *generalizability* function for which 'smooth' or 'normal' data are required.

An example in my research, which illuminates the generative nature of disrupted data, is the electricity project that was abandoned because of the closure of schools in a particular area due to a teachers' strike and the inability of the student teacher to implement the project elsewhere. By taking the disruption seriously, rather than discarding it, we are able to observe the context-bound nature of projects developed within the social, cultural, and political approach to the curriculum, as well as the essential role of protracted negotiations between the student teacher and the teachers in the schools for implementation. The data produced during the teachers' strike, in the other projects, also yields insight about how student teachers position themselves, and get positioned, in schools during teaching practice as well as what is construed as mathematics teaching and learning in schools by the various participants. For example, student teachers were allowed to continue with certain activities, such as teaching and learning about measurement, outside the classroom during the strikes.

Confronting the disruptions in the methodologies can also mean making radical and creative changes to the research design as the changes in the context unfold. I had to accept that I could not follow any one project in totality. I decided to try my best to be present in as many projects as possible for as much of the time as possible. I kept in constant telephone contact and made relevant entries in my research journal. This, of course, had consequences for the kinds of data produced and the processes for producing it, but it also impacted on my relationship with the students—especially those students I had observed the least and who felt neglected and left out. I was forced to make a decision in the middle of the research, to focus more on some projects than others—for instance, when interview and observation times coincided with each other. I was not present at two of the projects at all. I redesigned the research to create the opportunity to follow the projects through other means. Student teachers were constantly reminded about making entries in their own diaries, they were asked to keep all other records such as lesson plans, and they were given detailed guidelines for the writing up of the project that they were expected to submit at the end. I introduced, into the research plan, the idea that student teachers should attempt to collect data, more systematically, in the projects themselves. This they did to different degrees, usually because of limitations of resources (tape recorders and electricity). This deeper involvement of student teachers in the research had a positive impact, and gave them a greater stake in the research process. It increased what I referred to as *democratic participatory validity* (discussed later). It also brought, to the fore, other issues, such as students themselves getting positioned differently in their relation to me and the impact on the research.

Disruptions increase the reliance of the researcher on the participants and mean that issues of reciprocity in research relations must be taken seriously and addressed, not only for their own sake but also because they can enhance the analysis. For the student teachers whose participation was voluntary, it was agreed that we would prepare a joint paper that they would present at a national conference on mathematics education. This was facilitated, in large measure, by their becoming more involved in the data production process of the research. This was a powerful experience for those students who did participate in the process, and their analysis also began to feed into my analysis. Some of the teachers viewed my position as a researcher negatively. In at least one instance, student teachers reported that teachers in the school made comments about how students and teachers are 'used' in research for the benefit of others. This comes from a historical South African research tradition where ethical issues were consistently marginalized in research. In anticipation of this, I offered to assist each of the schools in any staff development initiatives they sought, and to assist the teachers in any curriculum development aspects. At least one school took up this offer, during the research, and two teachers asked my advice about their own further studies. Contexts characterized by disruptions require a re-examination of research relationships, which can become more equitable since each has something to offer the other—in a more realistic sense—in what is inherently an unequal knowledge power relationship.

Rethinking Criteria for Quality and Relevance in Mathematics Education Research

Of the many criteria applied to research in mathematics education, I have drawn attention to two—generalizability and validity—for debate in contexts in which disruptions in data occur. A few remarks about the alternative notions of 'generativity' and 'participatory validity' follow.

Disruptions may be seen as a natural feature of researching situations about *what could be*. Researching a social, cultural, and political curriculum approach through project work in a critical perspective in South Africa may be regarded as just such a situation. Through studying *what could be* (rather than *what is*), the opportunity is created, according to Kvale (1996):

> . . . to envisage possibilities, to expand and enrich the repertoire of social constructions available with respect to both theory and practice. Rather than *telling it like it is*, the challenge is to *tell it as it may become*. A generative theory is designed to unseat conventional thought and thereby open new and desirable alternatives for thought and action. Rather than mapping only what is, or predicting future cultural trends, research becomes one means for transforming culture. (p. 235)

A generative theory, as alluded to by Kvale and used to refer to research that creates new possibilities for thought and action, may be particularly relevant in contexts marked by disruptions. Instead of seeking generalizability of the findings, a study could be considered in terms of its capacity for generating ideas. In this way, not only can disruptions be seen as normal, but including them in the analysis process may be considered crucial as they allow the generation of knowledge that could otherwise be left unexplored. This is one of the strongest arguments for taking the disruptions seriously in the research process—generativity is essential to explain and justify disruptions in data.

In the conception of '*democratic participatory validity*', as proposed here, the concern has moved far from a focus only on the validity of conclusions drawn from an analysis to a validity concern that permeates the research process. It is a shift from a focus on the validity of the research process preoccupied with 'looking for fit', to one that also includes a concern for the participants in that process and the nature of relationships embedded in the process. The argument for participatory validity can be made from the perspective of critical research, with its focus on democratic forms of inquiry. However, it can also be argued to be an essential consideration in situations of disruption because the researcher is forced to rely on research participants in a different way in the research process. In these contexts, 'co-learning agreements' are set up rather than 'data-extraction agreements' (Wagner, 1997). This creates an imperative for the researcher to open, to scrutiny, the relationship between the researcher, the research participants, and the research process. Establishing some kind of 'democratic participatory validity' becomes crucial, especially for the South African research situation. This form of validity allows questions about the extent to which opportunities are created for a democratic form of participation in the research process; the extent to which participants actually come to own and shape the research process in its entirety; and how far the eventual findings are from those to which the different participants agree. Elements of choice, negotiation, and reciprocity may be seen as essential in research designs—not only as a political and ethical consideration but as critical to improving the quality of research itself—in its capacity to generate knowledge about whatever is under investigation. While the issues about what the content and meaning of participatory validity could be remain open to discussion, proposing such criteria in research begs the question of whether or not we still, in fact, speak of validity and in what sense we need validity in educational research.

Conclusion

To make advances in theory and practice in mathematics education, there is also a need to make advances in the methodologies used to understand those theories and practices. This means that we have to deal with the challenges posed in research directly, openly and honestly within contexts like those of South Africa. This may mean that we need to theorize methodology differently, and need to develop different criteria for rigour, relevance, and quality, so that we ask and address real and authentic research questions that advance knowledge in ways that are meaningful and improve the lives of those who live in those contexts. Notions of democratic participatory validity and generativity may be developed to occupy central positions in a critical mathematics education research methodology. However, we constantly need to question whether they are appropriate, what meaning they can come to have in research, and what other criteria we should consider.

References

Kincheloe, J. L., and McLaren, P.L. (1994). 'Rethinking critical theory and qualitative research.' In N.K. Denzin and Y.S. Lincoln (Eds.), *Handbook of qualitative research* (pp. 138–157). Thousand Oaks, CA: Sage.

Kvale, S. (1996). *Interviews: an introduction to qualitative research interviewing.* Thousand Oaks, CA: Sage.

Lather, P. (1986). 'Research as praxis.' *Harvard Educational Review*, 56(3), 257–277.

Lather, P. (1991). *Getting smart: feminist research and pedagogy with/in the postmodern.* New York, NY: Routledge.

Roman, L.G., and Apple, M.W. (1990). 'Is naturalism a move away from positivism: materialist and feminist approaches to subjectivity in ethnographic research?'. In E.W. Eisner and W. Peshkin (Eds.), *Qualitative inquiry in education* (pp. 38–74). New York, NY: Teachers College Press.

Scheurich, J.J., and Young, M.D. (1996). 'Coloring epistemologies: are our research epistemologies racially biased?'. *Educational Researcher*, 26(4), 4–16.

Sjöberg, G. (1971). *Ethics, politics, and social research.* Cambridge, MA: Schenkman.

Skovsmose, O. (1994). *Towards a philosophy of critical mathematics education.* Dordrecht, Netherlands: Kluwer Academic Publishers.

Vithal, R. (1998). 'Disruptions and data: the politics of doing mathematics education research in South Africa.' In N.A. Ogude and C.A. Bohlmann (Eds.), *Proceedings of the sixth annual conference of the Southern African Association for Research in Science and Mathematics Education* (pp. 475–480). Pretoria, South Africa: Unisa.

Wagner, J. (1997). 'The unavoidable intervention of educational research: a framework for reconsidering researcher-practitioner cooperation.' *Educational Researcher*, 26(7), 13–22.

Acknowledgements

I take full responsibility for the ideas expressed here. However, I must thank the following people for commenting on the ideas expressed here: Bunny Naidoo, Ole Skovsmose, Norma Sibisi, Jill Adler, Herbert Khuzwayo, Maga Moodley, Allan Tarp, Cassius Lubisi, and Jebbe Scott. I would also like to thank Jonathan Jansen for reading an earlier draft.

Notes

1. This chapter is reprinted from the 1998 *Proceedings of the sixth annual conference of the Southern African Association for Research in Science and Mathematics Education*, N.A. Ogude and C.A. Bohlmann (Eds.), pp. 475–480, Pretoria, South Africa: Unisa.
2. This is distinguished from the notion of an 'emergent design' in which a deliberate decision is made to allow the research strategy to unfold in the process of doing the research, or in which a tentative plan serves as a good guess for the research strategy.

4

Education for What? Discourses and Research in the South

Anil Khamis

Introduction

This chapter presents a theoretical stance, drawing on conceptualizations from research projects, to address the central thesis of this volume. Broadly, these studies have considered the nature and process of teacher development and educational change.

The approach and representation here echo that of Miles and Huberman (1994) who note: 'We see ourselves in the lineage of "transcendental realism" [. . .] That means we think that social phenomena exist not only in the mind but also in the objective world—and that some lawful and reasonably stable relationships are to be found among them' (p. 4). And further:

> The paradigms for conducting social research seem to be shifting beneath our feet, and an increasing number of researchers now see the world with more pragmatic, ecumenical eyes. Our view is that sharing more about our craft is essential, and that it is possible to develop practical standards—workable across different perspectives (and contexts)—for judging the goodness of conclusions. (Ibid., p. 5)

Pring (2000) considers the nature and purpose of research, which he argues are based on beliefs that lead to the formation of structures (of knowledge), as the activity to propose methods for interpretation that render the description of such belief structures a social undertaking. That is, as a reflexive activity, research aims to illuminate deeply held beliefs. Thus, it is necessary to start with the learner—the essential subject of the educational enterprise and, therefore, of educational research. This entails, concurrently, a need to consider what learning is—which has not always been the central focus of educational investment for most of the last 50 years. Such a starting point, for the educational researcher, poses pertinent concerns: what is the purpose of the research and how is such research used, by whom, and how does it relate to the teaching and learning we construct in school?

The effect of socio-economic factors, within a broader frame of geo-politics that either enables or conspires against educational development, is obvious to all educators. For instance, children in the UK who are less able educationally, but from better off socio-economic backgrounds, overtake their higher achieving but less well off peers by the end of primary schooling and do considerably better in secondary school (Feinstein, 2003). A recent government report notes that privilege and socio-economic status tend to play an important part when correlated with access to better schooling. In turn, this leads to access to the best available higher education, and subsequent entry into the professions—ones that effectively bar those from the lower socio-economic levels (Panel on Fair Access to the Professions, 2009). This vindicates Bourdieu and Passeron's (1990) exposition of *social capital* that argues that beyond what may be considered an entitlement in society, subtle factors such as family background and access to privilege lead to a formation of networks that aid and abet inequality in society. One example of this sustained barrier is the case of Muslim graduates in the UK who do not gain entry into graduate level employment at the same rate as their white counterparts (Hodge, 2005). So, from the viewpoint of such prospective candidates, inequality upon inequality disadvantages them.

So, the outlines of the debate come into relief: what is the nature of the reality that we wish to research; how best do we approach this type of study; and whether different contexts, with their intellectual histories and interactions with other contexts, require different approaches. We will proceed to address this series of questions with a focus on teachers in the broader field of educational development in order to come to some understanding.

Research Methodologies in the South: The Case of Teacher Education

Research beginning with Coleman (1966) noted that the benefits accruing from further teacher education, beyond a certain point, were limited. This finding is now called into question and recent work casts doubt on the original research's approaches (Darling-Hammond, 2006; Hanushek and Wößmann, 2007).

Coleman found that investments in further teacher education yield negligible improvement to student learning outcomes. Heyneman (1997), in a meta-review of the research, working in the context of sub-Saharan Africa, questions Coleman's conclusions. He finds that in resource-depleted contexts, more teacher education along with the provision of textbooks plays a positive role and can significantly improve the quality of learning. In a similar vein, Darling-Hammond notes that, for all teachers, there is no substitute for robust pre-service provision accompanied by in-service or continued teacher development. She further notes that the professionalization of teachers, whereby the teaching body constitutes an overseeing agency to guarantee and monitor teacher quality, is the crucial and necessary development for improvement of education at the systemic level.

Hoxby and Leigh (2004), Rockoff (2004), and Davies and Iqbal (1997), while acknowledging the multiple and variegated influences of the school environment and other accompanying factors such as school leadership, attest that the main in-school factor, correlated with student achievement, is the teacher. A competently trained and experienced teacher can have a much greater positive variance on student outcomes. Put differently, the claim is that an experienced teacher can teach children in primary school in half a year, what an untrained or inexperienced teacher would teach over a year or more. In the middle years of primary schooling, this difference would yield a gap of over two years in terms of learning and achievement for student cohorts taught by experienced teachers compared with untrained teachers.

Studies by Khamis and Sammons (2004, 2007), Khamis and Jawed (2006), and Khamis (2009) in the context of Pakistan, along with the findings of Heyneman (1997), show that in-service teacher education should be the central focus of educational development, albeit not at the expense of continued investment in initial teacher preparation. This obviously then requires that attention be paid to the cadre of teacher educators, their conditions of service, and the competing demands placed upon them. Anderson and Kumari (2009), building on this work, consider the purpose and nature of education provision, arguing for the need to articulate developments with the Education for

All [EFA] movement (see UNESCO, 1990, and the subsequent Declaration and Framework for Action [UNESCO, 2000]). This, they hold, requires the provision of secondary schooling in disenfranchised areas if EFA targets are to be achieved in a meaningful way.

Let us take stock of what is emerging and trace the outlines of the debate. At the outset, it is to be noted that Coleman, who generated the initial thesis on the value of teacher education, and attendant educational development research and investment did so in the context of 1960s North America—an industrial giant fully aware of its strength and stability and of its primary role to lead with a rich resource base that it marshalled to maintain its dominant global position. Indeed, one outcome of the Coleman report was specifically to require all US government-funded projects to assign a percentage (approximately 10–15 per cent) to evaluation activities. This was a conscious decision, to learn lessons from a stable state that foresaw ongoing improvement elsewhere. This context was also representative of an ideological base that was inspired by the modernization thesis that gave rise to the human capital theory (Schultz, 1961), to which we now turn.

Human Capital Theory

The ending of the Second World War led to the realization that the world, as a whole, needed to progress together and that if such progress was uneven, it would adversely affect all parts of the globe. Nowhere was this realization stronger than in the financial markets. The 'victors' of the war, the United States of America and Britain, resolved in 1944 to create a defence against global economic turbulence; and so, the International Monetary

Fund (IMF) and the International Bank of Reconstruction and Development (IBRD), or World Bank as it is commonly called, were formed—together known as the Bretton Woods Institutions. One of the principal objectives of these organizations was the reconstruction of Europe and Japan following the war, with the intent of creating global centres of stability.

The role of state sponsored schooling also changed markedly in this post-war period. One example is the 1944 Education Act, in England and Wales, which emphasized universal education in an era when education was the preserve of the few (education up to the age of 14 had been compulsory from 1918, was increased to 15 in 1947, and to 16 in 1972). The idea that only the particularly gifted, who were of 'good' (i.e., wealthy) families, should have access to schools was a pre-Enlightenment concept: education was only of value to the cultural elite, whose role it was to propagate the best of humanity and transmit it to the next generation and thereby reproduce society harmoniously (Fagerlind and Saha, 1989).

The 1950s and 1960s heralded profound change, the reverberations of which are still being felt. This was the time of independence: a time that saw the emergence of nation states, from the yoke of colonial empires, in Africa and Asia. This was also the time when the Human Capital Theory (HCT) was proposed. Theodore Schultz and Gary Becker revived Adam Smith's ideas from *The Wealth of Nations* (1776), based on data compiled in the United States (Schultz, 1961), for which they won the Nobel Prize in economics. The keystone of the theory was that education or schooling was the missing factor that explained economic growth. In developing country contexts, this meant that universal schooling would have the commensurate effect on the elimination of poverty. Although HCT is currently being challenged by the Capability Approach, developed by another Nobel Prize winning economist, Amartya Sen (1999), it is the dominant force underpinning education policy formation across the world.

The World Bank and Standardization of Education

Since education, it was argued, accrued value for all of society and not just the elite and since, furthermore, this value could be measured in economic terms or rates of return, the World Bank promoted HCT for all contexts. This was despite the fact that the data to support the theory was developed in the American context and never tested in developing countries' contexts. Nevertheless, the Bank entered the field of education with its first lending projects in the early 1960s, with a focus on developing human capital. Such 'education' projects were to lead to practical outcomes as they were economic investments. Therefore, no investment was encouraged in pre-school or general secondary education as such programmes were not considered to yield valuable benefits within the manpower planning models developed by the World Bank (Heyneman, 1999). Notwithstanding the criticism that emerged in the 1970s, with the oil crisis that imperilled the economies of many developing countries, HCT maintained its dominance in educational planning. HCT-inspired education programmes, in turn, spawned a whole industry of rates of return to education (RORE) and cost-benefit analyses, with its international overseeing body—the Institute for International Economic Policy—which built on earlier ideas of technical rationale thinking or positivism (Bennell, 1995).[1]

Investment in schooling meant that an input–output model suffices to explain the phenomenon of education. If one were to measure the combined cost of investments: number of schools, number of teachers, pupil/teacher ratio, and material/textbooks, then it would be possible to measure the output of schools in terms of those who occupy various jobs, the increased income of individual graduates, and their net contribution to the economy (particularly in terms of gross national product or GNP). This input–output model formed the basis of major monitoring and evaluation programmes for over four decades. Thus, Lockheed and Verspoor (1990)—both of the World Bank—in their pursuit of RORE research, with its concerns to develop evidence for educational policy to be adopted by developing countries, categorically state that the returns to primary schooling are in the order of 1:7. That is, every dollar invested in primary school returns seven dollars to the economy. Indeed, investment, particularly for girls' schools, also yields lower fertility rates, and directly contributes to escaping from crushing poverty and better health for families. Such investment is unrivalled; investment in secondary, or higher, education does not yield such benefits.

Thus, underinvestment in higher levels of education was the clear outcome, leading to further impoverishment of the education system as a whole (Bloom, Hartley and Rosovsky, 2006). However, a much more serious outcome was that such research ignored two salient aspects of education: the motivation and circumstances that individuals bring to their learning, and the actual learning on offer (or what is inside the 'black box' of the classroom). The net result has been to focus only on access to primary school, which has led to concerns about the relevance and quality of education on offer.

Cross-Cultural Education and Reform

At the behest of donors in the 1980s and 1990s, developing countries adopted technological processes to improve their school systems, based on the principles of planning developed in the Western countries. This resulted in large cohorts of undereducated and untrained teachers in developing countries engaging in curriculum development and subject specialization based on revision of textbooks:

> Efforts to implement major quantitative changes (borrowed from Western culture) in Third World curricula [. . .] have frequently met with less than anticipated success in practice and, while Western curriculum change strategies continue to be enthusiastically exported, less critical attention has been devoted to the potential and limitations of international transfer of such models themselves (Crossley, 1984, p. 77).

The combined result of resource outlay from the North, channelled via the World Bank, within the HCT framework—which held sway from the 1960s—was hegemonic dominance over the development discourse. Developing countries have acquiesced to certain donor conditions, as noted below, to secure the requisite investment in education. This investment has come with a cohort of experts who were charged with a monitoring or oversight role. Briefly, the condition is that people in the South must engage in 'development' or 'modernization'. This has come to mean that certain people (in low and middle income countries) engage in different or discontinuous activities; for example, structural reforms, governance and democratization, the 'Fast Track Initiative', and investment in productive sectors, whilst others (in rich countries) continue with their programmes in stable state conditions. With HCT underpinning planning, and progress being intrinsically linked to economic development (within the context of industrializing nations), we have come to the position today that:

(i) we have no consensus on what we mean by development; however, development spans economic, sociological, political, psychological, and cultural aspects of human societies;

(ii) development has traditionally focused on low and middle-income, or poor, countries; this seems to be no longer tenable as we contend with globalization, and cultural and demographic transformations;

(iii) methodological concerns remain paramount: there is a struggle between the retrenchments toward basic research; that is, economic and quantitative approaches, raising concerns about their applicability and empirical base to make judgements;

(iv) trajectories of the 'development process' are open to variation.

The table below contrasts the situation between the developed and developing countries, that has remained unchanged for the past fifty years.

Table 1: Developed and Developing Countries—Some contrasts	
Developed Countries	**Developing Countries**
Stable democracies	Unstable regimes
Continuity of dominance as a colonial power or imperial oversight	Post-colonial state establishing independence
Resource rich or net consumer	Resource poor or net producer
Innovator or creator of models	Recipient of innovation or required to comply with models of development
Culturally dominant	Cultural aspirant
Knowledge generator	Knowledge consumer
Target setter	Accountable for meeting target
Position of oversight	Position of scrutiny

The situation, from the turn of the millennium, is a departure in rhetoric from both modernization and HCT discourses. The ongoing research in teacher education, school improvement, and educational change has raised awareness of the limitations of the earlier paradigm as noted by Hargreaves:

> Faith in more generalised and scientifically known principles of school effectiveness has begun to be superseded by commitments to more ongoing, provisional and contextually sensitive processes of school improvement (Hargreaves, 1996 p. 54).

The task of educational improvement is not akin to an industrial process with technical–rational approaches but is highly complex and dynamic, involving the human will of individuals who interact in unpredictable ways. Work spearheaded by Haq (1995) and Sen (1999, 2007), building on earlier philosophical and social justice concerns, led to the development of the Capabilities

Approach (CA): 'Having greater freedom to do things that one values is: (1) significant in itself for a person's overall freedom, and (2) important in fostering the person's opportunity to have valuable outcomes' (Sen, 1999, p. 18).

Whereas the HCT model called for stable systems thinking, the Capabilities Approach calls for a dynamic equilibrium in environments of constant flux; whereas HCT called for the development of input–output models or processes, CA calls for an exploration of individuals' motives to engage in learning; and, whereas HCT called for the meeting of pre-established or *a priori* targets, CA calls for an unfolding or evolution of choices that have open or multiple trajectories. The CA fits well with the research of the 1990s, referred to above, that noted, particularly, the importance and centrality of social justice considerations: race, equity, and gender imbalances. These aspects, with their attendant power domains, need expression in the school curriculum and should be germane to the agendas of educational change, school improvement, curriculum development (including assessment regimes), and teacher education.

Having discussed the points of debate and departure heralded by CA, above, I will now consider what this implies for the nature of research in the South as opposed to the North, and reflect on the question itself: researching in the South versus the North, or research approaches in the South and North.

EFA: The New Education Discourse

The EFA Declaration (UNESCO, 1990) and Framework for Action (UNESCO, 2000), as part of the UN Millennium Development Goals, which is now the dominant force in education, can be subjected to Bernstein's (1999) analysis of hegemonic power and knowledge discourse setting. The international architecture that sustains and confers legitimacy on the enterprise begins with the Human Rights Declaration:

> The right to education is articulated clearly in Article 26 of the Universal Declaration of Human Rights (1948). This recognizes the intrinsic human value of education, underpinned by strong moral and legal foundations. Seen in this light, education is also an indispensable means of unlocking and protecting other human rights by providing the scaffolding that is required to secure good health, liberty, security, economic well-being, and participation in social and political activity (UNESCO, 1990).

This architecture, or to use the terms proposed by Bernstein (1999), a vertical (hierarchical) discourse spawns other localized national policy level manifestations or horizontal discourses, which create and sustain its authority. The arrogating of legitimacy results in the creation of a supposedly self-evident reality or of manifestly positive aims for education policy and programmes, which now have global reach or power. A global programme, such as EFA *à la* Bernstein, creates systems of knowledge transfer and commensurate power relations.

Bernstein's discourse analysis finds resonance in educational planning literature:

> Schriewer analyses the emergence of *das internationale Argument* in policy discourse and educational research. He finds that precisely at those moments when educational policies and practices become contested, policy makers and educational research resort to *das internationale Argument*; that is, use experiences in other educational systems as source of authority (Steiner-Khamsi, 2009, p. 69).

The alignment of educational planning and finance, with the superstructure of the Education for All Declaration (UNESCO, 1990) or 'movement' as it is sometimes known, offers 'access' to formal schooling. This is precisely what Gramsci (1971) referred to as the ideological basis of hegemony: education—formal 'modern' schooling—is effectively the adoption of the civilization from which formal schools draw their heritage, and a rejection of local or indigenous traditions. UNESCO and its partners greatly appreciated the implications of the Education for All movement by asserting, at Dakar in 2000, that along with access to schooling, the quality and relevance of the education on offer should have equal emphasis (UNESCO, 2000).

The results, for example the numerous Education Sector Reform Assistance (ESRA) and Fast Track Initiatives (FTI) programmes, are portrayed as meeting the needs of local contexts.[2] However, on closer scrutiny it is noted that the policy formation process has antecedents which, when unpacked or deconstructed (to use Foucault's term), manifest other discourses (see Chapman and Quijada, 2009). Bernstein shows that knowledge, when subjected to various levels of transfer in both vertical and horizontal domains, has a core which renders the chance of there being particular knowledge to local contexts very remote.

Together with Pring (2000), this chapter holds that research methods, along with their epistemological and ontological heritages, cannot be different in the North and the South. It is more the context, with its cultural and structural particularities, that require different questions to be asked.

In the post-Jomtien world, from 1990 onwards, the problematic issue is the uniform and entrenched standardized target of state-sponsored formal schooling for all. The features of the EFA Declaration, while holding individual countries accountable, actually reinforce the North's dominant position and hold the South up as an exemplar of underachievement. This is particularly so as funding regimes for overall achievement of EFA targets are controlled by the countries of the North; the model of schooling that is pursued was developed in the countries of the West at the onset of industrialization, and was imported via the to the colonies imperial powers (Alexander, 2000); and, the overwhelming educational expertise, training, and monitoring capacity exists in the North (Crossley and Tikly, 2004).

Education Discourses and Research in the South

We now turn to which questions are asked and why. The main point of debate is that it is the context and level of development of the system that identifies the questions to be asked and researched, as opposed to the different research approaches or methodologies that pertain to the South and the North. This then requires us to delve into what questions are asked and why, which questions are not identified, and what might be considered to be the limits to possible research. Here, we enter into philosophical speculation or paradigmatic thinking.

The dominant paradigm that has influenced the identification of questions that can be asked, or which are indeed permissible, has been developed by the logical positivists. This view holds that the nature of reality could only be determined as a result of what could logically be identified, as opposed to metaphysically determined, thereby enabling more knowledge to be unfolded.[3] This has led to an increased move towards the secularization of society, with an emphasis on social governance in an effort to transform society (De Sousa Santos, 2003).

In education, the influence of logical positivism is evident in the curriculum that is developed, the pedagogy that is advocated, the assessment systems in use, and the further training and investment on offer. Thus, the aims of education—its intended outcomes—and particularly the focus on cognitive development and what is considered to be successful, have seen an uncanny alignment across the world (Alexander, 2000). This is reified in the EFA movement. The consequence of this standardization is noted by the lead agency responsible for the oversight of the EFA movement: UNESCO notes that the global move to meet EFA targets has increased access to schooling at the expense of quality (UNESCO, 2005). This has led UNESCO, and its partner agencies, to rethink the position of formal schooling, the role of alternatives, and the involvement of what might be deemed non-experts in the provision of education.[4] We, therefore, see the rise of community-based schools, parental oversight and involvement, and the return of non-scientific discourse influencing the curriculum on offer. This is most evident in the North, with the rise of homeschooling by families concerned at the singular focus on evolutionary biology, at the expense of religious explanations for the origin of humanity, in schools (Micklethwait and Wooldridge, 2009).

When research and evaluation studies are undertaken with vigour and independence, we find that programmes developed on technical–rational thinking have had very limited success, or worse, where the unintended outcomes have at times been further knowledge–poverty, economic decline, environmental degradation, and disease and starvation (Lynch, Modgil and Modgil, 1997).

In the context of Pakistan, Warwick and Reimers (1995) found that the most successful educational development programme that increased access to education, albeit not without raising concerns, was the mosque school innovation. They hold the view, along with Lynch, that a greater understanding of local cultures, knowledge, and informal institutions is central to development programmes. Numerous such programmes, in developing country contexts, can be cited: complementary and alternative medicine, employment and income generation such as microcredit, and women's empowerment programmes. Such programmes appear to be far more successful when local culture and needs, as well as ownership and participation by the intended beneficiaries, are the central premise of the provision, and where the trajectory of the programmes is both open-ended and there is a long-term engagement.

The above analysis on education shows, with regard to developing countries, a maintenance of power and structural agency that divided the world into developing and developed, particularly in terms of models of education to be emulated or funding to be allocated. Similar analysis could be undertaken with regard to Muslims and the position of Islamic studies in the UK.[5]

To return to the matter of which questions can be asked and which are sensible, it is now evident that the post-Enlightenment modernity project that had pursued uniformity across the world, and which promised much to all the world's people, has not delivered what it promised. This is particularly so for those who were not involved with the modernization project in the early industrialization of the North: those in the South, and those who have been recipients of the North's unwanted attention. Chronic poverty and disenfranchisement exist largely in the South, where more than one billion people live in unacceptable conditions that have been worsened by the imposition of North-inspired development programming (Collier, 2007). This is further exacerbated with regard to the Muslim communities in the South who make up the majority of the poor (Khamis, 2010).

Conclusion

The idea of possible multiple modernities is all the more attractive in an era of globalization and hyper-communication and dissemination of information. For instance, we have witnessed that one dominant role of schools has been to reproduce inequalities in society—this has been a major lesson learnt from the last 50 years of educational development. In wanting to create more equity and harmony, whereby the world's population enhances others' life chances rather than operating on a zero-sum basis (my loss is your gain), disadvantage and disenfranchisement must be prioritized. This means, in current intellectual thinking, that we abandon the idea of only one route to development—which has its roots in post-Enlightenment Europe—as the model for the whole world.

We now live in a highly interdependent world. This applies to financial markets, as witnessed by the recent credit crunch that affected the global economies, and which harks back to the conditions that prompted the establishment of the Bretton Woods Institutions, or to the virtual world of instantaneous information communications technologies, or even the environment that is one shared biosphere. But, it applies even more in respect to the personal interactions that we might be unaware of, as evidenced by the worldwide Mexican swine influenza pandemic—which demonstrated the human agency in vector biology that enabled the global spread of the virus within a matter of days. Our extensive and unpredictable intercourse across national or ethnic boundaries, social or racial class divides, and economic or political societal stratification is a fundamental fact of the twenty-first century. As educationists and researchers, we should pause to consider the fast-paced changes—demographic and other—that constantly shift educational priorities and needs; and the (knowledge generating and research) approaches we advocate, the (developmental) agendas we privilege, the actual voices we choose to hear, the sense we make of their actual intent, and the effect of our responses.

The debate, then, is not whether research in the North or South is different. It is about the intent of our work and its outcomes, and the choice of robust and powerful methods available to us and their conscientious use:

> Human beings are not 'things' to be studied in the way one studies rats, plants, and rocks, but are valuing, meaning-attributing beings to be understood as subjects and known as subjects. [The researcher] deals with meaningful actions, and the understanding, explanation, analysis, or whatever, must be made with consideration of these meanings that make the ordering of human action possible . . . To impose positivist meanings upon a realm of social phenomena is to distort the fundamental nature of human existence (Hughes, 1976:25).

References

Alexander, R. (2000). *Culture and pedagogy: international comparisons in primary Education.* Oxford, UK: Blackwell.

Anderson, S. and Kumari, R. (2009). 'Continuous improvement in schools: understanding the practice.' *International Journal of Educational Development,* 29(3), 281–292.

Bennell, P. (1995). *Using and Abusing Rates of Return: A Critique of the World Bank's Education Sector Review.* Brighton, UK: University of Sussex Institute of Development Studies.

Bernstein, B. (1999). 'Vertical and horizontal discourse: an essay.' *British Journal of Sociology of Education,* 20(2), 157–173.

Bloom, D.E., Hartley, M., and Rosovsky, H. (2006). 'Beyond private gain: the public benefits of higher education.' In J.F. Forest and P.G. Altbach (Eds.), *International handbook of higher education* (pp. 293–308). Dordrecht, Netherlands: Springer.

Bourdieu, P., and Passeron, J.-C. (1990). *Reproduction in education, society and culture* (R. Nice, Trans. 2 ed.). London, UK: Sage.

Chapman, D. and Quijada, J.J. (2009). 'An analysis of USAID assistance to basic education in developing countries, 1990–2005.' *International Journal of Educational Development,* 29(3), 268–280.

Coleman, J.S. (1966). *Equality of educational opportunity study (EEOS) report.* Washington, DC: United States Department of Education.

Collier, P. (2007). *The bottom billion: why the poorest countries are failing and what can be done about it,* New York, NY: Oxford University Press.

Crossley, M. (1984). 'Strategies for curriculum change and the question of international transfer.' *Journal of Curriculum Studies,* 16, 75–88.

Crossley, M. and Tickly, L. (2004). 'Postcolonial perspectives and comparative and international research in education: a critical introduction.' *Comparative Education,* 40, 147–156.

Darling-Hammond, L. (2006). Constructing 21st century teacher education.' *Journal of Teacher Education* 57(X), 1–15. DOI: 10.1177/0022487105285962.

Davies, L. and Iqbal, Z. (1997). 'Tensions in teacher training for school effectiveness: the case of Pakistan.' *School Effectiveness and School Improvement,* 8(2), 254–266.

De Sousa Santos, B. (2003). 'The World Social Forum: toward a counter-hegemonic globalisation.' In J. Sen, Anand, A., Escobar, A., and P. Waterman (Eds.), *Challenging Empires* (pp. 336–343). New Delhi, India: Viveka Foundation.

Fagerlind, I. and Saha, L.J. (1989). 'Education and Development: the Emerging Confidence in Formal Schooling as an Agent of Change.' *Education and National Development* (pp. 32–64). Oxford, UK: Pergamon.

Feinstein, L. (2003). 'Inequality in the early cognitive development of British children in the 1970 cohort.' *Economica*, 70(277), 73–97.

Gramsci, A. (1971). *Selections from Prison Notebooks of Antonio Gramsci* (Q. Hoare and G.N. Smith, eds. and trans.), London, UK: Lawrence and Wishart.

Hanushek, E.A., and Wößmann, L. (2007). *Education quality and economic growth*. Washington, DC: World Bank.

Haq, M. (1995). *Reflections on Human Development*. New York, NY: Oxford University Press.

Hargreaves, A. (1996). Transforming knowledge: blurring the boundaries between research, policy, and practice. *Educational Evaluation and Policy Analysis*, 18(2), 105–122.

HEFCE. (2008). *International approaches to Islamic studies in higher education: a report to HEFCE*. Bristol, UK: HEFCE.

Heyneman, S.P. (1999). 'Development aid in education: a personal view.' *International Journal of Educational Development*, 19,183–190.

Heyneman, S.P. (1997). 'Economic growth and the international trade in educational reform.' *Prospects*, 27(4), 501–530.

Hodge, M. (19 July 2005). 'Keynote speech.' Seminar on Muslim Graduates in the Labour Market, held at the Royal Horticultural Halls, London, UK. Retrieved on 18 March 2005 from http://www.emetaskforce.gov.uk/pdf/MuslimGraduates_revised.pdf.

Hoxby, C., and Leigh, A. (2004). 'Pulled away or pushed out? Explaining the decline of teacher aptitude in the United States.' *American Economic Review*, 94(2), 236–240.

Hughes, J. (1976). *Sociological analysis: methods of discovery*. London, UK: Nelson.

Khamis, A. (2009). 'Cultures of learning.' In A.B. Sajoo (Ed.), *A Companion to the Muslim World* (pp. 237–262). London, UK: I.B. Tauris/Institute of Ismaili Studies.

Khamis, A. (2010). 'Teacher education in Pakistan.' In K.G. Karras and C.C. Wolhuter (Eds.), *International handbook on teacher education worldwide: training, issues and challenges for the teaching profession.* Athens, Greece: Atrapos Editions.

Khamis, A., and Jawed, S. (2006). 'Teacher education and school improvement: a case study from Pakistan.' In I. Farah and B. Jaworksi (Eds.), *Partnerships in educational development,* (pp. 171–182). Didcot, UK: Symposium.

Khamis, A. and Sammons, P. (2004). 'The development of a cadre of teacher educators: some lessons from Pakistan.' *International Journal of Educational Development,* 24(3), 255–68

Khamis, A., and Sammons, P. (2007). 'Investigating educational change: the Aga Khan University Institute for Educational Development teacher education for school improvement model.' *International Journal of Educational Development,* 27(5), 572–580.

Lockheed, M.Ed. and Verspoor, A.M. (1990). *Improving Primary Education in Developing Countries.* Washington, DC: World Bank.

Lynch, J., Modgil, C., and Modgil, S. (Eds.). (1997). *Education and development: tradition and innovation* (Vol. 1: Concepts, approaches and assumptions). London, UK: Cassell.

Micklethwait, J., and Wooldridge, A. (2009). *God is back: How the Global Revival of Faith is Changing the World.* Harmondsworth, UK: Allen Lane, The Penguin Press.

Miles, M.B., and Huberman, A.M. (1994). *Quantitative data analysis: a sourcebook of new methods* (2 ed.). Thousand Oaks, CA: Sage.

Panel on Fair Access to the Professions. (2009). *Unleashing aspiration: the final report of the Panel on Fair Access to the Professions (Milburn Report).* London, UK: Cabinet Office.

Pring, R. (2000). *Philosophy of educational research.* London, UK: Continuum.

Rockoff, J.E. (2004). 'The impact of individual teachers on student achievement: evidence from panel data.' *American Economic Review,* 94(2), 247–252.

Schultz, T. (1961). 'Investment in human capital.' *American Economic Review*, 51(1), 1–17.

Sen, A. (1999). *Development as Freedom*. Oxford, UK: Oxford University Press.

Sen, A. (2007). *Identity and Violence: The Illusion of Destiny*. Penguin, London.

Steiner-Khamsi, Gita (2009). 'Knowledge-based regulation and the politics of international comparison.' *Nordisk Pedagogik*, 29(1), 61–71.

UNESCO. (1990). *World declaration on Education for All: our framework of action to meet basic learning needs*. Paris, France: UNESCO.

UNESCO. (2000).*The Dakar framework for action. Education for all: meeting our collective commitments*. Paris, France: UNESCO.

UNESCO. (2005). *EFA global monitoring report: the quality imperative*. Paris, France: UNESCO. Paris

Warwick, D.P. and Reimers (1995). *Hope or despair? Learning in Pakistan's primary schools*. New York, NY: Praeger Press.

Notes

1. The influence of Logical Positivism, developed in the 1920s, can be detected in these planning models and regimes, with their dependence on empirical data. This position holds that all problems are challenges to be solved by technical means. That is, the challenge is to find appropriate, already available solutions to problems, with the aim of modernization (see Lynch et al., 1997).

2. ESRA programmes are, in the main, funded by USAID. The largest recipient countries are Nigeria, Egypt, Pakistan, and Indonesia. Importantly, these countries, which are the largest Muslim majority countries in the world, are also classified as developing countries.

3. The late nineteenth and early years of the twentieth century was a time of great development in mathematics (Russell and Ramanujan), physics (Einstein), and biology (Darwin). They developed systems of logic, which relied on empirical data that could be tested and verified.

4. See Khamis (2009) for a full discussion, with respect to educational development in Muslim civilizations and possible trajectories in the future.
5. See HEFCE (2008), which seeks to unfold its own vertical and horizontal discourses to fashion Islamic Studies in the UK.

5

Researching Very Different Societies: An Impossible Task?

Richard Pring

Context

The context for what follows is that so much research, even in the South, is either conducted by researchers from a very different culture or dominated by research traditions within a different culture. How can people from one culture really understand the problems and contexts of a very different society?

The seriousness of this question is highlighted by the 'evidence-based' research, funded by international agencies, on the basis of which support is given to economically less advantaged countries but on certain terms. The perspective (through which problems are identified, issues explored, and solutions offered) is dominated by assumptions about how society functions and how individuals relate with each other—which may not be how very different societies actually work. How can researchers from one tradition get inside the minds of people and societies from very different traditions? And furthermore, if they do, how can they communicate that understanding to people who have not attained the insights that the researchers' reports depend upon?

To take a politically significant example, both the focus of research and the tradition through which the research is conducted could be that of a democratic way of life. Indeed, a more democratic form of life might be a condition of international aid, and therefore its development over time be the object of research. But, is not 'democracy' a very loaded word, embodying a distinctive tradition of decision making which may not tally with the much hallowed decision-making processes of the society being researched? And is not 'democracy' itself a word that picks out different traditions that have emerged over time? (If that were not the case, there would be little room for political philosophy or theory.) There can so easily be an unquestioned imposition of values, distinctive of a dominant culture that is shared by the researcher, but which ignores or does not take into account the very different values of the society being researched.

Stating the Problem

This problem, however, could be tackled at different levels.

The first level is of an empirical nature: whether, *as a matter of fact*, there is a problem that could be avoided with greater care. It is simply a matter of the researcher recognizing the complex nature of understanding another society or a very different culture, and so working hard to overcome barriers, to get rid of prejudices, and to see things from the point of view of those being researched—for there certainly exists the problem of researchers who quite uncritically assume that those researched think and act in much the same way as people do in the researchers' own societies. They simply have not tried to understand things from the others' point of view—the understandings, customs, and values which shape the ways in which the objects of the research see the world. People operate within different social and moral traditions. These have to be factored in if sense is to be made of what they do.

At another level, however (and this underpins some of the contributions to this book), the accusation is that cultures are so different—different in the conceptions of human nature, of the nature of society, of human flourishing—that understanding them is impossible and the language will reflect these differences. Hence, there is a logical impossibility in, both, getting to understand a very different culture from within, and then (if one does) of translating this insider understanding into terms that are shaped by a very different language and by very different social customs. Only the researcher who is part of a given society can really understand it. Therefore, he or she alone should be responsible for conducting the research within it.

This problem is not a new one. Winch, in *The idea of a social science* (Winch, 1958) and then in his later paper 'Understanding a primitive society' (Winch, 1964), addressed the problem of how researchers can understand a society very different from their own—so different that there seems to be nothing recognizable in their social life. The social world of those being researched, constituted through very different social rules, could not be captured in the concepts, language, and social rules of the researcher.

This chapter argues for the *logical* possibility of such unity of understanding, while recognizing the *practical* difficulty. The apparent logical difficulties are no different from those of a middle-class, middle-aged, male researcher from the south of England researching working-class, female adolescents from the north of England—very different cultures, interests, aspirations, and social practices. Or, again, the logical difficulties (that is, the difficulties in understanding other people and societies which are constituted of very different ways of seeing the world) seem no different from those of the historian trying to make sense of events in the distant past. The historian and philosopher, Collingwood, in *The Idea of History* (Collingwood, 1946), saw the imaginative re-enactment of the past, constantly tested through criticism and further evidence, as essential to the understanding of history. One might understand why Caesar crossed the Rubicon because, in the light of evidence and what we know of Caesar's character, one is able to 're-enact imaginatively' that event. Of course, one may be wrong, but so might one be wrong in ascribing explanatory motives to one's own friends and companions. It is well-justified understanding that one is seeking, not grounds for certainty; that is never attainable.

The problems, therefore, which gave rise to this debate,—where they stem from very different (ideologically different, perhaps) views of the political, social, and religious worlds—are often exaggerated and are philosophically unsound.

Understanding, Explaining, and Social Context

The major aim of research is to understand a situation or phenomenon, very frequently with a view to explaining why it happened, or how it can be avoided in future, or how the situation might be improved. If the elimination of poverty is the reason for calling in researchers, then that research should endeavour to understand the nature, extent, and causes of that poverty and what needs to be done to alleviate it. If there is a mistaken understanding of the extent and nature of the poverty, then the solutions offered might well fail. The same could be said of illiteracy, which is often associated with poverty.

However, problems that can so easily arise through lack of cultural understanding are immediately apparent. Poverty is not necessarily understood in the same way in different societies, or indeed in the same society over a period of time. A person considered poor in present day England might not have been considered so 40 or 50 years ago. The *criteria* for being considered poor have changed, not just officially but more importantly in the implicit and everyday understandings of the people themselves. The criteria logically relate to further values about a good life and human flourishing, and the indispensability of a certain level of material goods for such a life. Different values entail different criteria of poverty. Our concepts, reflected in the words we use (or indeed shaped by the words we have learnt to use), have a history. They change and adapt over time. There is both continuity and change in meaning. How else could the full version of the Oxford English Dictionary be so long, reflecting as it does the changing meaning of key words?

Hence, the understanding of the physical and social worlds—which we try to make sense of through research—depends on the language we use; that language has both a history and a complex set of meanings related to wider social, moral, and economic understandings.

However, it is now commonplace, in the context of research, to point to the difference between understanding (and explaining) physical phenomena and understanding the behaviours of persons, although those differences are exaggerated too often through the uncritical dichotomy between 'positivist' (now a 'boo word' amongst educational researchers) and 'interpretive' research. But it is true that, to understand a person and to explain his or her behaviour, one needs to know the intentions behind the behaviour. Two behaviours (identical in terms of what is open to observation) might be understood very differently in terms of the intention that informs them. A wave of the hand could *mean* a friendly gesture, a request for attention, or the signal to start a revolution. To put it crudely, one needs to 'get inside the mind of the actor'—observation is not enough.

Let us take the interpretation of the hand-waving as requesting attention. It is not simply a matter of getting into the inside of that person's mind in order to understand what is happening—to get at the 'subjective meanings' of the actor, as so many PhD theses mistakenly assume. That wave of the hand has meaning only in so far as it can be interpreted by others as a call for attention. The intention to get attention, and the behaviour through which attention is gained, depend upon a set of social rules by which others will come to understand the gesture for what it is. One cannot disassociate the meaning of behaviour from a social context and from the set of social rules (usually understood though only implicitly) through which interpersonal relations are established and communication is made possible.

One can see, therefore, the complexity of understanding other people, and how that is made yet more complex and difficult where those people are living within very different social contexts.

First, what appear to be the same words for describing situations might well, as a result of different ways of life and different values, take on significantly different meanings. The potential for misunderstanding increases manifold when those words are translated into a different language—which itself has evolved in very different economic, religious, and social circumstances, reflecting what Wittgenstein referred to as 'different forms of life'.

Second, those words 'perform' against a different set of social rules and norms which are implicit and which, as far as the researcher is concerned, need to be discovered. They are not written down. They are known implicitly and practically by the people under investigation, but they themselves might well not be able to recognize them explicitly, let alone describe them to the researcher.

Third, however, those social rules need to be understood against a wider account of the values and aims that are built into the society's way of life. An obvious example of this would be a broadly conceived religious set of beliefs that enter—implicitly—into the norms of appropriate living, the gestures and behaviours of the practitioners, and the relationships between people and within families. But one could also point to democratic ideals and assumptions that 'explain' the dominance of certain values and ways of behaving.

A Word of Caution

Research practitioners from the South claim, critically, that the problems I have outlined make it difficult or impossible for researchers from very different contexts to engage in research within their cultural context. However, the problems, as stated, are equally valid within countries which appear to the outsider to be culturally homogeneous—as they are across countries that appear to be culturally heterogeneous.

Let us, once again, take the example of religion. The philosopher Charles Taylor describes, in *A Secular Age* (Taylor, 2007), how a broadly understood and accepted religious understanding of society (reflected in various symbols of office, singing of hymns at school, rituals at key stages of life and death, etc.) in the West has given way to a secular culture (not necessarily anti-religious—see the United States) where religious practice is no longer the 'default position'. Those who do believe in God and practise a religion are expected to explain and justify themselves and their beliefs to the unbeliever, rather than vice versa. Society becomes divided between those with secular assumptions, who have gained the high ground, and those who retain a religious dimension to their lives which affects how they understand and feel about the world they live in. It is interesting to note that many Muslims in England are happy to have their children educated in Catholic schools; there is a greater sharing of understanding between the two religious communities, than there is between either of them and those who espouse a secular foundation to their lives and to society. Therefore, would a Catholic researcher from the West have an insight into the practices of the Muslim societies of the South—an insight that a researcher with no religious understanding or insights would not have? Given the central importance of religious belief and practice to societies in Muslim countries, how could a non-believer understand the social practices, the customs, the motivations, the understandings, or the relationships that characterize the societies being researched into?

Let us take a further example: that of a white, middle aged, middle class researcher trying to understand the criminal behaviour of gangs of black youth in a highly disadvantaged and economically undeveloped part of an English city which is in a state of industrial decline. There has arisen a different language, a musical tradition that is quite alien, a form of comradeship and gang loyalty in opposition to that from which they have been rejected, and a set of shared values. Trying to understand and explain their behaviour (with a view to changing and improving it) the researcher would no doubt call upon the language and understanding of behaviour and social norms through which he or she makes sense of the social world. But, the world of the gangs of alienated and criminal youth, reflecting a very different form of life, could not it might seem, be captured in the language and explanatory system of the researcher.

The point is that the logical difficulties, which underpin the criticisms of those from the South who point to the problem of external researchers trying to make sense of their societies and their problems, are no different from the difficulties encountered *within* any society which is divided on class, religious, or ethnic grounds. How can one understand people and communities very different from one's own?

Understanding Other Societies

One preliminary comment must be that 'understanding' is only 'more or less' attained; there is always room for 'deeper' understanding, or for a more comprehensive explanation of events—in the physical sciences as well as in the understanding of other people and of the societies they belong to.

To understand (more or less) other people is, as I explained above, first, to understand things from their point of view—the intentions that lie behind the observed behaviour. Even so, one must be a little cautious in stating this. People can be self-deceived; sometimes, the observer understands the motives of the agent better than the agent himself or herself. We perceive

Macbeth as ambitious and Othello to have acted out of jealousy, though neither character would have recognized those motives in himself.

Second, to understand other people is to understand the language and the concepts through which they make sense of their behaviours and interpret the world. And, different cultures have come to conceptualize that world in relevantly different ways. Take, for example, the list of virtues through which we evaluate our own and others' actions. These vary from age to age, as well as from society to society. The Aristotelian virtue of 'magnanimity' or 'magnificence in spending' finds no place among the beatitudes; acting out of honour (as in 'honour killing') is totally alien to many yet self-evident to others; 'obedience' has given way to the recently arrived virtue of 'autonomy' in the neo-liberal tradition; and 'enterprise' has become the most recent virtue as an object of educational nurturing. Not only, therefore, do researchers have to 'get on the inside' of the other persons' minds. They also, in so doing, have to apply the concepts and 'language' through which the researched, but not necessarily the researcher, describe and evaluate the physical, moral, and social worlds they inhabit.

Third, the understandings of the researched—the ways in which they perceive things including their own motives and aspirations—are themselves acquired through learning a language and through participating in the social practices of those around them, their parents, friends, village and town folk. Those social practices will have evolved over much time, particularly reflecting the economic conditions in which they live and the religious and ideological perspectives through which the respective communities make sense of their lives. These understandings are embodied in a range of social rules, only some of which are made explicit. In the absence of such social rules (for example, of showing respect, of 'saving face', of signalling disapproval, of cementing relationships as in marriage) it would be impossible to engage in any form of social life and indeed to communicate with others. Remember the example of hand-waving in order to attract attention: the interpretation by others depends upon an implicit understanding of shared social rules whereby someone else is able to interpret it in the intended way.

The problem is this: how can researchers from a very different society and culture—with different ways of describing the world and of evaluating actions and motives, and with different social rules through which daily communication takes place and relationships are formed—understand a society and culture that does not share these? Surely they will interpret what is observed, not in the terms of those being researched, but mistakenly in their own terms—hence, the prevalence of misinterpretation and misunderstanding, and the constant failure of researchers from the 'North' to understand the problems and possible solutions to those problems of the South.

There are two answers to the question posed thus. The first is 'with difficulty'—and with a difficulty that is rarely grasped. The most effective way of understanding a different social practice is to immerse oneself in it. The outsider must become—at least to some extent, depending on the research questions—an insider, understanding the language through which sense is made of the physical, social, and economic worlds, and appreciating the social rules through which everyday communication and relationships are conducted.

The second answer, however, is that it is not impossible; the gulf between cultures can be exaggerated. A non-Muslim might not, easily, fully grasp the social practices of a Muslim society, but many of these practices would not seem alien to those similarly brought up in a religious tradition—an understanding of prayer and worship. The list of virtues might be different, but there is, inevitably, a great deal of overlap and a capacity to see how virtues relate to different economic and social conditions. Wittgenstein's notion of a 'form of life', within which actions can be understood and language takes on specific meanings, can be pitched at different levels. There is the 'Catholic form of life' or the 'Muslim form of life', constituting a range of practices which embody, though only implicitly, beliefs and values and ways of relating to each other. But there is also the 'human form of life' through which, deeper than specific forms of life, we can make connections with people from very different cultures. In recognizing someone as human, I recognize him or her as capable of joy and sadness, hurt and pleasure, fear and hope, hunger and thirst, love and hatred, virtue and vice. One recognizes, too, the need for a prolonged childhood in which there will be different ways of initiating the young into adulthood—related, no doubt, to the economic conditions in which they have to survive. One comes to recognize how authority is exercised as part of the necessary enforcement of social rules. It would be difficult to conceive of a society where there were not implicit rules for regulating relationships—though what we call 'marriage', however, might take on different forms.

But, this simply argues for the possibility of understanding. To gain that understanding—to enter into the different traditions through which a society can be understood—requires a deeper immersion in the 'other society' than is often undertaken by the researcher.

References

Collingwood, R.G. (1946). *The idea of history*. Oxford, UK: Oxford University Press.

Taylor, C. (2007). *A secular age*. Cambridge, MA: Harvard University Press.

Winch, P. (1958). *The idea of a social science and its relation to philosophy*. London, UK: Routledge and Kegan Paul.

Winch, P. (1964). 'Understanding a primitive society.' *American Philosophical Quarterly*, 1(4), 307–324.

6

Who Pays the Price?
The Ethics of Vulnerability in Research

Rashida Qureshi

Introduction

In biomedical science research, some conventions regarding the notion of 'vulnerability' are hard to miss. First, vulnerability is defined literally, i.e. the state of being weak; susceptibility to attack or injury; being not well-defended. Second, vulnerability afflicts research participants only. Third, the vulnerability of research participants stems from their inability to act/react in certain situations. As a result of these conventions, the discourse of bioethics revolves around informed consent and the issues related to voluntary participation of research participants. The implicit assumption of the discourse is that a researcher is a fully 'autonomous' being who knows what is right and wrong and does the right thing. However, in social sciences, where different notions of knowledge, rigour, and research are prevalent, the imposition of these bio-ethics conventions is problematic on two accounts:

i) First, theoretically, social science research is a contextually-bound social interaction where potential sources of vulnerability for both parties are part of the context. The conventional vulnerabilities of a research participant may be present in such a context, but researchers may also be susceptible to some constraints as they 'need to develop better understandings of the politics and contexts within which ethics are regulated' (Israel and Hay, 2006, p. 10). The possibilities of misunderstanding the 'ethical environment' (Black, 1999) of a particular context, and the resulting conflicts, cannot be ruled out—which can constrain the autonomy of a researcher and increase his/her vulnerability.

ii) Second, as the whole discourse of ethics in research flows from the North to the South, the ethical guidelines for dealing with vulnerabilities create practical issues for, and increase the vulnerability of, social scientists working in the South.

These two sets of issues, which are related to the application of bioethics standards to the social sciences, are distinct but interrelated. In the first category are the issues that arise from a discourse of the biomedical and social sciences. At the heart of these issues is the subjugation of the social sciences, in particular where the bioethics research discourse is held as the professional standard. The second set of issues, on the other hand, relates to the flow of knowledge from the North to the South, with a concomitant subjugation of what the South has to offer in terms of knowledge and notions of research, with implications for appropriate procedures of ethics in research. Taken together, the two sets of issues highlight the vulnerabilities of social science researchers in general and of those working in the South in particular. Therefore, in order to understand the notion of vulnerability from a Southern perspective, the ethics of research discourse in the social sciences needs to be located within the larger framework of the North–South divide because the South suffers from layers of vulnerabilities because of the historical process of marginalization. Being a vulnerable context, the vulnerabilities associated with research processes in the South are not limited to research participants only but also affect the autonomous decision-making of researchers working in such contexts.

This thesis is developed in the present chapter. The basic premises of the argument are as follows:

i) The bioethics discourse may need modifications when applied to social science research on theoretical and practical grounds. Theoretically speaking, the notion and nature of vulnerability differs in these disciplines and, practically speaking, holding bioethics standards as models marginalizes social science researchers.

ii) The South as a context, because of its historical experiences of exploitation through imperialism and colonialism, is still vulnerable.

iii) Not only are the research participants vulnerable, but so too are the social science researchers working in the South.

The chapter is organized around these themes. Following the comparison of vulnerability in biomedical and social sciences, the term is re-defined for the social sciences. Described next are the historical experiences of the South. The chapter ends with the peculiarities of the ethics of vulnerability in such contexts.

Vulnerability in Biomedical vs. Social Science Research

In the aftermath of the Second World War, research involving humans was seen as a moral enterprise; the indicator of 'ethical' research was its strength, in terms of getting 'voluntary consent', because the Nuremberg trials were based on the premise that German scientists used humans as the objects for conducting the research. Hence, the autonomy, respect, and dignity of the research participants were the key concepts for the Nuremberg Code, and the other codes of ethics that were based on the Nuremberg Code, for conducting research with humans. From the formulation of the Nuremberg Code of research ethics in August 1947, and its expansion into the first declaration of the World Medical Association at Helsinki,[1] to the creation of the CIOMS Guidelines in 1993, the whole discourse of research ethics (or more correctly, bioethics, which still dominates), revolved around the issues related to informed consent.

Moreover, since the research participants were forced to take part in research trials/experiments in the Nazi era, and had paid a heavy price due to their unfavourable circumstances, the notion of 'vulnerability' in biomedical research became associated with 'those special circumstances of the C–S [candidate–subject] that call into question the efficacy of consent in effecting the permissibility of research' (Kipnis, 2001). Consequently, the literature on research ethics mainly focuses on issues related to the vulnerability of the research participants in terms of their consent.[2]

Unlike the biomedical sciences, there is no 'world' body to provide universal guidelines in the social sciences but the Declaration on Professional Ethics, which was adopted in August 1985 by the International Statistical Institute (1985), has served as a set of universal regulations 'from which most social science codes are derived' (Hutton, Eccles and Grimshaw, 2008, p. 6). If we consider this Declaration as the parent document for social sciences' ethical guidelines, then the ethics discourse for the social sciences parts company with the biomedical sciences in the most fundamental way. The Declaration on Professional Ethics has four sections on obligations: to society, to funders and employers, to colleagues, and to subjects. Inferences to potential sources of vulnerability can be drawn from each section, but this is not the task for this chapter. For the present discussion, suffice it to say that the circumstances creating threats—which call into question the permissibility of research—are not limited to the informed consent and voluntary participation/withdrawal of research participants, which are the central points for biomedical discourse. The threats encompass much wider concerns, which are acknowledged in the following passage from the Declaration document:

> It [the Declaration] is framed in the recognition that, on occasions, the operation of one principle [of statistical inquiry] will impede the operation of another, that statisticians—in common with other occupational groups—have competing obligations not all of which can be fulfilled simultaneously. Thus, implicit or explicit choices between principles will sometimes have to be made. (International Statistical Institute, 1985, p. 2)

It is important to note that the circumstances under which these 'implicit or explicit choices' are made are, by and large, part of the research context for a social science researcher, particularly for those who are working in a qualitative paradigm, which is not generally used in biomedical sciences. In the post-Nuremberg

Code era, social scientists pointed out the need to reconsider not only many of the prevailing notions of the scientific research paradigm, but also the applicability of bioethical standards to the social science disciplines (Israel, 2005). A detailed discussion of this discourse is not warranted here,[3] so I will be selective in highlighting only the points needed to build my discussion of vulnerability in social science research.

The very first point concerns the definition of 'human subjects'; the bioethical model considers humans as 'subjects' about whom, and from whom, data is gathered, mostly in the quantitative paradigm. The status of the researcher is that of an outsider and an authority on the subject. Responsibility for conducting research in an ethical manner lies with the expert, who is seen as an autonomous being. In contrast, in social science research settings, data is often collected in a qualitative paradigm where humans are not the 'subjects' of the study but are active participants. This 'going from "human subjects" to "co-researchers and collaborators"' (Mohr, 2001, p. 7) involves a paradigmatic shift that Mohr describes as 'the parting of the Red Sea' (loc. cit.).

In such a setting, the relationship between a researcher and his/her 'collaborators' are multi-dimensional, fluid, and ever-changing, requiring constant negotiation and re-negotiation. Moreover, the distinction between 'authority' and 'subject' is not as sharp as it is in biomedical sciences; in the social sciences, research in general, and qualitative research in particular, is a meaning-making activity where new knowledge is being generated together. Hence, both the researcher and the researched experience the perils of research exercise as the process exposes them to uncertain situations where 'It doesn't need an academic to say what vulnerability is. We can all see it, much more often than we care to.' (Schroeder and Gefenas, 2009, p. 115). If it comes to paying a price in research, then the possibility of such a burden falling on both parties cannot be ruled out.

Similarly, the notion of 'voluntary consent' for social scientists is a matter of gaining their collaborators' trust, and not simply 'getting permission'. Not only do researchers need permission to gain entry into the field, but also need to maintain it by building mutually respectful relations with their collaborators. Hence, 'consent', 'participation', and 'withdrawal' are not one-time gestures but are part of an ongoing negotiation/re-negotiation process that increases the vulnerability of researchers as they are constantly monitoring the barometer of their social acceptance by the participants.

Furthermore, the notion of 'justice' in bioethics relates to the selection of subjects in the medical domain—where the physician has more choice about including or excluding a sample as, in most cases, the physician–researcher relates with the 'subject' in a one-to-one setting. In social science research projects, on the other hand, a researcher mostly deals with a group; for instance, in teaching and learning projects, a teacher–researcher has little freedom to decide who to include or exclude from a classroom.

Lastly, there are the notions of 'risk' and 'harm': according to bioethics, the indicators are visible and concrete. In the social sciences, they are neither visible nor concrete. A researcher will have to negotiate and re-negotiate with his/her 'collaborators' to define and re-define what constitutes risk. Therefore, the definitions are not set but evolve, and are shaped and re-shaped as the research activity progresses, because—unlike bio-medical research—social sciences' research is mostly inductive. Hence, vulnerability in social sciences' research involving humans is neither limited to research participants, nor to the issues of consent only. Research in the social sciences' disciplines is a multifaceted process where researchers 'pay' the price for conducting research—which is a 'moral enterprise' according to Vazir (2004), a social practice for Simons and Usher (2000), and a political process for Vithal (2008). As an enterprise/process, it involves both parties; the issues associated with vulnerability, according to Mitchell and Irvine (2008), 'have relevance for both participant and researcher well being and also have a number of ethical implications for both parties' (p. 32). However, the issues are little examined in the literature on research ethics in the social sciences.

Vulnerability Redefined for Social Sciences

Kipnis (2001), in his article entitled 'Vulnerability in research subjects: a bioethical taxonomy', has categorized different types of vulnerabilities. Although, like fellow researchers in bioethics, Kipnis has focused on the special circumstances of research participants' consent issues, with slight modification the defini-tion can accommodate other ethical concerns as well. Hence, I have adapted Kipnis's definition of vulnerabilities as those *special circumstances of a research context that call into question the efficacy of both parties in effecting the permissibility of research*. By deleting the 'C–S', (candidate–subject) and leaving out 'consent', the concept of vulnerability links up to the broader context in which the process of research unfolds. This broadening of the definition of vulnerability enlarges the ethical domain covered by the concept of vulnerability to accommodate not only the specificities of the stakeholders but of the research context as well, which is especially important for researchers working in the qualitative paradigm that is predominant in the social sciences disciplines. Unlike quantitative research studies (most prevalent in medical and natural sciences), the purpose of qualitative research studies is generally to understand the meaning of a person's or group's experiences, rather than to develop or contribute to generalizable knowledge. Hence, qualitative approaches to research are based on a 'world view' that is holistic and has the following beliefs: (i) there is not a single reality; (ii) reality is based upon perceptions that are different for each person, and these perceptions change over time; (iii) what we know has meaning only within a given context (Ross, 1999). The manner in which social scientists view reality provides the social research setting, with a broader physical as well as theoretical context, with multiple sources of vulnerabilities that can impact the stakeholders.

Roberts and Roberts (1999) have identified three kinds of vulnerabilities that may impair research participants' capacity to make informed choices in a particular research context. These are intrinsic vulnerability, extrinsic vulnerability, and relational vulnerability. Although Roberts and Roberts (1999) discuss these vulnerabilities for research participants with psychological illnesses, the logic of their argument can be extended to other groups as well (see Asif, 2010, for further discussion). For instance, an individual with mental or physical illness may lack personal competence, which will increase his/her intrinsic vulnerability. Likewise, an individual living in poverty and social deprivation may also lack personal competence, because of a lack of opportunities to develop it. Similarly, situations like confusion or coercion (real or perceived) will increase the extrinsic vulnerabilities of research participants with or without mental or psychological disorders. For researchers, pressures are implicit in their academic culture (e.g. publish or perish, acquire research grants to get promoted within a limited time period) that increase their extrinsic vulnerabilities. Furthermore, relations like that of captive populations expose individuals to relational vulnerabilities. For the purposes of the present chapter, I extend the discussion of the latter two types of vulnerabilities—extrinsic and relational—beyond individuals at two levels. First, the discussion of theoretical issues needs to be widened to cover the vulnerability of the context itself. The special circumstances of a developing context like Pakistan increase the extrinsic and relational constraints of such a context in the global discourse of knowledge (including research). The historical process of marginalization of the South, which still continues, should be part of the larger discourse on the ethics of vulnerability because, according to Holmes and Crossley (2004), the global discourse of knowledge still threatens the non-Western contexts as 'new forms of capitalism are increasingly colonizing the non-material worlds of knowledge, ideas and research' (p. 201). Hence, the extrinsic and relational vulnerabilities of the South, as a whole, need to be discussed in order to locate the vulnerabilities of researchers and research participants with reference to their practical issues (Qureshi, 2006). This is the second level of discussion, relating to the application of academic guidelines within the framework of research ethics that deal with the extrinsic and relational vulnerabilities of both parties (research participant and researcher) involved in a social research setting in a context like Pakistan.

The South: A Vulnerable Context

The legacy of colonialism and the impact of the rhetoric of modernization in the post-colonial era have been part of the special circumstances contributing to the marginalization of knowledge (research included) in the South. In the post-Second World War era, the notion that knowledge is not only a prerequisite for modernization but also a practical and intellectual resource for development was promoted by the North. As development in the name of modernization is a 'central myth of Western society' (Tucker, 1999, p. 4), which is rich in all meanings of the term, people living in non-Western cultures were perceived to be living in poverty including that of knowledge.

This impoverished image of non-Western contexts was created in the Marshall Plan—which was proposed by the USA to rehabilitate the war-devastated areas of Europe and 'other' parts of the world. Under this plan, the US Secretary of State, George Marshall, divided the world into 'developed' and 'underdeveloped' blocks of nations. The message, sent by this gesture, was that the 'backward' people of the undeveloped societies of Asia, Africa, and Latin America would learn from the superior culture and civilization of the 'developed' world (Bezanson, 2000). Hence, the whole post-colonial discourse of development surrounding the forms of knowledge, and of the production, reproduction, and usage of knowledge, was that of standardization which 'prioritize[s] Euro–American conceptions of research that can devalue much of the traditional knowledge and expertise that exists in the South' (Holmes and Crossley, 2004, p. 202). As societies in the South were 'living in conditions approaching misery' (Rist, 2002, p. 259), their socio-political status was frozen in the lowest ranks of the global system of social stratification because, under the modernization rhetoric, the non-Western contexts were labelled as backward, traditional, and non-rational (Tucker, 1999).

This division of the world into two blocks—developed and underdeveloped (or North and South, respectively)—had far reaching implications for the South. First and foremost, the very act of branding the non-Western contexts as backward embodied the power imbalance between the North and South. By stating 'we must embark on a bold new program for making the benefits of our scientific advances and industrial progress available for the improvement and growth of underdeveloped areas', US President Harry S. Truman (quoted in Rist, 2002, p. 259) communicated in the language of the early colonizers who considered it a 'white man's burden' to civilize the 'uncivilized' natives of Africa, Asia, and Latin America. Their crusades led to a long era of colonialism and the attendant destruction of native cultures (Ofori-Attah, 2006; Milligan, 2003; Esposito, 1999; Ntuli, 1999; Vakily, 1996). Although the post-Second World War era witnessed the formal end of colonialism, the essence of the relationship between the former colonial masters and the newly independent states did not change as the Euro–American alliance under the Marshall Plan unleashed a new wave of colonialism. The condescending mind-set of the North, that 'we should make available to peace-loving peoples the benefits of *our sum of technical knowledge* in order *to help them realize their aspirations* for a better life' (Truman, quoted in Rist, 2002, p. 259, emphasis added), was equally imperialistic. The flow of 'superior' technical knowledge from the North accentuated the contours of an ideological partition between the North and South. Over time, the local forms of knowledge were neglected and the production, reproduction, and usage of such knowledge were undermined (Chilisa, 2006).

Therefore, not only did the North create a socio-economic, and politico-ideological, split between the 'developed' North and the 'backward' South; it also denied the heterogeneity of the South's cultural experiences and realities 'under the rubric of "traditional society"' (Tucker, 1999, p. 4). The newly independent countries were struggling, in the post-colonial era, to regain or reformulate their lost identities: 'For instance, the struggle for what constitutes African philosophy, African literature and African religion, and the language argument are among the most burning issues that confront us' (Ntuli, 1999, p. 186). The issue of 'contesting identities' (Ntuli, 1999, p. 186) was not unique to Africa. The rich heritage of the Asian and Latin American colonies was also ignored, and even destroyed, during the process.

Contrived from the post-colonial global discourse on knowledge was the label, 'non-rational', for the South. The era was dominated by the kind of knowledge that, by Habermas's classification, would qualify 'as guided by a technical interest' (Carr, 1995 p. 12), because it was 'instrumental' and had a 'means-ends character' (ibid). The dominant research paradigm was also instrumental and rational which was, and is, especially favoured by the West (Tucker, 1999). This paradigm is believed to yield valid and reliable information that is scientific: 'Allegiance to "positivism" has been claimed to give the blessing of objectivity, hypothesis testing and verification, careful operationalization of concepts, testing and measurement pictured as leading to even-handed versions of truth' (Davies,

2002, pp. 4–5). Thus, research under this paradigm is considered to be designed to develop or contribute to universally accepted knowledge (Black, 1999; Maddock, 1997). This definition of research, by and large, rejects the kind of knowledge that is guided by a 'practical interest'—that is, 'an interest in guiding, informing and educating readers by interpreting the world and our understandings of it'(Carr, 1995 p. 12). Subsequently excluded are qualitative research approaches that make use of, and create, local knowledge that is considered un-scientific and thus 'less privileged' (Yanow, 2004). While it may be true that such an 'un-scientific' knowledge may not lend itself to universal generalizability, nonetheless, it does help in understanding the meanings of a person's or group's experiences. Such perceptive and 'thick descriptions' (Geertz, 1973) can only be generated by approaches to research that are based on a 'world view' that is holistic and has meanings only within a given context (Ross, 1999). Appreciation for such world views is especially important for understanding the social realities of developing countries that have been historically marginalized. However, not only did the North label the non-Western contexts as backward, traditional, and non-rational, but it also distorted the indigenous world views that were supported by local beliefs and practices (McKeever, 2000).

In such a milieu of lost knowledge and lost identities reflecting the legacy of colonialism and the impact of modernization rhetoric, not only does the integrity of the researcher come under the shadow of doubt, but so does the entire research process also becomes questionable. McKeever (2000) has very aptly described the perils of such a context: 'Conducting research in a postcolonial context can be like a game of snakes and ladders.

The only way to proceed is to cling to the ladders of the oppressed while trying to avoid the snakes of the colonial past.' (p. 101). The vulnerable position in which a researcher finds himself/herself is not because of intrinsic factors (such as his/her personal competence or extrinsic factors) but because of the subordinate status of his/her context in the global market. But, the inferiority of a Southern context is not limited to markets: 'Scientific inquiry, in its current form, is derived from the hard (imperialistic) sciences that are proclaimed to be the benchmark of academic rigor and trustworthiness' (Bhattacharya, 2007 p. 1109). The vulnerabilities of the researchers working in the South increase because of the academic culture's lack of confidence in the South's ability to produce authentic knowledge. The weak academic culture (perceived or real) undermines the trustworthiness of the meanings constructed, and the interpretations made, for any consequential knowledge production in that context.

The Ethics of Vulnerability in the South

The second level of discussion, on the ethics of vulnerability, involves the application of professional ethical standards to social science research settings within the above context. In the majority of cases, these professional standards are formulated in the North and do not match the ground realities of the South (see Qureshi, 2006; 2010, for further discussion). It is not my intention to deal with all the practical issues that confront researchers working in various social science disciplines for obvious reasons of space and because of the variety and enormity of issues involved also, these concerns have already been voiced by different researchers (Simons and Usher, 2000; Welland and

Pugsley, 2002; Bhattacharya, 2007; Shamim and Qureshi, 2010). I will select a few applications to illustrate the vulnerabilities of both the parties. For example, one of the requirements, for the ethical conduct of social science research, is that research participants be informed about the purpose and procedures of the research (Strike, Anderson, Curren, Geel, Pritchard and Robertson, 2002). In contexts like Pakistan, researchers find it difficult to share the purpose and procedures of research with participants who may not be able to grasp the real meaning of the activity—either because of no/low literacy or because of a weak research culture (see Qureshi, 2010, for further discussion). But, on the other hand, the researchers' inability may be partially attributed to the fact that Western language and terminologies dominate the discipline of research, making the meaning of research itself hard to explain. The professional standards that social scientists from the South are expected to follow, in order to be recognized as experts of their own context, are not home-grown; the global discourse on knowledge tends to marginalizes indigenous knowledge and alienates the South and the expertise residing in it. Also, the knowledge of the South, and from the South which is to be published in the North, has to be guided by the ethical guidelines of the North—based on Western values and norms. Often, these 'alien' professional standards become a pretext for violating research participants' right to information, thus increasing their extrinsic vulnerability. Not only does the infringement of research participants' right to information increase their extrinsic vulnerability, but it also has deep implica-tions for the enactment of other rights. For instance, informed consent becomes a token activity: if they did not have enough information, what did they consent to? Moreover, participants may be put at, or put themselves at, risk if they have not been given complete information about such aspects of the research; hence, research participants are more vulnerable by not having enough information.

Researchers are also vulnerable because of the procedural aspects of research, especially if it is a commissioned assignment (Pugsley, 2002). For instance, with limited time available for undertaking the research, researchers need to complete the formal procedures to get started and finished on time. Hence, implicit and explicit pressures to conform to, and perform according to, professional standards make them vulnerable in the context of an academic culture which may or may not be in line with the social culture of their research context. The researchers may have to tell participants 'half truths' which, according to a group of researchers, is 'not deception but just the right kind of information for participant(s) to understand the purpose of our activities if not the purpose of our research' (Qureshi, 2010).

Furthermore, the nuances of researchers' relational vulnerability have not been fully discussed in the literature on research ethics, and yet these have implications for the process of research in developing country contexts. For instance, McKeever (2000) in South Africa was vulnerable because of her race: 'The first question is whether I, as a white person, have any right to research black experience' (p. 102). The relational positions of researcher (part of the colonizer race) and researched (the subjugated population) threatened to undermine the epistemological stance of her research. By the same token, the authenticity of cross-cultural research studies is also undercut because of the hierarchical positions of the researchers and researched. Now, if the Northern discourse of research ethics and Western instruments are considered inadequate to capture the life experiences of the South, and if the researchers from the North are perceived to be unable to relate to Southern realities, then the horizontal relations do not make the situation simpler either because of the presence (perceived or actual) of 'subjectivity'. Can a researcher, distant from his/her research context and the meaning making activity taking place within that context, make any meaningful claims? And if such claim is made by him/her then whose meanings are we referring to?

In addition to the theoretical dimension of relational vulner-abilities for researchers, the practical side also needs to be considered in Pakistan and in similar contexts where the cultural codes governing human interactions are relational. Thus, the range of choices and the degrees of freedom available to researchers are determined by how they are introduced to community members, and what relational category/categories are assigned to them (Thapar-Bjorkert, 1999; Makkar, 2002; Ashraf, 2010). Asif (2010), herself from Multan, Pakistan, while conducting her research there became 'a "Multani researcher" who was familiar with the local cultural norms and was, therefore, expected to understand and respect the right of the research participants to behave in whatever way *they were* [emphasis added] comfortable with'. In order to accommodate her participants' comfort level, Asif had to alter her research plans. Similarly, Bhattacharya (2007), originally from India, describes her vulnerabilities as she explored the experiences of two Indian female graduate students in the US. The research participants, because of their 'trust' in their 'elder sister', would not 'do elaborate member checks . . ., read transcripts, and provide feedback . . .' (p. 1097). But, Bhattacharya, as a researcher, was worried because of the implications of this trust and sisterhood on the quality of her work:

> How might our relationship be affected if I insist on our formal agreement for academic rigor? Am I willing to sacrifice academic rigor for maintaining the blurred relationships of sisterhood, friendship, mentorship, and the researcher and researched? How else can academic rigor and trustworthiness be redefined when consenting, kinship relations and shared cultural understandings intersect in transnational feminist research? (p. 1098).

Similar experiences of constraints, posed by the insider/outsider status of researchers, have been shared by other researchers as well (from Pakistan, Pardhan, 2007; Shamim, 1993; Asif, 2010; from Kenya, Rarieya 2010; and Makkar, 2002, from Brazil). Common to all these experiences are the pressures on researchers to apply Northern professional standards of ethics to Southern social settings and the struggles involved in making ethical choices. However, more evidence from the field and the voices of the researchers (from the North and South, and bioethics and social science ethics alike) are suggesting reconsideration of the 'one size fits all' philosophy of the universal application of ethical guidelines (Fisher, 1997; Levine, 1996; Blue, 2000; Leaning, 2001; Resnik, 2004. Rhodes, 2005; Qureshi, 2010). In light of the theoretical concerns and practical evidence, the bioethics discourse may need modification when applied to social science research. I agree with the position taken by Bhattacharya (2007) against the application of 'a lens of universalized understanding' (p. 1108) to research, and (by implication) to the ethics of vulnerability in the South. My contribution to this point is that ethics, ethical guidelines, and ethical standards are part and parcel of what Blackburn (2001) calls 'the ethical environment' of a specific context. Hence, the nuances of the researchers' and research participants' vulnerabilities are embedded in their own contexts, and vary from context to context. While it is true that there are common ethical principles as well, the interpretation of these principles is not neutral or value free. To conclude, Bhattacharya (2007) offers an opposite summary:

Reducing the participant to universally agreeable categories would have been impossible. Whose knowledge do I use as a benchmark to set up anticipated agreements? To whom do I look to anticipate head nods? Whose science do I borrow? Whose science is 'legitimate science' for understanding the production and negotiation of the participants' experiences? Whom do I silence when I align with what is deemed scientific in current discourses that attempt to regulate ways of knowing? (p. 1108)

Conclusion

In this chapter, I have argued that the ethics of vulnerability in social science research needs to be problematized at three levels: (i) on a theoretical level, there are issues that arise from the clash between the discourses of bio-medical sciences and social sciences, as the former is imposed on the latter; (ii) on a historical level, problems emerge with the perception that the flow of knowledge is from North to South, as this promotes a concomitant subjugation of what the South has to offer in terms of knowledge; (iii) on a practical level, concerns surface because of the implications of theoretical issues and historical experiences for appropriate ethical procedures in research. I have also pointed out that evidence emerging from the North and South brings problems to light that are inherent in applying universal guidelines to social science research processes, as the interaction between the researcher and research participants occurs in a natural setting which is context bound. If the context makes research participants vulnerable in social science research, the danger exists for the researcher as well—as has been demonstrated by the documented voices of researchers from the South who also pay a price as they, too, are vulnerable.

Acknowledgement

I would like to thank my colleague, Ms Azra Naseem, for her critical feedback on the earlier draft of this chapter.

References

Ashraf, D. (2010). 'Using a feminist standpoint for researching women's lives in the rural mountain country in Pakistan.' In F. Shamim and R. Qureshi (Eds.), *Perils, pitfalls and reflexivity in qualitative research in education* (pp. 101–126). Karachi, Pakistan: Oxford University Press.

Asif, S. (2010). 'Obligations, roles, and rights: research ethics revisited.' In F. Shamim and R. Qureshi (Eds.), *Perils, pitfalls and reflexivity in qualitative research in education* (pp. 59–77). Karachi, Pakistan: Oxford University Press.

Bezanson, K. (2000). *The Development Decades in Encarta Encyclopedia.* Millennium Edition Microsoft.

Bhattacharya, K. (2007). 'Consenting to the consent form: what are the fixed and fluid understandings between the researcher and the researched?'. *Qualitative Inquiry*, 13(8), 1095–1115.

Blackburn, S. (2001). *Being good: a short introduction to ethics.* Oxford, UK: Oxford University Press.

Black, T. (1999). *Doing quantitative research in the social sciences: an integrated approach to research design, measurement and statistics.* London, UK: Sage.

Blue. I. (2000). 'Individual and contextual effects on mental health status in São Paulo, Brazil.' *Revista Brasileira de Psiquiatria*, 22(3), 116–123.

Brody, B.A. (1998). 'Research on the vulnerable sick.' In J.P. Kahn, A.C. Mastroianni and J. Sugarman (Eds.), *Beyond consent: seeking justice in research* (pp. 32–46). New York, NY: Oxford University Press.

Carr, W. (1995). *For education: towards critical educational inquiry.* Buckingham, UK: Open University Press.

Chilisa, B. (2006). 'Educational research within postcolonial Africa: a critique of HIV/AIDS research in Botswana.' *International Journal of Qualitative Studies in Education*, 18(6), 659–684.

Corbie-Smith, G. (1999). 'Continuing legacy of the Tuskegee syphilis study: considerations for clinical investigation.' *The American Journal of the Medical Sciences*, 317(1), 5–8.

Davies, B. (2002). 'Is action research good for you?'. In T. Welland, and L. Pugsley (Eds.). *Ethical dilemmas in qualitative research* (pp. 1–18). Farnham, UK: Ashgate Publishing.

Esposito, J. (1999). *The Islamic threat: myth or reality?* New York, NY: Oxford University Press.

DuBois, J.M. (2007). *Ethics in Mental Health Research, Principles, Guidance and Cases.* Oxford: Oxford University Press; New York.

Fisher, C.B. (1997). 'A relational perspective on ethics-in-science: decision making for research with vulnerable populations.' *IRB: Review of Human Subjects Research*, 19(5), 1–4.

Geertz, C. (1973). *The interpretation of culture.* New York, NY: Basic Books.

Grinnell, F. (2004). 'Subject vulnerability: the precautionary principle of human research.' *American Journal of Bioethics*, 4(3), 72–74.

Holmes, K., and Crossley, M. (2004). 'Whose knowledge, whose values? The contribution of local knowledge to education policy processes: a case study of research development initiatives in the small state of Saint Lucia.' *Compare*, 34(2), 197–214.

Hutton, J.L., Eccles, M.P., and Grimshaw, J.M. (2008). 'Ethical issues in implementation research: a discussion of the problems in achieving informed consent.' *Implementation Science*, 3(52), 1–8.

International Statistical Institute (1985). 'Declaration on professional ethics.' Retrieved on 18 March 2010 from http://isi. cbs. nl/ethics. htm.

Israel, M. (12 January 2005). 'Research hamstrung by ethics creep.' *The Australian (Higher Education Supplement,* 30.

Israel, M., and Hay, L. (2006). *Research ethics for social scientists.* Thousand Oaks, CA: Sage.

Kipnis, K. (2003). 'Seven vulnerabilities in the pediatric research subject.' *Theoretical Medicine,* 24, 107–120.

Kipnis, K. (2001). 'Vulnerability in research subjects: a bioethical taxonomy.' In National Bioethics Advisory Commission (Ed.), *Ethical and policy issues in research involving human research participants* (pp. G1-G13). Bethesda, MD: National Bioethics Advisory Commission.

Kipnis, K. (1979). 'Full Consent and the Legitimacy of Experimentation on Prisoners.' In L.T. Sargent, (Ed.), *Consent: concept, capacity, conditions, and constraints* (pp. 181–188). Wiesbaden, Germany: Franz Steiner Verlag.

Leaning, J. (2001). 'Ethics of research in refugee populations.' *The Lancet,* 357(9266), 1432–1433.

Levine, C., Faden, R., Grady, C., Hammerschmidt, D., Eckenwiler, L., and Sugarman, J. (2004). 'The limitations of vulnerability as a protection for human research participants.' *American Journal of Bioethics,* 4(3), 44–49.

Levine R.J. (1996). 'International codes and guidelines for research ethics: a critical appraisal.' In H.Y. Vanderpool HY (Ed.), *The ethics of research involving human subjects: facing the 21st Century* (pp. 253–59). Frederick, MD: University Publishing Group.

Maddock, T.H. (1997). 'Habermas, Carr and the possibility of a science of education.' *Interchange,* 28(2–3), 171–182.

Makkar, B.D. (2002). 'Roles and responsibilities in researching poor women in Brazil.' In T. Welland, and L. Pugsley (Eds.), *Ethical dilemmas in qualitative research* (pp. 75–93). Farnham, UK: Ashgate Publishing.

Malaspina, D., Corcoran, C., Kleinhaus, K.R., Perrin M.C., Fennig S., Nahon D., Friedlander Y., and Harlap, S. (2008). 'Acute maternal stress in pregnancy and schizophrenia in offspring: A cohort prospective study.' *BMC Psychiatry,* 8(1), 71.

McKeever, M. (2000). 'Snakes and ladders: ethical issues in conducting educational research in a postcolonial context.' In H. Simons and R. Usher

(Eds.), *Situated Ethics in Educational Research* (pp. 101–115). London, UK: Routledge.

Milligan, J.A. (2003). 'Teaching between the cross and the crescent moon: Islamic identity, postcoloniality and public education in the Southern Philippines.' *Comparative Education Review*, 47(4), 468–492.

Mitchell, W., and Irvine, A. (2008). 'I'm okay, you're okay? Reflections on the well-being and ethical requirements of researchers and research participants in conducting qualitative fieldwork interview.' *International Journal of Qualitative Methods*, 7(4), 31–44.

Mohr, M. (2001). 'Drafting ethical guidelines for teacher research in schools.' In J. Zeni (Ed.), *Ethical issues in practitioner research* (pp. 3–12). New York: Teachers College Press.

Nichol, G., Huszti, E., Rokosh, J., Dumbrell, A., McGowan, J., and Becker, L. (2004). 'Impact of informed consent requirements on cardiac arrest research in the United States: exception from consent or from research?'. *Resuscitation*, 62(1), 3–23.

Ntuli, P.P. (1999). 'The Missing Link between Culture and Education: Are We Still Chasing Gods that Are not Our Own?'. In M. Makoba (Ed.), *African renaissance: the new struggle* (pp. 184–199). Cape Town, South Africa: Mafube Publishing.

Ofori-Attah, K.D. (2006). 'The British and curriculum development in West Africa: a historical discourse.' *Review of Education*, 52(410–422).

Pardhan, A. (2007). 'Methodological issues and tensions: reflections on conducting ethnographic research with women in Booni valley, Chitral district, Pakistan.' In R. Qureshi and J. Rarieya (Eds.), *Gender and education in Pakistan* (pp. 237–256). Karachi, Pakistan: Oxford University Press.

Pugsley, L. (2002). 'Putting your oar in: moulding, muddling or meddling?'. In T. Welland, and L. Pugsley (Eds.). *Ethical dilemmas in qualitative research* (pp. 19–31). Farnham, UK: Ashgate Publishing.

Qureshi, R. (2010). 'Ethical standards and ethical environments: tensions and a way forward.' In Shamim, F. and Qureshi, R. (Eds.), *Perils, pitfalls and reflexivity in qualitative research in education* (pp. 78–100). Karachi, Pakistan: Oxford University Press.

Qureshi, R. (3–4 November 2006). 'Whose ethics? Global guidelines and local realities.' *Proceedings of the Multidisciplinary International Conference on Qualitative Research in Developing Countries: Opportunities and Challenges* (pp. 144–151). Karachi, Pakistan: University of Karachi.

Rarieya, F.A. (2010). 'Perils and pitfalls of qualitative research in developing countries: A Case from Kenya.' In F. Shamim and R. Qureshi (Eds.), *Perils, pitfalls and reflexivity in qualitative research in education* (pp. 127–147). Karachi, Pakistan: Oxford University Press.

Resnik, D. (2004). 'Research subjects in developing nations and vulnerability.' *American Journal of Bioethics*, 4(3), 63–64.

Rhodes, R. (2005). 'Rethinking research ethics.' *American Journal of Bioethics*, 5(1), 40–42.

Rist, G. (2002). *The History of development: from Western origins to global faith* (2 ed.). London, UK: Zed Books.

Roberts, L.W., and Roberts, B. (1999). 'Psychiatric research ethics: an overview of evolving guidelines and current ethical dilemmas in the study of mental illness.' *Biological Psychiatry*, 46(8), 1025–1038.

Ross, J. (1999). 'Ways of approaching research.' Retrieved 25 June 2009 from http://fortunecity.com/greenfield/grizzly/432/rra3. htm.

Schroeder, D., and Gefenas, E. (2009). 'Vulnerability: too vague and too broad?'. *Cambridge Quarterly of Healthcare Ethics*, 18, 113–121.

Shamim, F., and Qureshi, R. (Eds.). (2010). *Perils, pitfalls and reflexivity in qualitative research in education.* Karachi: Pakistan: Oxford University Press.

Shamim, F. (1993). Teacher-learner behaviour and classroom processes in large ESL classes in Pakistan. Unpublished PhD dissertation. Leeds, UK: University of Leeds.

Silvers, A. (2004). 'Historical vulnerability and special scrutiny: precautions against discrimination in medical research.' *American Journal of Bioethics*, 4(3), 56–57.

Simons H., and Usher, R. (Eds.). (2000). *Situated ethics in educational research.* London, UK: Routledge.

Strike, K.A., Anderson, M.S., Curren, R., Geel, T.V., Pritchard, I., and Robertson, E. (2002). *Ethical standards of the American Educational*

Research Association: cases and commentary. Washington, DC: American Educational Research Association.

Thapar-Bjorkert, S. (1999). 'Negotiating otherness: dilemmas for a non-Western researcher in the Indian subcontinent.' *Journal of Gender Studies*, 8(1), 57–69.

Thompson, R.A. (1992). 'Vulnerability in research: a developmental perspective on research risk.' In S. Chess, M.E. Hertzig, A. Thomas (Eds.), *Annual progress in child psychiatry and child development* (pp. 119–143). Philadelphia, PA: Psychology Press.

Tucker, V. (1999). 'The myth of development: a critique of a Eurocentric discourse.' In R. Munck and D. O'Hearn (Eds.), *Critical Development Theory* (pp. 1–26). London: Zed.

Vakily, A. (1996). 'The spiritual leadership, promotion of Shari'a and political movement in the Bantin revolt of 1888 in Indonesia.' *Muslim Education Quarterly*, 13(2), 61–67.

Vazir, N. (2004). 'Research ethics: significance, application, and obligation to the practice of research.' *Journal of Educational Research*, 7(1/2), 3–11.

Vithal, R. (3–4 December 2008). Research Methodologies in the 'South'. Keynote address at a Conference on 'Research Methodologies in the "South",' Karachi, Pakistan.

Welland, T. and Pugsley, L. (Eds.) (2002). *Ethical dilemmas in qualitative research*. Farnham, UK, Ashgate Publishing.

Wolff, H., Epiney, M., Lourenco, A., Costanza, M., Delieutraz-Marchand, J., Andreoli, N., Dubuisson, J.B., Gaspoz, JM., and Irion, O. (2008). 'Undocumented migrants lack access to pregnancy care and prevention.' *BMC Public Health*, 8(1), 93.

Yanow, D. (2004). 'Translating local knowledge at organizational peripheries.' *British Journal of Management*, 15(Supplement 1), S9-S25.

Notes

1. The Nuremberg Code of research ethics was formulated in August 1947. In June 1964, in Helsinki, it was expanded into the first declaration of The World Medical Association. This declaration has been revised in 1983, 1989, 1996, 2000, and 2008. In 1993, the Council for International

Organizations of Medical Sciences (CIOMS) created the CIOMS Guidelines, which were updated in 2002.

2. For instance, Kipnis, 1979; Thompson, 1992; Roberts and Roberts, 1999; Grinnell, 2004; Levine, Faden, Grady, Hammerschmidt, Eckenwiler and Sugarman, 2004; Resnik, 2004; Silvers, 2004; have all referred to circumstances where the ability of the research 'subjects' to freely give, or withhold, consent seems to be compromised. Others include: patients in general (Brody, 1998), minority patients (Corbie-Smith, 1999), subjects with life-threatening illnesses (Nichol, Huszti, Rokosh, Dumbrell, McGowan and Becker, 2004), patients with mental health problems (DuBois, 2007), pregnant women (Wolff, et al., 2008; Malaspina et al., 2008), and minors (Kipnis, 2003).

3. The interested reader is referred to papers from a seminar on Emerging Ethical Issues in Social Science and Cross-Cultural Research held at the University of Sussex, 5–6 May 2005, available at http://www. ncrm.ac.uk/ research/other/NMI/2005/www. sussex. ac. uk/soccul/1-3-2-3-1. html.

7

Ethnographic Field Methods in Research with Women: Field Experiences from Pakistan

Almina Pardhan

This chapter draws out key methodological issues with which I have struggled while using ethnographic field methods largely defined within the prevailing Northern academy in two studies related to women and education in the Southern context of Pakistan. Although girls' and women's education heads the list of government priorities in Pakistan, great gender disparities persist, resulting in girls and women being more disadvantaged. Furthermore, development contexts like Pakistan remain largely silent around the gendered nature of the ideologies, programmes, and processes in education (Stromquist, 1996).Through my research, I wanted to bring to the fore the complex issues faced by women as learners and teachers in Pakistan, in an attempt to explore the underlying processes that result in different patterns of gendered educational experiences. The first study, for my master's thesis, explored how the recent advent of schooling in the remote, mountainous, rural village of Booni Valley, Chitral District, Pakistan, is affecting women's lives (Pardhan, 1995). In my second study, I explored the lived experiences of women kindergarten (pre-primary) teachers in the urban context of Karachi, Pakistan, (Pardhan, 2009).

In line with prevailing standards of conducting research, much of the preparation for these two studies drew on research strategies described in qualitative books and articles predominantly informed by the Northern academy. There were moments, as I engaged in fieldwork in Pakistan, when the qualitative process was just as these books and articles had described. However, it was also much more. Negotiating codes and guidelines in the organization of indigenous societies, like Pakistan, took on a whole new set of meanings, with relatively little in the less dominant Southern academy to inform my experience (Dev Makker, 2002; Swadener and Mutua, 2007). I often found myself on a lonely journey, uncertainly navigating predicaments in diverse aspects of the research design that I encountered in the lived world of the rural and urban research sites of a Southern context. Added to this challenge were the limited accounts of other researchers, who may have encountered similar quandaries and from which I could draw both comfort and a sense of certainty to negotiate various dimensions of the fieldwork process. As the contextual issues impacted my research process in a fundamental way, the research methods and techniques required modification from those traditionally noted in literature. To this end, this chapter provides personal details of complex, messy, perplexing situations I encountered and negotiated in an attempt—to assist others facing similar predicaments. The qualitative tradition recognizes the peculiarities in fieldwork rooted in the researcher's position and researcher–participant relationships which constantly requires the engagement of reflexivity. My reflective account is, therefore, meant to inspire, rather than to serve as a universal formula, for others to reflect upon their intimate experiences navigating complex situations in similar contexts. This chapter marks an important contribution to the knowledge base by foregrounding and affirming indigenous epistemologies and ways of knowing in-field sites of the South that often remain masked within the dominant qualitative research traditions of the Northern academy.

The chapter begins with a brief overview of the research context in relation to women and education. I then discuss the influences that have guided my educational research with women in Pakistan, including my insider/outsider position. A brief overview of 'ethnography' and the 'ethnographic field methods' in my research with women in Pakistan, including the critical role of reflexivity, ensues. I then reflect upon the tensions of negotiating traditional research norms and practices within the codes and guidelines that organize the rural and urban research settings in the Southern context of Pakistan. In particular, I discuss complexities around selecting research sites, the intricate process of building relationships, and notions of research, particularly during the interview process. Although the chapter foregrounds research methods and methodological issues, excluding mention of my position as a female researcher in the visibly patriarchal context of Pakistan, rife with socio-political instability as well as ethical tensions, has been difficult. These issues and challenges during my fieldwork are, therefore, interwoven in discussing the research process. Finally, I bring the chapter to a close by highlighting the possibilities of using ethnographic field methods in educational research with rural and urban women in Pakistan, and the implications for policy and practice in diverse cultural settings. I also consider the broader relevance of notions related to research, space, and researcher–participant relationships in Southern contexts, like Pakistan, that differ from the mainly Northern contexts from which these are derived.

Context and Background

Pakistan's cultural fabric is characterized by a patriarchal organization of social institutions, including the family, school, and society. Gender segregation, with deep-rooted gender roles and expectations, and unequal gender power relationships are prevalent. Local variants of Islam in Pakistan usually lead to the adherence of strict rules regulating the behaviour of girls and women whose behaviour is linked to family honour (Ashraf, 2004). Men's roles are to be the producers, providers, and decision-makers. They occupy the outside-home spaces. Women occupy the household domain and have the roles of caregiving and domesticity. In rural contexts, like the remote, barren, mountainous region of Chitral District where I conducted my study, women's lives are complicated by harsh geographic conditions as well as their additional involvement in agricultural activities (Pardhan, 1995, 2007).

In education, gender disparity in resource allocation and enrolment, to the disadvantage of girls and women, is evident. Significant gaps between male and female, and urban and rural, literacy rates have persisted over the years (Farah and Shera, 2007). Of the approximately 8.61 million children in the three to five year age group, the net participation rate of pre-primary education was only 25 per cent, of which 31 per cent was male and 18 per cent was female (Ministry of Education, 2003).

Nationally, the net primary enrolment rate for boys is 71 per cent and for girls 62 per cent, with high dropout rates—particularly of girls—beyond primary school due to lack of opportunities, mobility issues, and cultural norms constraining girls' access to higher education, especially in the rural areas (Government of Pakistan, 2002). For example, in Chitral District, schooling for girls was unavailable prior to the 1980s largely due to gender norms. Most secondary schools are single sex, with parental preference to send their daughters to girls-only schools with women teachers[1] (Warwick and Reimers, 1995). A significant barrier to girls' education in rural communities is the difficulty of recruiting women teachers.

Pakistani women play an important role in the provision of pre-primary and primary education. Approximately 45 per cent of primary school teachers are women (Ministry of Education, 2007). In the public sector, primary teachers also teach pre-primary classes as no pre-primary teachers have been reported (Ministry of Education, 2007). Out of a total 3,405 private sector pre-primary teachers reported, 2,950 are women (Ministry of Education, 2007). Teaching pre-primary and primary is considered culturally appropriate and respectable for women. However, these teachers have little training and a low status, and are among the lowest paid and work in under-resourced classrooms. Private, English-medium schools, particularly in urban centres, are preferred for their relatively comfortable, conducive, and facilitative work environments compared to the under-resourced and run-down government schools and the hardship of the rural areas (Heward, 1999).

Gender and education, and the impact of women teachers, have been considered from the perspectives of achievement and enrolment. However, as yet there has been little discussion of the lived experiences of Pakistani girls and women and their daily negotiation of gender roles and identities in their schools, families, and communities (Kirk, 2003). Through my research, therefore, I wanted to bring to the fore the different and diverse dimensions of rural and urban women's lives, to better understand their specific educational experiences.

My desire to engage in qualitative research with women in Pakistan required the process of forming relationships with the participants within the ideological framework of the context. This reality impacted the research process in both studies in fundamental ways. In particular, it necessitated a modification of the research methods, rooted in the dominant discourse of the Northern academy around qualitative research, that had formed a large part of my thinking prior to entering the field.

Ethnographic Field Methods

Both my studies involved long-term immersion in the field. collecting data using in-depth interviews and participant observation with women in Pakistan. Employing these field methods—which are drawn from the ethnographic tradition of attempting to understand how people within a cultural group construct and share meaning—was empowering for the participants. In Southern contexts, like Pakistan, numbers are often used within educational policy and planning to discuss gender issues related to educational access, retention, and achievement. These numbers largely dilute the intensity of issues and mask the plight of women who remain largely vulnerable, disadvantaged, and unheard. My two studies, employing ethnographic field methods, provided women with space to voice their experiences and to share the daily negotiations of their identities, roles, and responsibilities in socio-cultural settings that often silence them (Fetterman, 1998).

Nevertheless, the process of using ethnographic field methods to gain insight into the rural and urban participants' experiences gave rise to a quagmire of complexities while navigating the organization of the indigenous rural and urban cultures of a Southern context. Contemporary ethnographic discourse, drawing predominantly on a Northern perspective, recognizes the partial, subjective nature of the research experience, and the influence of the role of power and authority. Yet, the hegemonic arrangements of this tradition remain, for the most part, silent about the ambiguities of the research enterprise, not least in the way power issues and subjectivity are played out in Southern contexts like Pakistan. In such contexts, prevailing constructions of knowledge, around the research process, call for alternate forms of production. The remaining sections consider this, in relation to an explicit reflection of my experiences confronting issues during fieldwork, within the ideological frameworks of rural and urban settings in Pakistan.

Engaging in Reflexivity through the Use of Ethnographic Field Methods with Women in Pakistan

Engaging in reflexivity was critical to the research process related to women and education in Pakistan. Reflexivity allowed me to make sense of my field experiences in a Southern context, where traditional documented ways of engagement in research are often rendered problematic and perplexing within indigenous values and norms. I was conscious of my location in a complex, and often contradictory, history that has influenced what I want to study and has guided and constrained the research process (Denzin and Lincoln, 2000).

My educational research, exploring the lives of women in Pakistan, intersects with my life in multiple ways. I am a Shia Ismaili Muslim immigrant of South Asian origin, born in Kenya. Much of my life has been spent in Canada, where I have pursued my education (including at the master's and doctoral levels) and my professional life as a teacher. Currently, I am professionally located in Pakistan, as a teacher-educator and educational researcher in the areas of early childhood education and gender. Nevertheless, I constantly travel within various countries.

The values underlying my scholarship are deeply rooted in the strong emphasis placed by my family and religious community on education and service to humanity, particularly to help and support the needy to live a dignified life. My travels to the Northern Areas of Pakistan. a cultural environment geographically and culturally close to Chitral District, nearly 18 years ago sparked my interest in researching women, development, and education in Pakistan. I grappled with the idea of girls' schooling. which was a relatively recent phenomenon in the region. and was moved by the women's courage who were attending schools while having to deal with such impoverished socio-economic conditions as well as such a challenging topographical and geographical environment. Through my master's research in Chitral District, I was keen to make the women's lives and experiences central by exploring how schooling was affecting them in relation to family roles, gender relationships, work, and long-held cultural values. Building on this in my doctoral work, I chose to explore the gendered life experiences and teaching practices of female urban pre-primary teachers based on my current work and research into early childhood education at a private university in Karachi, Pakistan.

The geographical, cultural, religious, racial, ethnic, linguistic, and class borders that I have crossed gave me particular perspectives on the experiences of women in the rural and urban contexts of Pakistan (Rarieya, 2007). I was aware that the representation I was making, of the women, was also a product of my interpretation. Reflexivity was, therefore, critical throughout my research, in exploring the dynamics between the participants and me, as we all came to these studies with our own multiple identities (Glesne, 2006; Rarieya, 2007; Young, 2003). I acknowledge the biases, values, and interests that I have brought to these studies. I believe that these have led to the multiple perspectives that have emerged from my research into understanding the experiences of women and education in the rural and urban contexts of Pakistan (Creswell, 2003; Rarieya, 2007).

The following sections describe the methodological issues employed in selecting research sites, and in building relationships in the studies with the rural and urban women in Pakistan. Highlighted, as well, are the implications of the constant tension negotiating my insider and outsider positions.

Selecting the Research Sites

Books on research often address the process of selecting research sites, and acknowledge that sound decision making is required for site selection even though there is no list of rules to guide these decisions (Glesne, 2006; Patton, 2002). Less attention is paid to the on-going sensitive considerations of making these decisions within the socio-cultural norms of settings in Southern contexts, like Pakistan, which are themselves so diverse. I, therefore, attempt to bring to the fore the complexities and considerations of approaching site selection during my two studies in Pakistan.

Considerations for Study 1: Exploring Women's Experiences of Schooling and Work in Booni Valley

Having limited experience in Pakistan, I relied on the support of the Aga Khan Education Services, Pakistan (AKES-P)—a non-government organization that has played a significant role in establishing schools (particularly for girls)—to select the research site for my study with rural women. My selection of Chitral District, as the research site, was largely driven by the organization's interest in the potential of such a study for its own purposes. Chitral District is a region where, until the 1980s, girls' access to school was extremely limited. Prior to my study, no research to explore the women's own perspectives about their educational and work experiences had been conducted in this region. Though I had never been to the Chitral District, I learned that this region is less developed than the Northern Areas that I had previously visited. Poor infrastructure, treacherous mountain roads, limited amenities, a region that remains cut-off from the rest of the country during the winter months,[2] and an environment that hardly favours women, would render fieldwork in this context complex and challenging. While I felt daunted, as a young woman—who had virtually no familial commitments—just embarking upon her career in academia, I was also excited to take the opportunity to carry out fieldwork in such a rugged, rustic context. I had not envisioned the significant impact that gender norms and socio-political structures within this context would have upon my study. Upon arriving in Chitral District, and during discussions with the AKES–P staff, the impact that my own gender would have on my research gradually began to dawn on me. Being a woman, the choices available to me for data collection would be limited; my mobility would be restricted culturally, geographically, educationally, politically, and linguistically (Pardhan, 2007). Within the prevailing gender norms of the context, I would require a male escort to accompany me while travelling from one village to another. Geographically, my mobility would be difficult. The roads connecting villages are poorly developed and landslides are not uncommon. In some villages, as well, girls' schooling was not yet available. This period in Pakistan's history was also characterized by political tensions, particularly between the two dominant religious groups in the region—Sunni Muslims and Shia Ismaili Muslims. As a Shia Ismaili Muslim from outside the district, it was critical to consider my security. As the advent of schooling was very recent, there were very few women who spoke English and could provide translation support, as I did not know the local language, Khowar. Booni Valley was one of the few villages that, therefore, seemed conducive to conducting research from a cultural, geographical, educational, linguistic, and political perspective. There was a woman in this village who spoke English and who was well-respected in the community through her involvement with women's issues in Chitral District; she would be my research collaborator, providing support with translation, locating participants, and understanding the local culture. In the village, there was a girl's hostel where I could stay comfortably and safely, and girls' schooling was available. Although both Sunni Muslims and Shia Ismaili Muslims live in this village, the AKES–P staff assured me that the two sects, for the most part, lived side-by-side in relative peace in this part of Chitral District. Conducting research in this village would also provide deeper insight into the gender experiences of women in this region from both religious sects.

Considerations for Study 2: Exploring the Gendered Life Histories and Teaching Practices of Women Kindergarten Teachers in Karachi

My fieldwork experience, dealing with contextual tensions in the remote mountainous valley of northern Pakistan, greatly facilitated the research process for my subsequent study exploring the experiences of women kindergarten teachers (Pardhan, 1995, 2007). While my first choice of research site was to return to Chitral District, and build upon my previous research, I chose to conduct research in a school in the city of Karachi, primarily for logistical reasons. I have been living and working in Karachi for the past few years and this is where my family currently resides. As a mother of two children in their pre-primary years, I hesitated to carry out research in the highly gender-segregated and harsh geographical region of Chitral. My multi-layered research design required my being in the school research site for one academic year; taking my very young children to Chitral would be difficult, as would being away from them for such a long period. In the Pakistani context, where the research culture is in its infancy, I was aware that conducting my study in a school affiliated with the private university where I was working would be easier; as a 'cooperating school', it would have a close partnership with the university. Moreover, the school would also be familiar with classroom and school-based research and, therefore, be more likely to lend its support to my study. My previous contact with a school, as a member of the faculty of this private university, would also be important to facilitate the research process. Conducting research with female teachers in urban private schools was also of interest to me, given the limited research about their experiences (Kirk, 2003). My research questions also required that the school have a co-educational kindergarten setting, that is, girls and boys learning together. Another important consideration was language. At the time, I had limited fluency in Urdu—the language most commonly used in Karachi—so it was critical that the school be English-medium. In my study with rural women, I felt that I had missed out on valuable information that had been lost through the translation process. The unpredictable and volatile socio-political climate of the country was also a consideration, in terms of neighbourhood security and unexpected school closures. I selected Rainbow School (a pseudonym) as my research site because it fitted my parameters for a research site. It is an urban, private, English-medium school, located in a relatively safe area of Karachi, and is affiliated with the private university. It educates boys and girls together until class five, and also has a pre-primary section.

I was aware that, in my two studies with women, there would be issues of representativeness based on my selection of research sites, but my choices were limited. Thus, I knew that in both studies, the women's experiences that I would gather would be specific only to the rural women of Booni Valley in my first study, and to the urban female kindergarten teachers of Rainbow School in the second study.

Negotiating an Intricate Web of Relations with Research Participants

The development of researcher–participant relationships is critical to the entire data collection process. According to Darling and Scott (2002), this relationship is subject to continuous negotiation that extends to the participants' trust in the researcher at every stage of the process. What it is critical to fore-ground in Southern contexts like Pakistan, where the research culture is gradually emerging, are the intricacies of positioning one's researcher-self and how one is positioned as a researcher in the web of relations within an indigenous research setting. I entered into the field with multiple identities: woman; researcher; teacher; teacher-educator; doctoral student; wife; mother; woman in an extended family; Ismaili Muslim; and Canadian with South Asian cultural heritage. All of these identities had an impact on the whole process of my interaction with the female participants who had their own multiple identities. I was deeply aware of my subjectivity, and of paying particular attention to aspects of power and ethics, during the fieldwork as I began relationships and as these relationships evolved.

Beginning Relationships

Throughout the research process, I negotiated an intricate web of relations with both the rural and urban women participating in my research. Building relationships with the research partici-pants, in both studies, was a hierarchical process, mainly through acquaintanceship and within the norms of the context. This was an important consideration in planning and accessing the research sites. I was particularly concerned about not causing any harm to my research participants by contacting them directly.

As I familiarized myself with the culture in Booni Valley, I realized that it would be difficult for me, independently, to select the research participants. As a woman, I faced cultural limitations in not being able to move freely in the community. As such, my research collaborator's networks became mine. I was aware that this would introduce an element of bias, not unknown to me as a researcher, but because of my gender and the prevailing cultural norms, I had no choice (Pardhan, 2007). Within the norms of this patriarchal context, contacting potential research participants also had to be carried out in a culturally sensitive manner. Although my research collaborator had been to school and was very active in the community, her mobility in the village was restricted by gender norms. We needed to rely on a male escort to move about the village. In many instances, one of my research collaborator's male colleagues also visited homes to explain the nature of my study to the men of the households and to seek their permission for me to interview the women. Once permission was received, my research collaborator and I would be escorted, by a male, to the women's homes for the interviews. This process of negotiation within the existing cultural norms required much patience. Moreover, it was both stressful and insightful, resulting in constant reflection about entering into and sustaining ethically acceptable research relationships with the women. Reflexivity was critical to ensure that no harm befell the women research participants, as well as the viability of the research process.

During my study with female urban kindergarten teachers, I also had to rely upon networks within the academic community to facilitate building relationships with potential research participants. Most schools are hierarchical in nature. Many individuals (principals/head teachers, coordinators) possess authority at different levels above the teachers, who are normally at the bottom of the hierarchy. The principal, at Rainbow School, was the first entry point into the school. Once she gave her consent, further negotiations for my research also had to be made with additional gatekeepers in the school hierarchy. In line with the experiences described by Burgess (1984), I quickly realized that the multi-layered research design of my study, which necessitated my presence in the field for an extended period, would require that I negotiate and re-negotiate my presence at the school until I left the research setting. This negotiation continued at different levels, with different gate-keepers, and with all of my research participants. It was important to respect the involvement of the research participants at the various levels in my study. I always negotiated the interview and observation schedule with the participants ahead of time.

Both experiences led me to question the pressure that the research participants might have felt to participate in my research studies. In this patriarchal context, much of the decision-making, including that concerning women's lives, is done by male family members and is upheld with little, if any, question. Did the women in Booni Valley feel compelled to participate in my study? Did the female kindergarten teachers in Karachi feel obliged to participate, given the prevailing norms of respect for authority in the school hierarchy? While it never emerged explicitly during the course of my fieldwork, I often wondered how many of these female kindergarten teachers may have also sought permission from their husbands and/or extended family members—within the prevailing cultural norms—to participate in my research. These situations, and many others that I would encounter during my fieldwork, posed dilemmas for me. It was important that I respect the ethical considerations of my university and the general social science community; at the same time, I also had to respect the local standards of conduct and ethics (Dev Makkar, 2002; Heath, Charles, Crow and Wiles, 2007). Practically, these considerations often became blurred (Dev Makkar, 2002).

Evolving Relationships—The Interview Process

In both studies, the interview process involved multiple negotiations and allowed for the reconstruction and interpretation of subjectively meaningful features and critical episodes in individual lives (Denzin, 1989). Throughout the research process, I wondered how the research participants placed me in their web of relations in a context where there is little, if any, notion of research.

Many of the research participants in Booni Valley had never been to school or had limited schooling. Having never left their village, it was difficult for them to have a geographic sense of 'Canada', let alone understand the concept of research and a thesis. I would explain that I was going to write a 'book' about their experiences. With the advent of schooling, the community placed great importance and value on education, in a manner that reflected an undervaluing of the significant roles of farming, agricultural, and domestic contributions. I perceived a sense of reverence, on the women's part, for my educational status and their bewilderment at why an 'educated' person like me would have any interest in their experiences. They felt that they had nothing of value to contribute to the study because they had never been to school or had limited schooling. In this culture, where most major decision-making is done by men and women are encouraged to say very little (Belenky, Clinchy, Goldberger and Tarule, 1986), some women wanted the male members of the household to speak on their behalf. I attempted to reassure the women that their life experiences and contributions to their families and communities were of great value and that their insights would be very important to the project. Furthermore, I explained that I wanted to hear about their lives and what was important to them, from their point of view, as women are rarely given such opportunities to share their experiences (Belenky et al., 1986). My research collaborator played an important role in facilitating the participants' confidence in the value, to the research, of their experiences in their own voices. Nevertheless, I was never certain of the extent to which the women participating in my studies felt completely at ease and comfortable.

During the interview process, the issue of language created many tensions in building relationships, particularly with the research participants in Booni Valley. Although I had a questionnaire to guide me during the unstructured ethnographic interviews, I wanted the women's stories to evolve. Not knowing the language, there were moments when I felt that I was missing out on valuable information as the women's stories unfolded. Often during interviews, a question or a probe that I asked would be translated—resulting in the research collaborator and research participants engaging in a lengthy conversation about common experiences and relationships. When I inquired what they were talking about, the research collaborator would explain that it was not related to the study. It was difficult for me to explain to her 'the interest that small details represent for (such) research, in the way they reflect the women's subjectivities' (Thapar-Bjorkert, 1999, p. 60). I had to be sensitive, patient, and trusting of the situation. Nevertheless, I felt that I had to cede power in how I directed the research and built relationships with the research participants. My research collaborator was aware of the cultural context and, thus, was at an advantage.

During my second study with female urban kindergarten teachers, I used semi-structured life history interviews—which allowed me both to probe deeply and to pick up on the topics and issues that the research participants initiated (Bogdan and Biklen, 1998). The interviews were mainly conducted in English; at times, the research participants switched to Urdu if they felt unable to express themselves in a meaningful way in English. Because most of the interviews were audiotaped, I could check the Urdu meanings later. Moreover, I felt that I had enough understanding of Urdu to make sense of what the teachers said within the context of the interview discussion. I also knew that I could ask them for clarification if I did not understand. For the most part, I found my primary role to be that of 'effective listener'. Intense concentration was required to keep track of the nuances of the teachers' stories and of the various relatives and other individuals, particularly within their extended family networks, who have played a role in their lives. I also had to keep track of different episodes in the women's lives and how they connected to each other. There were moments when I was uncertain about when and how to probe for more detail—to clarify a point or to return to the focus if I felt that we had gone away from the topic. The extreme heat in Karachi, particularly during the first, and some of the second, set of interviews, added to the challenge of remaining focused and alert.[3]

The in-depth interviews exploring the participants' life experiences since childhood left me feeling quite overwhelmed with the level of disclosure. Some interviews also left me feeling emotionally unsettled. I felt like a 'counsellor' listening to the women express pent-up feelings of frustration, pain, anger, and loneliness. Two research participants mentioned that they had shared, with me, experiences about which no one except a few family members were aware. The participants' comfort with the interview process left me pleased, though uncertain at times about handling my researcher role. The interview process seemed 'cathartic' for them. Consequently, I often felt torn between allowing them to continue speaking about experiences I sensed they needed to voice, and bringing them back to the research agenda. The teachers mentioned feeling better and lighter after each interview, and lamented having few such individuals in their lives with whom they could interact. Many of the teachers were often reluctant for an interview to end; I was conscious about having to remind them when our agreed time was about to end.

These experiences led me to question how a researcher can reconcile the various identities the research participants perceive her to have, particularly in a context where people have little concept of what research means or involves. Where did the participants place me in their web of relations? At what point was my researcher role visible and/or invisible? There were moments when I felt quite burdened with the kind of information being shared with me. In many respects, they had placed themselves in a vulnerable position, which I had to handle sensitively and ethically, particularly during data interpretation and representation. In retrospect, I wonder if a similar situation might have arisen during my interviews with the women in Booni Valley had I been able to understand and speak Khowar— the local language of Chitral. Had these women's lengthy conversations with my research collaborator been a 'cathartic' experience for them? Like the women in Booni Valley, the kindergarten teachers often asked whether their stories would be of any value to my study. I acknowledged the worth of their life experiences, inviting them to celebrate their worthiness as women in an attempt to demystify the prevailing myth of the deficit model of women (Acker, 1994). I would express my gratitude to them for sharing their experiences, which would make valuable contributions. This seemed to reassure and comfort them.

The interview process led me to experience, and deal with, a range of emotions. Some of the women's experiences resonated with my own experiences as a Muslim woman, with a South Asian ancestral heritage, currently living and working in Pakistan. Some of their experiences left me awed at the strength and courage they demonstrated living in the visibly patriarchal context of Pakistan. I pondered over the support a researcher might require to deal with her or his own emotions after an interview. But, more importantly, it left me wondering about the support the research participants might require in dealing with pent-up emotions, feelings, and memories of experiences that they had brought to the surface and voiced during an interview. As much as I was obliged to promise minimal risk to the participants, as a result of participating in this research, I realized that it was very difficult to enter into this kind of agreement with them (Rarieya, 2007). Moreover, while attempts to build rapport with the participants appeared to be successful, and I was able to gather rich, insightful data, I remained sensitive to the importance of interpreting and representing the research participants' experiences in an ethical manner.

Insider/Outsider Status in Building Relationships

Both studies with women in Pakistan presented continuous shifts in terms of how the research participants perceived me. There were moments when I experienced a sense of 'belonging', or being an 'insider', particularly as a woman and sharing a similar religious (i.e. Muslim) and cultural (i.e. South Asian) heritage. At other times, I was also confronted with the challenge of negotiating my 'otherness', or being an 'outsider'. My Canadian education—including my master's and doctoral studies—and my work experiences contributed to the participants' views of my privileged position. During my doctoral studies, for example, this became particularly uncomfortable when participants older than me referred to me as an 'expert' and wanted to learn more from me. In our shared cultural experience, respect for elders and their wisdom through their life experiences is paramount. I was cautious about not offering advice to my participants unless it was asked for. My suggestions and thoughts were always prefaced by my mentioning that what I was sharing might or might not be in line with the established policies and practices at their school. Moreover, it was not my place to interfere in such matters nor did I want to do that. I was grateful for the school's cooperation with my study, and did not want to cause any tension between the administration and the teachers in the way they planned and taught. My identity as a Muslim woman, teacher, mother, wife, daughter, and daughter-in-law with South Asian ancestral heritage, living and working in Pakistan, enhanced my role as researcher. Sharing common interests and experiences facilitated the building of relationships of trust with the women kindergarten teachers: food; clothing; raising and educating our children; furthering our professional development; being effective and contributing members of the community and of our families; religious festivals; contextual concerns like the intense heat, electricity and water problems, and heavy traffic in the city due to construction, as well as common illnesses.

The women in Booni Valley often compared their lifestyle with their perception of my lifestyle, mentioning that they 'were not like me'. They viewed themselves as 'dirty' because they work with 'cattle', and perceived me to be 'clean' because I had been to school and could 'sit', 'read', and live a 'clean life'. Such comparisons were awkward for me, and though I would tell them that their work was valuable and important for their families and communities, I wondered how much this actually changed how they felt about themselves. While most of these women wanted to relate to me as a Muslim first, my being Canadian with South Asian ancestral heritage was intriguing (Pardhan, 2007). They were awed that my family would allow me, a young unmarried woman, to travel alone to Chitral from Canada as, in their cultural context, women's mobility, particularly if they are not yet married, is restricted. Their initial impression, from my South Asian features, was that I was Pakistani. I faced the challenge of trying to explain my multiple identities, spanning diverse geographical contexts, to them—which, from their frame of reference, was difficult to comprehend. This complicated the process of building a relationship of trust and understanding.

Moreover, they were bewildered as to why a woman from Canada would be interested in Chitrali women's experiences. Nevertheless, they felt honoured that I would visit them and listen to their experiences in their homes. As our culture is known for its hospitality and the value placed on guests in our homes, I had to be sensitive to this—in the rural context—where financial resources are limited. Ultimately, I feel that my shared experience as a Muslim, and as a woman, transcended many apparent differences between the research participants and myself. Furthermore, my research collaborator's respected status in the community facilitated the process of building relationships of trust with the women.

Occasionally, I shared my own life experiences and turning points with the research participants, complying with the principle of 'reciprocity in research' (Glesne, 2006). I usually shared these experiences if the participants inquired about them. I also sensed that sharing my own stories was appropriate in certain instances. With the female kindergarten teachers, this generally happened after I had spent some time in the field and had developed a relationship with them. Talking about my own experiences was important, in building a relationship of trust with the participants, and made me more genuine in their eyes. It was also an attempt to eliminate power patterns between us. Nevertheless, I was always careful about the way in which I spoke of my experiences. I was concerned that my stories might influence the way the women responded to, or viewed, me. I was also constantly aware of the position of privilege they perceived me to have as a Canadian woman with Western education.

Conclusion

In this chapter, I have attempted to provide an overview of the tensions—using ethnographic field methods defined within the prevailing Northern academy—in two studies with rural and urban women in the Southern context of Pakistan, where significant gender disparities persist in education. Ethnographic field methods were critical in studying these women's experiences in a developing context where an educational/social research culture is in its infancy and where women are rarely studied or provided with space to voice their issues. Ethnographic field methods created the possibility of going beyond the numbers often used within educational policy and planning, to unveil the complexity of gender ideologies and processes in education experienced by the rural and urban women in my studies. Their voices and actions were placed in their broader educational, social, geographical, religious, economic, cultural, and historical contexts to better comprehend their specific experiences.

Nevertheless, my research with rural and urban women in the Southern context of Pakistan has also highlighted the complexity of research sites and research relationships, which are often problematic to articulate and which tend to remain under-examined in academia. Navigating the research process within the social, political, cultural, economic, educational, and gendered frameworks in rural and urban settings of Pakistan required modification of the research methods and techniques traditionally found in literature. My being a female researcher, as well as my insider/outsider status, were critical to the constant negotiation and re-negotiation during the research process. As this chapter highlights, this was particularly evident in relation to the notion of research, space, and building of relationships in the visibly patriarchal context of Pakistan. While no universal formula can be applied to negotiating the subjective and complex labyrinth of meanings in field work, this chapter has provided a reflective account to assist others encountering similar quandaries.

My experiences, using ethnographic field methods, have brought home the complexity of the research process in Southern contexts like Pakistan, where current hegemonic research traditions cannot be transferred piecemeal. Crossing geographical borders has immense potential for developing educational insights. Nevertheless, it is also critical to reflect on, and carry forward, the sensitive considerations of ideological frameworks in diverse research settings, which entail alternate approaches to research processes. As Swadener and Mutua (2007) write, 'particular culturally framed genres of research and methodology are necessary and should reflect indigenous epistemologies, languages, and expressive forms in relevant ways' (p. 202). My field experiences also point to the importance of foregrounding deliberations over ethics in fieldwork—ones that consider and respect social relations and practices in diverse cultural contexts of Southern contexts to ensure participant well-being. This, therefore, entails a conscious and continuous examination of gaps in the current traditions of carrying out research, to reflect the complexity of the research process when considering indigenous ways of knowing. Recognizing these complexities in specific local enactments, which can draw from a substantial diverse body of global knowledge, increases the possibility of relevant and more comprehensive constructions of knowledge.

References

Acker, S. (1994). *Gendered education: sociological reflections on women, teaching and feminism*. Toronto, ON: OISE Press.

Ashraf, D. (2004). *Experiences of women teachers in the Northern Areas of Pakistan*. Unpublished Ph.D. dissertation, Toronto, Canada: University of Toronto.

Belenky, M.F., Clinchy, B.M., Goldberger, N.R., and Tarule, J.M. (1986). *Women's ways of knowing: the development of self, voice, and mind*. New York, NY: Basic Books.

Bogdan, R.C., and Biklen, S.K. (1998).*Qualitative research in education: An Introduction to Theory and Methods* (3rd ed.). Boston, MA: Allyn and Bacon.

Burgess, R.G. (1984). *In field: an introduction to field research*. London, UK: George, Allen and Unwin.

Creswell, J.W. (2003). *Research design: qualitative, quantitative and mixed approaches* (2 ed.). Thousand Oaks, CA: Sage Publications.

Darling, Y., and Scott, D. (2002).*Qualitative research in practice, stories from the field*. Buckingham, UK: Open University Press.

Denzin, N.K. (1989). *The research act: A theoretical introduction to sociological methods*. Englewood Cliffs, NJ: Prentice Hall.

Denzin N.K., and Lincoln, Y.S. (2000). 'The discipline and practice of qualitative research.' In N. Denzin and Y. Lincoln (Eds.), *Handbook of qualitative research* (2nd ed.) (pp. 1–28). Thousand Oaks, CA: Sage Publications.

Dev Makkar, B. (2002). 'Roles and responsibilities in researching poor women in Brazil.' In T. Welland and L. Pugsley (Eds.), *Ethical dilemmas in qualitative research* (pp. 75–93). Hants, England: Ashgate Publishing Limited.

Farah, I., and Shera, S. (2007). 'Female education in Pakistan: a review.' In R. Qureshi and J. Rarieya (Eds.), *Gender and education in Pakistan* (pp. 3–40). Karachi, Pakistan: Oxford University Press.

Fetterman, D.M. (1998). *Ethnography: step by step* (2nd ed.). Thousand Oaks, CA: Sage Publications.

Glesne, C. (2006). *Becoming qualitative researchers: An introduction* (3rd ed.). Boston, MA: Pearson Education, Inc.

Government of Pakistan. (2002). *National policy for development and empowerment of women.* Ministry of Women Development, Social Welfare and Special Education, Islamabad, Pakistan.

Heath, S., Charles, V., Crow, G., and Wiles, R. (2007). 'Informed consent, gatekeepers and go-betweens: negotiating consent in child- and youth-orientated institutions.' *British Educational Research Journal*, 33(3), 403–417.

Heward, C. (1999). 'Introduction: The new discourses of gender, education and development.' In C. Heward and S. Bunwaree (Eds.), *Gender, education and development: beyond access to empowerment* (pp. 1–14). London, UK: Zed Books.

Kirk, J. (2003). *Impossible fictions? Reflexivity as methodology for studying women teachers' lives in development contexts.* Unpublished Ph.D. thesis, Montreal, Canada: McGill University.

Ministry of Education. (2003). *National Plan of Action on Education for All (2001–2015) Pakistan.* Islamabad, Pakistan: Government of Pakistan.

Ministry of Education. (2007). *National curriculum for early childhood education* (Revised). Islamabad, Pakistan: Government of Pakistan.

Pardhan, A. (1995). *Women, schooling and work in Booni Valley, Pakistan: Chitrali Muslim women's perceptions.* Unpublished master's thesis, Edmonton, AB: University of Alberta.

Pardhan, A. (2007). 'Methodological issues and tensions: reflections of conducting ethnographic research with women in Booni Valley, Chitral District, Pakistan.' In J. Rareiya and R. Qureshi (Eds.), *Gender and education in Pakistan* (pp. 237–256), Karachi, Pakistan: Oxford University Press.

Pardhan, A. (2009). *Women kindergarten teachers in Pakistan: their lives, their classroom practice.* Unpublished Ph.D. thesis, Toronto, Canada: University of Toronto.

Patton, M.Q. (2002). *Qualitative Research and Evaluation Methods* (3rd ed.). Thousand Oaks, CA: Sage Publications.

Rarieya, J. (2007). *School leadership in Kenya: the lived realities of women heads of schools.* Unpublished Ph.D. thesis, Keele, UK: University of Keele.

Stromquist, N. (1996). 'Gender delusions and exclusions in the democratization of schooling in Latin America.' *Comparative Education Review*, 40(4), 404–425.

Swadener, B.B., and Mutua, K. (2007). 'Decolonizing research in cross-cultural contexts.' In J.A. Hatch (Ed.), *Early childhood qualitative research* (pp. 185–205), New York, NY: Routledge.

Thapar-Bjorkert, S. (1999). 'Negotiating otherness: dilemmas for a non-Western researcher in the Indian sub-continent.' *Journal of Gender Studies*, 8(1), 57–69.

Warwick, D.P., and Reimers, F. (1995). *Hope and despair? Learning in Pakistan's primary schools*. Westport, CT: Praeger Publishers.

Young, M.D. (2003). 'Considering (irreconcilable?) contradictions in cross-group feminist research.' In M.D. Young and L. Skrla (Eds.), *Reconsidering feminist research in educational leadership* (pp. 35–79). Albany, NY: State University of New York Press.

Notes

1. Where private co-education is offered at the secondary level, girls and boys usually sit in separate sections reflecting cultural values that discourage interaction.

2. During the long, harsh winter months, the entire district is virtually cut off from the rest of the country. The Lowari Mountain Pass—which makes vehicular access into and out of the district possible—is blocked by snow, and air travel is severely affected (Pardhan, 2007).

3. Each classroom had four fans. Sometimes, only two fans would be working if there was 'load-shedding' (rolling blackouts) in the city and the school was using its own generator.

8

Auto/Biographical Research in the South: A Lived Experience

Ayesha Bashiruddin

Introduction

I have been involved in conducting auto/biographical research in general, as well as self-study research (see Bashiruddin, 2002; 2006; 2007) and narrative inquiry (Bashiruddin and Retallick, 2008). Taking these two as examples, in this chapter I will present my lived experiences of conducting and facilitating auto/biographical research in Karachi, Pakistan. The chapter specifically considers issues related to the methodological aspects of auto/biographical research. It also points out some practical issues faced in the field.

The chapter is divided into four parts, each of which discusses a particular issue that arose during my research and which is likely to be an issue for any auto/biographical research conducted in a traditional, multilingual, technologically less-developed context that is often encountered in the South. The four issues are: (a) notions of 'respect' exist that inhibit questioning authority, and therefore pose specific challenges to critical understanding of the development of teaching; (b) the infrastructure of research is weakly developed generally and understanding of auto/biographical research is almost non-existent, thus creating conceptual and logistical barriers for research; (c) the language of encoding and documenting the research is often not the first language of the research participants and therefore poses some, possibly intractable, challenges—even in a setting with a strong and rich tradition of story-telling; (d) it is difficult to establish regular communication and to build relationships with the research participants because of contextual factors, such as unreliable telephone systems. Examples of each of these are provided, and the chapter concludes with some reflections on these issues.

Critical Understanding of the Development of Teaching

In the South in general, and in school contexts in particular, it is generally seen that notions of 'respect' inhibit the questioning of authority and therefore pose specific challenges to a critical understanding of the development of teaching. During my research, I noticed many such incidents which limited the gathering of data. For example, while doing narrative inquiry, both the teachers were unable to comment critically on the way they taught and were taught. One of them, reluctantly, said that now, after her own teaching experience and after attending a workshop, she felt that the way she had been teaching had not been very helpful to her students. However, she could not critically comment on her teachers and the way they taught. On further exploration, she very carefully noted that she respected her teachers and, therefore, would not be able to comment on the way they taught. This, in a way, limited the information that would have been valuable to me as a researcher. Another teacher said that she teaches in the same way as she herself was taught by her 'ideal teacher'—which was through a very traditional 'grammar translation' method. However, during her teaching, I observed that, on many occasions, she taught using a more learner-centred approach. When I further probed about the differences between the approach that her 'ideal teacher' took and the ones she herself sometimes took, on the one hand, and about some of her more learner-centred lessons, on the other hand, she said that both were fine. However, she appeared to have great difficulty in critically discussing the difference between the two.

Similar examples were noted when the participants were involved in self-study research (SSR). One of the participants spoke to me, while writing his stories about becoming a teacher in the northern part of Pakistan, about the way he viewed teaching now. He stated that he could not criticize his elder colleagues and teachers because it would be very disrespectful towards them. Secondly, he said that he could not critically evaluate their teaching since they had never had the opportunity to study or go beyond the villages that they were working in, and so had no exposure to newer teaching methodologies.

Creating Conceptual and Logistical Barriers

In the settings in which I researched, I found that the infrastructure of research was generally weakly developed and understanding of auto/biographical research was almost non-existent—thus creating conceptual and logistical barriers to research. To overcome these barriers, the first step in conducting auto/biographical research was to educate the stakeholders and research participants. One example is that of access. Before starting the narrative inquiry in the two schools—one a private school and the other a public school—negotiating entry was a major issue. It took a lot of time, explaining the research methodology—what the research entailed; its importance; and its benefits to me as the researcher, to the participant, and to educational research—to the key stakeholders. In particular, many stakeholders (including the Educational Directors and principals of the schools) were not convinced by the idea of storytelling as research and were sceptical about the methodology. One of them asked me, 'How can stories of teachers' practice be research? Research is something which is done through experiments.' The long duration of the research was also an issue because, according to one of the principals, a teacher would waste a lot of her time by merely telling me her stories. After several extended discussions of the merits of such research, I managed to convince the stakeholders that I was not there to evaluate the teachers or the school, or indeed its management, but to understand the teachers' teaching development. I also promised the stakeholders that they would get a copy of the research findings. Although some were still sceptical, they did allow the research to go ahead.

Similarly, when I was introducing self-study research to some in-service teachers, who were enrolled in a Master's in Education (MEd) programme at a private university, they found it difficult to see themselves as research participants. Their concept of research was that the researchers were experts who were there to conduct research. This could be because, in our educational institutions—even in higher education—students are not introduced to research. Most of the masters and bachelors courses are based on course work in which the students read research that has been carried out by others. Therefore, the students who study at this university for their MEd degrees are unlikely to have received any training in research. They learned through reading about self-study research, reviewing examples of self-study research, and getting involved in the process of writing stories about their own professional development. There were other reasons why the teachers on in-service programmes were initially sceptical. One was that they had not learnt to value themselves as knowledgeable teachers capable of learning from themselves—neither in their schools nor in their teacher education institutions. A second reason was that they were reluctant to disclose stories that might upset others, due to a fear that headteachers or other senior individuals might hear about them and take offence.

Language of Encoding and Documenting the Research

Stories have, as narrative inquirers say, an 'invitational quality' (Connelly and Clandinin, 1990, pp. 7–8). Since we, in Pakistan, have an oral culture of folklore as well as stories with a moral or religious base, and travel stories, involving research participants in telling or writing stories was a natural and interesting activity.

In my research, as the language of encoding and documenting was mostly English—which was not the first language of the research participants—this posed some challenges, even in a setting with a strong and rich tradition of story-telling. In qualitative auto/biographical research, the participants are involved in writing or telling stories of experience. One of the most important tools for data collection in narrative inquiry is the semi-structured in-depth interview. At first, during the interviews, I talked to the participants in English but I soon realized that both my participants preferred to respond in Urdu. As I felt that, if I insisted on using only English, I might not glean sufficiently rich data in the form of stories of teaching practice, I told the participants I was happy for them to use Urdu, English, or a mixture of English and Urdu. However, this posed problems for me, as the researcher, while transcribing the data and attempting to make sense of it.

In the self-study research that I conducted, participants were asked to write their stories in English—which obviously created difficulties where this was not the language in which participants could best express themselves. One of the participants, during the self-study research workshops, suggested to his peers, who were finding it hard to write the stories, that they should imagine themselves telling these stories to their children. He said he was reminded of storytelling sessions with his grandfather, and imagined himself in his village, sitting close to the fire in winter, and listening to his grandfather's stories. Similarly, at the very initial stage of writing in self-study research, the participants wrote a number of stories about their journeys towards becoming teachers. One of the participants reported that he could not stop thinking about the stories—he had so many—and he kept sharing them orally, including with his peers. Oral story telling is a traditional form of developing and transferring knowledge. However, writing is always difficult for a variety of reasons. The students might not be used to writing, especially in English; while students at universities, they may have had little or no experience of writing on their own—there were always books or notes (that could be bought from the teacher) that they had to memorize in order to pass their examinations. They rarely had the opportunity of independent writing whereas, in self-study research, they had to write several stories and, indeed, several drafts of each story.

Establishing Regular Communication and Building Relationships

The fourth and final issue that I wish to discuss is the difficulty in establishing regular communication, and building relationships, with the research participants because of contextual factors.

In qualitative auto/biographical research, the participants are involved in writing or recounting stories of experience. The main tool for data collection in narrative inquiry is semi-structured in-depth interviews. In my research study I planned six oral life history interviews, each of two hours' duration. However, I learnt that one of the participants was teaching most of the time. Her daily school routine allowed her to be free for only one period a day, during which she had to correct her students' work. I negotiated, with the principal, that she be allowed some time off for the interviews: two days a week, when I could have two hours with her. However, when I went to the school, I was told that the teacher who was supposed to substitute for her had gone on long-term leave, and so she could not possibly leave her classes in order for me to interview her. Since my research was at stake, I used whatever time was available—which was rarely more than 40 minutes of the participant's time. Extended in-depth interviews provide time and space to develop relationships and to recall stories of teaching and learning from memory. Even when I did interview this particular teacher, she was either too tired to recount her stories, or was distracted by other pressures. A problem of working with only one teacher in the public sector was that the school did not have a telephone—through which I could contact her, or she could make contact me, if she was unable to attend school on a particular day—nor did she have access to a mobile phone. Such issues related to institutional structures, discipline and governance, and access can become significant problems for any research that requires a lot of time with participants, as is clearly the case with narrative research.

As a researcher, I had to continuously look for threads that would help me understand the teachers' stories of their practices. This was not a straightforward or linear process, but rather a complex, cyclic process. I needed to find how one story of teaching connected to another, and so on, and some threads needed to be explored further. It was a process of determining what the teachers knew or believed about their teaching, and how their understanding of their work might itself be understood. The amount of information that I collected had to be processed at every stage—so that I could make sense of, and make connections within, the stories. Listening to the teachers' stories was an exercise that developed my skills in listening, in processing what I heard, and in making meaning of their stories.

In order to access their stories of teaching, I gave the teachers some stories from my own journal to read. Thus, the research process was a two-way communication in which the teachers read my stories and I listened to theirs. In fact, there was another layer to this learning and talking. As a researcher, I could use what I learnt from one of them to form questions to better understand the other. In this way, I almost became a mediator between the two teachers. That, in itself, was a learning experience. I could probe and ask about experiences that one of the teachers had, from the perspective of the other teacher.

Engaging in such in-depth exchanges of stories requires a trusting relationship between the participants and the researcher. This was my first school-based research experience, and also the two participants' first opportunity to participate in any kind of research. Neither school in which I conducted my research had ever had a researcher work in it before; hence, it was also the schools' first experience of having a 'guest' (as one of the principals described my status), talking to the teachers and observing classes for such an extended period of time. I had to build a relationship of trust with the teachers, with the principals of the schools, and with the Director of Education of each school system. This was crucial to my study, and a great source of tension. Building a relationship of trust with the Director of Education and the principals meant trying to answer their frequently asked questions: How will the school benefit from the research? What are you going to teach the teachers? Why do you want to be in the school for so long? I observed that trust can never be taken for granted, and that it was necessary to bring issues out into the open—such as issues of confidentiality, anonymity, and the assurance that I was not there to 'evaluate' but to 'understand' their practices. I realized that working on the relationships needed constant attention. Establishing a relationship does not just depend on a singular event or incident; it is an ongoing process.

Similarly, 'meaning making' was difficult for the teachers engaged in the self-study research project. To help them make meaning of their stories, I paired them up and gave them some questions for critical reflection. The teachers had very rarely questioned their journey or what they taught, how they taught, and why they taught the way they did. They had never had to do so in their school contexts; their job was to teach and get good results. During the SSR workshop, I showed them examples of my own stories and how I analysed them, what questions I asked myself, and how I critically evaluated and synthesized the stories.

This process, although it took a great deal of time, did, I believe, help the teachers make sense of their own stories.

Significance for Me as a Researcher

The rich experience of learning from the teachers' stories could only be done through long and detailed conversations. The experience made me realize how important such conversations are, and how much knowledge teachers have to share. The conversations involved the teachers sharing their individual feelings and ideas about important issues related to the development of their classroom practices, which in turn provided me with extended opportunities to reflect on these developments. As a researcher, the one initiating the conversation, I became aware that I was neither neutral nor passive; I actively facilitated and sustained conversations so that the participants could make sense of their experiences (Lampert, 1985).

This research study has given me an opportunity to understand how teachers learn from the telling of their stories. Listening to, and sharing, stories of learning and teaching provided the teachers with an opportunity to learn from their own storytelling, as well as from my stories of teaching development—which I shared with them during data collection. One of the teachers pointed out that it was very 'interesting and heartening' to know that there are people in Pakistan, like me, who are involved in such research projects and have been continually involved in professional development.

For me, as a researcher and a teacher educator, our interaction provided a new experience of getting insights into teachers' understanding of their own development. It was an opportunity for me to grow and learn by understanding them. It has encouraged me to plan teacher education programmes that would fully appreciate, identify, and help teachers in their professional growth in their respective contexts.

My own involvement, in teaching teachers how to undertake self-study research, provided me with various opportunities for learning about the participants' ways of thinking and about the ways in which different people in the same country develop as teachers and teacher educators. Reading their stories, and their interpretations of the stories, gave me an in-depth understanding of the subjective understanding of teachers who have been involved in teaching for a long time. As a researcher, I developed ways of facilitating the teachers, both on a one-on-one basis and in general.

Significance for the Participants of the Study

Auto/biographical research was of significance for the teachers too—for example, the narrative inquiry was a significant experience for the two teachers of English. Both greeted me with enthusiasm before our conversations. They both reported that they had never had such opportunities to discuss or talk to anyone—not even to their colleagues—since they felt that no one was interested, nor were they expected to discuss their teaching methods; teaching was just taken for granted. They were both keen to review their teaching and learning, and to develop themselves as professionals, and so particularly appreciated the time spent on talking about their teaching and to interpret, think, and reflect.

The overall reflections of the students, who were involved in the self-study research, demonstrate that although they found self-study research rather tedious initially, they benefited immensely from the process of writing, re-writing, and 'making meaning' of their stories. One of the teachers said that she had never looked into her life and had never been able to explore her own development as a teacher. She also acknowledged that, by being involved in her own stories, she had been able to examine her professional journey. This, she emphasized, was very important as she had never previously realized how one can learn from one's own experiences.

Conclusion

The above discussion demonstrates that conducting auto/ biographical research in the South, specifically in Pakistan, is possible but that a lot of effort is required to develop an environment and understanding of research if such initiatives are to succeed. It is also important that, while conducting such research, cultural and school norms are kept in mind. The backgrounds of the research participants also play an important role.

References

Bashiruddin, A., and Retallick, J. (Eds.) (2008). *Becoming a teacher in the developing world: a monograph.* Karachi, Pakistan: Aga Khan University-Institute for Educational Development Publications.

Bashiruddin, A. (2007). 'Becoming a teacher educator: a female perspective.' In R. Qureshi and J. Rarieya (Eds.), *Gender and Education in Pakistan* (pp. 43–59).Karachi, Pakistan: Oxford University Press.

Bashiruddin, A. (2006). 'Pakistani Teacher Educator's Self Study of Teaching Self-Study Research.' *Studying Teacher Education,* 2(2), 201–212.

Bashiruddin, A. (2002). 'Seasons of my learning.' In J. Edge (Ed.), *Continuing professional development: some of our perspectives* (pp. 104–114). Kent: IATEFL Publications.

Connelly, F.M., and Clandinin, D.J. (1990). 'Stories of experience and narrative inquiry.' *Educational Researcher*, 19(5), 2–14.

Lampert, M. (1985). 'How do teachers manage to teach? Perspectives in problems in practice.' *Harvard Educational Review*, 55(2), 178–194.

9

Mathematics Education between Utopia and Reality: Examining Research in Contexts of Conflict, Poverty and Violence

Paola Valero and Alexandre Pais

As I walked up the hill, I started feeling the bad smells because in that shantytown there was no sewage system. Terrible! When I got there, four colleagues welcomed me and showed me my classroom. It didn't have a floor, just the bare ground. There were 45 children. They hadn't got a teacher. The children were in terrible conditions, dirty, extremely dirty! The room stank. I approached and started asking their names. At least I am going to make a list, I thought, and give them some recommendations about their personal care, their appearance, how we are going to organize the classroom—because all of them were like packed in a corner. Next day, when I came, they at least knew I was going to be their teacher. It was a first grade class. The children haven't had any previous school immersion experience. I had to start from scratch and give them some introduction, but fast because I also had to prepare them to read, write, and calculate. There were older children with plenty of problems. That day I started noticing their reality when I called the list. I called for somebody. He is not here. Why didn't he come? Does somebody know why he didn't come? Yes. Last night, his father came back home extremely drunk and beat the whole family, so they haven't slept. And I don't know how many similar situations were frequent. Harsh. Very harsh. That moved me deeply. I started to realize that life was not easy. I started to feel that I had to do something, that those children had been put in my hands and that I had to help them. And basically, the only thing I could give them was affection. I particularly remember Daniel, who was so good for doing calculations but could not read. He dropped school soon after I came but I saw him around in the neighbourhood. I always wondered about him. I still remember many of those kids. I have them here in my heart despite that it has been now twenty years since I first met them. (Mercedes, Interview set 1).

These are the words of Mercedes—a Colombian secondary school mathematics teacher—describing her first teaching experience at a public school in a shantytown on the outskirts of Bogotá (Valero, 2002). Mercedes refers to an early experience that impacted her history as a teacher, and narrates the encounter she had with a group of students at a public, under-resourced school, during her first job just after graduating as a mathematics teacher. The story also reveals the material and emotional life conditions of the students at that particular school, as well as expressing Mercedes' awareness of the mission that she perceived for herself as a teacher—a mission that went beyond the school curriculum, and had to do with providing her students with a basic sense of affection. The narrative also signals the deep impression that the experience left on her. Although Mercedes' words are the story of a particular, real teacher in a Latin American country, they allow us to think about the everyday experiences of many teachers in Colombia, and in many other parts of the world where similar life conditions characterize teachers' and students' contexts. Mercedes' words also represent the tension that many educators experience, between a belief in one's work making a difference and contributing towards a better world, and the crude and harsh reality of which teachers and students are a part.

Following Jaramillo's observations (Jaramillo, Torres, and Villamil, 2006), the work of teachers, in situations where the harshness of life is evident, invites us to conceive of educational activity as a constant movement between *Utopia* and *reality*. With these terms, we want to signal the sharp contrast between the formulation of many ideal, almost unachievable, hopes for practise that tend to guide educators, and the realization of the material and structural conditions that shape teachers' and students' lived experiences of education. Utopia and reality can vary depending on the contexts in which they are dreamt up and experienced. For some teachers, Utopia can be related to a dream of having all their students learning more (and more advanced) mathematics—but recognizing that their efforts sometimes fall on 'unproductive ground'. For many other teachers around the world, Utopia may be having the hope of seeing their students grow and become adults in the middle of a reality where even life may be seriously threatened. There are many Utopias and many realities in education. We are particularly interested in the contrast between the Utopia(s) that mathematics education research constructs and the possibilities for real classrooms. We see a very sharp contradiction between the discourses that dominate in theory and methodology, and their responsiveness towards situations of conflict, poverty, and violence.

In this chapter, we explore how the fact that educational practice is a cause of tension between utopia(s) and reality/ies is made (in)visible in mathematics education research. We want to suggest elements, for a research agenda, that address the difficulties faced by teachers in situations of poverty and conflict. We will argue that dominant mathematics education research creates utopia(s) related to the idealization of the teachers' and students' lives and situations. This utopian view of classrooms constructs a strong, unachievable demand for teachers to tailor their practices to the desirable, idealized prescriptions emanating from research. This demand is unachievable because—especially in situations of conflict and poverty—the problems faced by teachers, in many ways, go beyond the problems predicted and addressed in such research. We argue that the acknowledgement and understanding of the constitution of mathematics education in these types of context is crucial, both for the teachers and the researchers.

We are not advocating the adoption of a fatalist view of education, but rather an awareness of the fact that education is constituted in the midst of deep inequalities and conflict beyond the scope of education. Nevertheless, if research intends to provide an understanding and interpretation of educational practices, that may eventually lead to some type of betterment, then research has to address the dominant ideas prevalent in the field vis-à-vis available theories and methodologies for the study of situations of conflict, poverty, and violence.

We start this chapter by making a closer examination of the forms of utopia, and their corresponding realities, that are prevalent in research discourses and practice. We address some elements of a research agenda, in terms of theoretical and methodological issues that need to be examined. We conclude with the significance of such agenda for the understanding of the work of teachers in these contexts.

Between Reality and Utopia

Mercedes' story is a narrative of a mathematics teacher. Although, in this fragment, it is not made explicit how this experience influenced her actions as a mathematics teacher, conversations with her showed how her teaching priorities were significantly altered when meeting children in difficulties. Mercedes' life story shows, clearly, how a mathematics teacher also navigates in the field of tension between utopia and reality. In fact, in her work as a secondary school teacher, Mercedes reported altering the mandated curriculum, and her teaching strategies in mathematics, to attend to the needs of one student who had returned to school after spending time on the streets with his father (Valero, 2002). Such evidence, of the life work of a mathematics teacher, seems to contradict public discourses that mathematics and mathematics education do not have a connection to the flesh and blood realities referred to by Mercedes. While many mathematics educators might consider that their students' life conditions do not impact their function as instructors of mathematics, for us, Mercedes' story is a clear reminder of the complex social and political constitution of school mathematics education. If this is the case, it becomes important for us to examine how the reality of classroom life changes the utopian perspective of mathematics education. Now, in a search for answers, we turn to research in mathematics education.

In a great deal of the research in mathematics education, there is a utopian view about the cognitive ability of students to think adequately and learn mathematics; for example, the discursive creation of students, as cognitive subjects, with the wish and desire to engage in mathematical learning (Valero, 2004). All the complexity of the social and political life of the student is ignored by the research; the student is reduced to a biological entity, likely to be investigated in a clinical way. This utopian perspective, which obliterates all the social and political life of the student, is set in contrast to the crude reality that teachers face when confirming that, in fact, very few students really get close to the cognitive being that researchers have been dreaming of. Pais (2010), building on his own experience as a teacher in deprived schools in Portugal, describes the dramatic encounter between the idealized students he met in the research literature and in teacher education, and the actual students that he encountered every day in his classrooms. Teachers realize that some of the nicely prepared plans that they had learned to engineer tend to fail because strange 'things', not supposed to happen in a classroom, actually happen very often. Those 'things', such as the ones described by Mercedes, have to do with the presence of many real children of flesh and bone, with fears, desires, problems, hopes, and needs, that definitely were not the ones teachers were educated to meet or ones they envisioned when preparing their classes.

The tension between utopia and reality may be defined in terms of the very well-known and documented problem of school failure and underachievement. When people operate in the tension formulated in these terms, a deficit discourse emerges as a possible explanation for the mismatch between expectations and achievement. The deficiency discourse blames students, teachers, or schools for possessing internal and intrinsic characteristics to which the mismatch is attributed. There are many examples of this discourse, as well as critical readings of it (e.g., Ginsburg, 1997). A brilliant example of such a type of discourse is the one constructing a parallel between (mathematics) education research and medicine. In this parallel, a low achievement student is like an 'ill patient', while educational research is the science of treatment—used to understand the symptoms that characterize the students' difficulties in learning mathematics—employed to propose the appropriate treatment: 'The evolving understanding of the *logic of errors* has helped support the design of better instructional treatments, in much the same way that the evolving understanding of the *logic of diseases* has helped the design of better medical treatments' (Silver and Herbst, 2007 p. 63, emphasis in original). Based on this logic, students are seen as patients in need of treatment, and the role of mathematics education research is to understand the students' problems and elaborate designs to treat their learning diseases.

This type of view, focusing on deficiencies, bears a tremendous symbolic violence—to use Bourdieu's term—in situations of poverty, conflict, and violence. In these situations, the perception of students as being in 'lack' is constructed by measuring them against the norms and interests of the schools' organizations, which adopt the value sets of a dominant, Western, white middle class. The students' failure is seen as the failure to achieve some desirable norm—in this case, the norm that attests that every child in the world should learn particular forms of school mathematics in particular ways. Therefore, by considering certain aspects of mathematics learning to be crucial for everyone, we are deploying a mechanism of normalization—and, thereby, of exclusion of all those people whose lived experiences diverge from the norm. School failure is secured by the discourse itself. The societal demand that everyone should be mathematically competent in particularly established ways functions as a norm that defines the terms of the schools' success. This fact has implications for the future of children, especially in situations where school still represents the only opportunity for gaining access to a minimal form of material improvement. In other words, the utopian discourse, based on the desire to achieve some kind of utopian state where all people will experience success in school mathematics, bears notions of 'normality' and 'deficiency'. These notions create a sense of failure among students and teachers whose daily experiences are far from fulfilling school mathematics expectations.

So far, we have been contrasting utopia and reality. We could go further by saying that it is also possible to imagine, and in fact identify, a *dystopian* discourse. While the utopian discourse conveys the idea that, through better teaching and learning practices, all students will be able to experience success in mathematics and thereby an improvement in their lives, a dystopian discourse accepts failure as a 'natural' attribute of schooling. This discourse is frequently heard, in practice, where teachers or school leaders express the view that children—like the ones in Mercedes' story—simply cannot learn. They are not good at anything, particularly not at learning mathematics. It is not rare to hear that certain teachers are also hopeless. Maybe they themselves, when young, were children like the ones in Mercedes' classroom . . . Some people would even argue that in conditions of poverty, conflict, and violence, it is impossible to educate and to learn since learning presupposes some kind of normalization and fulfilment of basic human needs. The dystopian discourse tends to sound highly realistic, deterministic, and also pessimistic. This type of discourse also brings with it a tremendous violence: millions of people and children in the world, who actually live in the midst of conflicts, would never have a chance. It implies that no matter what teachers or schools do, there is little prospect of any improvement in the life-chances of individuals; that their future is pre-ordained to be the same as that of their parents. And, even if this may be true from the point of view of the possibilities for resolving endemic structural inequalities and conflicts in the world, the discourse of dystopia is unacceptable from an educational standpoint. It is unacceptable, not because education should be the utopian promise for resolving everything including inequalities and conflicts, but rather because the acceptance of dystopia would set a closure on human agency within structures.

The reliance on either of these two types of discourses, outlined above, leads to an inadequate approach to the tension. In the utopian discourse, the idea that teachers and schools can solve the problem of failure in mathematics imposes an impossible demand—of providing success for all students—on them, leading to a constant state of (students') failure and (teachers') anxiety. In the dystopian discourse, acknowledgement of the extent and depth of the inequalities, low achievement of specific groups of students, and school exclusion and conflict can easily result in students and teachers feeling powerless and indifferent, and resigned in terms of facing their state of affairs; the possibility of social change would be denied to them. From the point of view of research, our suggestion is to articulate both discourses with the reality in which such discourses are made operational. This implies the search for a language that allows us to move within the tension, without staying at either of its extremes. Such language would allow us to understand and interpret mathematics education practices that bring, to the forefront, their social and political constitution.

Elements of a Research Agenda

It seems, to us, that a central point at stake, while researching mathematics education in situations of poverty and conflict, is the way in which we theorize, empirically document, and analyse the connection between mathematics education and its context. In utopian discourses, the context is assumed to play no role. Utopia, in order to be accepted as such, must eliminate from its enunciation all the antagonisms that, if made visible, would ruin the utopian belief. Teaching and learning processes in mathematics, children's mathematical thinking, or teachers' instructional practices can easily be researched independently of what 'surrounds' them. This act of political disavowal (Žižek, 1991) conceals the crude reality of a society organized around exclusionary principles. When the focus moves to situations of learning that have evidently been affected by their context, the same neutrality cannot be assumed (Vithal and Valero, 2003). Here, we address a number of points that we see as fundamental in advancing research in situations of poverty and conflict.

The theories that have been used, to study mathematics learning, build on a fundamental assumption of continuity and progression in the flow of interaction and thinking leading to learning: the material world of the learner, the stimuli and interactions, and the conditions for thinking are assumed to exist and be available to the learner. Definitions of learning, as a *process*, reflect these assumptions. Although we acknowledge the importance of these theories, in acquiring our current knowledge about ways of improving the processes used in teaching and learning mathematics, we argue that by taking the concrete situations in which education takes place for granted, these theories can end up reducing education to a technical enterprise. In Pais, Stentoft, and Valero (2009), we developed an analysis of how theory is used in mathematics education research, and concluded that, in most cases, solutions to educational problems are being reduced to finding better methods and techniques to teach and learn, to improving the use of technology, to assessing students' performance, etc. Education has progressively been reduced to becoming a controllable, designable, *engineerable*, and operational framework for the individual's cognitive change. This approach has left important problems, faced by the educational communities in their everyday practices, unaddressed. We argue that, in order to bring these problems under the scrutiny of serious research, we need a broader theoretical frame that allows us to understand theory not just as 'theory of learning', but also as 'theory of education' (Biesta, 2005).

A theory of education acknowledges that education cannot be reduced to a technical matter. Education is not only a matter of teachers improving their teaching skills and researchers developing designs to improve teaching and learning possibilities. To say that we need educational theory—instead of just learning theory—recognizes that education is a political task that primarily touches the constitution of subjectivities, even when the education has to do with mathematics. It addresses the issue of the kind of people being developed in mathematics classrooms—that is, why people engage in the teaching and learning of mathematics. Ultimately, we can engage in a discussion about the kind of world being constructed and sustained by the research in mathematics education. Therefore, a theory of mathematics education, and not just of mathematics learning, places educational practices in a wider political context—where mathematics and mathematics education are neither neutral nor innocent. Such a theory makes it possible to raise deep educational questions about the teaching and learning of mathematics in the social, political, economic, cultural, and historic contexts in which they are immersed.

When 'learning' is studied in a situation characterized by drastic change or sudden destruction—or intermittent and disruptive provision—of material and human resources, the available concepts and language to describe education and learning seem to be inadequate. When they are simply applied, without further examination, the result has often been the creation of a dystopian disengagement, as examined above. The question then arises of how one should redefine mathematics 'learning', so that a better language can be developed to grasp the conditions and characteristics of education and thinking in situations where continuity and progression cannot be assumed. Children and human beings continue to direct their growth, to think and to cognize even school mathematics, but probably in ways that we have not considered before.

Some socio-cultural theories of learning resolve the issue, about the role of the macro-social world in individual thinking, by formulating the thesis that cultural tools and artefacts mediate the relationship between the individual, his/her thinking, and his/her cultural environment. Neo-Piagetian theories—focusing on the role of the social world and social interaction, and individual learning—formulate the thesis that, in social interactions in which learning takes place, the macro-social world enters individual thinking through social marking and the evoking of social representations (De Abreu, 2000). In other words, it is assumed that the macro-social world enters the micro-social world of mathematics learning interactions in some sort of symbolic, fuzzy way. However, it seems to us that the missing teacher, the leaking roof, the bare dusty floor, the blue beaten arms of a child, or the lack of food are more materially present in situations of poverty and conflict than the 'symbolic, mediational presence' that these theories assume. The macro-context, and its harshness, is vividly present—sometimes almost physically present—in many classrooms. If this is the case, research that re-conceptualizes the impact of the macro-social world, in the micro-social world, is necessary.

Thirdly, and as a consequence of the two previous points, it is important to develop theoretical tools and corresponding strategies of analysis that allow us to grasp the complexity of the way in which mathematics education practices occur, and to gain meaning in both micro- and macro-contexts—where poverty and conflict are constitutive elements of those practices. Viewing mathematics education as a network of socio-political practices (Valero, 2009) could be a way of providing a broader landscape for understanding the multiplicity of forces involved in forging mathematics education in contexts fraught with violent disruption and an acute lack of resources.

As far as methodology is concerned, it is important to consider the characteristics of the practices that educational research is addressing. Reality is contradictory, full of curves and spins, unpredictable, sometimes dangerous, and profoundly unfair. There is no way of fully grasping all the complexities that surround us in our daily problems as teachers and researchers. If we assume a post-structuralist position, we can say that all the discourse and, more fundamentally, all the language is not a representation of reality but a condition for its constitution. Our discourses construct the reality in which we live. In this way, discourses are immersed in power by delimiting the ways in which we conceive our problems and address them. The methodology that intends to address reality, in all its complexity, is the one that tries to find a language in which it can express the contradictory features of reality in a way that does not neglect or sanitize them—by setting aside the conflicts and constraints so that the research may be presented in a harmonious and positive way. Rather, such discontinuities need to be made the focus of research.

If we take Mercedes' story, and the desire to create an understanding of her practice, it does not make sense to construct a research strategy where the problems of the ill-smelling facilities, the lack of hygiene of her students, the poor school installations, the violence and alcoholism in the students' families, and so on, become obliterated so that the research can only focus on the (mathematical) learning process of the students. The only way we can address these problems is by dealing with them, not as abnormalities, marginalities, or details of an unequal society, but as core problems of many schools around the world that keep deferring what could be a utopian state of mathematics for all. Therefore, the first strategy of a methodology concerned with these problems is to assume that what are usually seen as marginal research vicissitudes become the central issues of research.

This methodological approach implies bringing what Žižek (2005) calls the *symptoms*—the points at which the hidden truths of a system emerge—under research scrutiny. This prevents us from engaging in salvation discourses that, by blindly mis-understanding the lived problems of mathematics teachers and students, only perpetuate existing realities. In Mercedes' case, these symptoms are the fact that Colombia is a highly unequal society, where poverty is a daily reality for many people and armed conflict is present in all its materiality (Valero, 2007). The majority of the research in mathematics education completely ignores these 'symptoms', or sanitizes them, for the sake of research. These symptoms demonstrate that the problem of failure in mathematics is, above all, a social and political problem that cannot be resolved within the boundaries of mathematics education alone. In other words, they demonstrate the in-consistency of a system that, on the one hand, demands mathematics for all but, on the other hand, uses it as a privileged mechanism of selection and credit (Vinner, 2007).

As a Conclusion

Some of the problems experienced by teachers in their profession, especially teachers working in situations of conflict and poverty, are not only problems related to finding better ways of improving students' mathematical learning from a micro-didactical perspective. They are also the socio-political problems that show the embeddedness of teachers' practices in a socio-political context. These problems are not present in the 'cognitive subject' or in utopian 'prototypical classrooms' (Skovsmose, 2006) that dominate discourses of mathematics education research. These problems are normally obliterated and made invisible. They are excluded, through the application of 'orderly' research methods and theories that need 'sanitized' environments (Vithal and Valero, 2003). We stress, again, that we are not suggesting that

we discard all the knowledge—on ways to teach and learn
mathematics—that research in the field has proposed. We are
simply arguing that all the knowledge lacks a broader theoretical
foundation—whereby we can perceive mathematics education as
a task that involves more than simply providing mathematical
learning to students and technical skills to teachers; it involves
addressing the social and political issues prevalent in the everyday school realities of the mathematics classrooms, particularly
for those in contexts of conflict, poverty, and violence.

If we take the example of Mercedes, we should garner the
courage to say that we (researchers or teachers) do not have the
solutions to her problems. The problems of conflict and poverty
go beyond mathematics education, and should be addressed as
social, political, and economic problems that are an intrinsic part
of our current society, and of the educational practices in it—and
not in the micro context of the classroom. This realization should
prevent us from blindly engaging in utopian discourses that
expect schools and teachers to bring about a miraculous
transformation. However, we should also avoid adopting a
fatalist discourse, assuming that we are simply puppets in a play
in which we can make no difference. The teacher can make a
difference, but this difference, besides being unpredictable, rests
on a lucid comprehension of the operations of the school system
in situations of conflict and poverty.

We want to 'deconstruct' the utopian discourse that conceives
of mathematics education as merely a technical issue of devising
better tools and designs to teach and enable students to learn
mathematics as effectively as possible. A teacher's work is
difficult; it involves the concrete situation of each individual
school and student, and cannot be totalized in a utopian

discourse. To deal with these problems, teachers have to constantly resort to strategies that cannot be predicted, nor can they be easily grasped, by a restricted research viewpoint. There are social and political dimensions involved in the teachers' work, which delineate the nature of problems faced in the schools. Teachers have no way of escaping these problems. The best they can do is to be prepared to understand the depth of these problems, so that they do not engage in exaggerated discourses that confer the role of society's saviours on the teachers. Teachers are not saviours, nor are they the masters who will guide the students and their mathematics education to a utopian state—they are people confronted with problems that are beyond their capabilities to solve. Working with the teachers—to critically comprehend their roles and possibilities in reality—is the best contribution mathematics education research can make to their work.

References

Biesta, G. (2005). 'Against learning. Reclaiming a language for education in an age of learning.' *Nordisk Pædagogik*, 25(1), 54–55.

De Abreu, G. (2000). 'Relationships between macro and micro socio-cultural contexts: Implications for the study of interactions in the mathematics classroom.' *Educational Studies in Mathematics*, 41(1), 1–29.

Ginsburg, H. (1997). 'The myth of the deprived child: New thoughts on poor children.' In A. B. Powell and M. Frankenstein (Eds.), *Ethnomathematics: challenging eurocentrism in mathematics education* (pp. 129–154). Albany: State University of New York Press.

Jaramillo, D., Torres, B., and Villamil, M. (2006). 'Interacciones en clase de matemáticas: una mirada desde la etnomatemática.' Paper presented at the Foro Educativo Nacional de Competencias Matemáticas.

Pais, A. (2010). 'Portrait of an influence.' In H. Alro, O. Ravn, P. Valero (Eds.), *Critical mathematics education: Past, present and future* (pp. 133–144). The Netherlands: Sense Publishers.

Pais, A., Stentoft, D., and Valero, P. (2009). 'Mathematics education as more than learning: A theoretical contribution.' Paper presented at II Congreso International de Investigación en Educacion, Pedagodía e Formación Docente. 25–28 August, Medellín, Colombia.

Silver, E., and Herbst, P. (2007). 'Theory in mathematics education scholarship.' In F. Lester (Ed.), *Second Handbook of Research on Mathematics and Learning* (pp. 39–56), New York: Information Age.

Skovsmose, O. (2006). 'Research, practice, uncertainty and responsibility.' *The Journal of mathematical behavior*, 25(4), 267–284.

Valero, P. (2002). *Reform, democracy and mathematics education. Towards a socio-political frame for understanding change in the organization of secondary school mathematics.* Unpublished PhD Thesis, Copenhagen, Denmark: Danish University of Education.

Valero, P. (2004). 'Postmodernism as an attitude of critique to dominant mathematics education research.' In M. Walshaw (Ed.), *Mathematics education within the postmodern* (pp. 35–54). Greenwich (USA): Information Age.

Valero, P. (2007). 'In between the global and the local: The politics of mathematics education reform in a globalized society.' In B. Atweh, A. Calabrese Barton, M. Borba, N. Gough, C. Keitel, C. Vistro-Yu and R. Vithal (Eds.), *Internationalisation and globalisation in Mathematics and Science Education* (pp. 421–439). New York: Springer.

Valero, P. (2009). 'Mathematics education as a network of social practices.' In V. Durand-Guerrier (Ed.), *Proceedings of the VI CERME*. Lyon: Université de Lyon—ERME.

Vinner, S. (2007). 'Mathematics education: procedures, rituals and man's search for meaning.' *Journal of Mathematical Behavior*, 26(1), 1–10.

Vithal, R., and Valero, P. (2003). 'Researching mathematics education in situations of social and political conflict.' In A. Bishop, M.A. Clements, C. Keitel, J. Kilpatrick and F.K.S. Leung (Eds.), *Second international handbook of mathematics education* (Vol. 2, pp. 545–592). Dordrecht: Kluwer.

Žižek, S. (1991). *For they know not what they do: Enjoyment as a political factor.* London: Verso.

Žižek, S. (1995/2005). *The metastases of enjoyment: Six essays on women and causality.* London: Verso.

10

Politics and Practice of Action Research

Rana Hussain and Anjum Halai

Introduction

Action research, as a methodology for generating knowledge and as a paradigm of change, is gaining prominence in the context of social and educational development. This is evident from the shifting emphasis of donor funding policy, towards fostering collaborative research in which partners—often from both the North and the South, aspire to participate on equal terms. The research community appears to recognize the significance of the social and political contexts in which new technologies and ideas are deployed, to reduce poverty and promote development; therefore, action research is recognized as an approach to bridging the divide between academia and practitioners.

Typically, action research projects in education aim to generate knowledge rooted in the reality of schools and classrooms—to provide nuanced understanding of local issues in education that also have more general relevance. The research process leads to the development of local innovations and strategies—for improvements in the quality of school and classroom processes and outcomes (Halai, 2004). This knowledge is empowering because it provides insights that offer possibilities for social transformation. Forging the world of the researcher and practitioner is also beneficial, because it creates a critical mass, within the community, to ensure that the process of change is sustained beyond the life of the project. However, alongside these advantages that recommend action research projects as an approach in the developing world, there are also certain challenges that need to be taken into account, some of which are presented in this chapter.

Depending on the purpose and nature of the inquiry, approaches to action research vary from technical, or practical, to emancipatory. Technical action research is product directed and concerned with efficient and effective practices. It promotes personal participation, by the practitioners, in the process of improvement. While the significance of personal and professional judgement, when coming to a decision about improving a social situation, is an important feature of practical action research, emancipatory action research promotes change through a critical consciousness and manifests itself in actions of a political nature which challenge the assumptions that underpin a social situation (Halai, forthcoming; Haggarty and Postlethwaite, 2003; Grundy, 1987).

Whichever approach is taken, a key question is what constitutes improvement in a social situation, and from whose perspective? These are inherently political questions because they can potentially challenge the status quo. For example, a significant purpose in encouraging practitioners at schools to participate in action research is to enable them to question deep-rooted assumptions that underpin their practice and raise issues related to traditional hierarchical school structures. This process can potentially lead to discomfort and negative consequences for the participants, thereby raising ethical issues. Likewise, clarity is needed about the ethics of engaging in research where the roles of researchers and practitioners are blurred so that anonymity and confidentiality are neither possible nor always desirable (Eikeland, 2006; Halai et al., 2008; Nolen and Putten, 2007).

In this chapter, methodological and philosophical issues in action research are presented and discussed—in particular, issues relating to the politics and practice of action research that emerged during the course of action research with teachers in rural unschooled communities in a low-income setting in rural Pakistan.

Context and Background

Pakistan's education system can be broadly divided into basic education (primary, elementary, and secondary levels) and higher education (post-secondary and graduate levels). Both are governed by separate ministries with distinct management and financial systems. Government-funded schools—or 'mainstream' schools as they are generally referred to—offer primary education from classes I to V (ages 5 to 9), then middle—or elementary[1]—schooling from classes VI to VIII (ages 10 to 13), and then secondary schooling in classes IX and X (ages 14 to 15) (for details see Ministry of Education, 2006).

In addition to the mainstream (government) schools, the private school system is becoming increasingly significant. There is immense variation in the types of private schools—they include the elite schools, not-for-profit schools run by community-based trusts, and private school systems run by large non-governmental organizations. One such private school system, the Pakistan Education Service, Pakistan (PES–P), complements the government education system in Pakistan through the establishment and management of more than 180 schools in the northern and southern regions of the country. A key feature of the schools run by the PES–P is that they offer support to teachers, for continuing professional development, through a system of Field Education Officers. These are highly trained professionals, appointed by the central PES–P system, who are associated with individual, or clusters of, schools.

Policy making in Pakistan, including the education policy and the setting of its strategic direction, is the responsibility of the federal government.[2] Policy implementation is mostly carried out by the provincial governments and, more recently, has been further devolved from provincial to district level. Curriculum development is within the purview of the federal government's Ministry of Education, and is undertaken through a consultative process with the provincial governments via their respective education departments. The District Government is responsible to the people and to the Provincial Government, for improvement of governance and delivery of services. Affairs of education, at district level, are looked after by the office of the Executive District Officer Education.

An Illustrative Action Research Project

To ground the findings and provide illustrative examples of issues, we have discussed an action research project (below), which looked at perceptions and practices in multi-grade teaching at the PES–P's schools.

PERCEPTIONS AND PRACTICE OF MULTIGRADE TEACHING

Multi-grade teaching describes a situation where students in different grades receive education from a single teacher in the same classroom. Such groupings are generally formed at schools located in sparsely populated—mostly rural—contexts. Although some studies have found that students learn more in multi-grade classes, than in mono-grade classrooms, others have found the opposite; there does not appear to be any strong evidence either way (Pridmore and Vu, 2006; Miller, 1989; Little, 2001). In the highly deprived and hard-to-access areas of northern Pakistan, multi-grade teaching was considered a strategy for providing education to a wider group of learners. Hence, the PES–P invested substantially in in-service courses for teachers, to help them improve their teaching of multi-grade classes. However, the courses focused on telling the teachers about multi-grade teaching, rather than supporting them in developing the necessary skills in their own classrooms. It was recognized that teachers in multi-grade settings are isolated, and therefore the PES–P had instituted a system of field education officers who visited the teachers. However, due to the difficult terrain, vast distances, and inadequate resources, these visits were relatively few and mainly of an administrative nature. As the multi-grade schools were for children from low income homes, they were supported by the Village Education Committee (VEC) in the form of some funds and resources.

A two-year action research project was undertaken, at the behest of the PES–P, in fifteen such multi-grade teaching schools within a 10–12 kilometre radius. A key focus of the study was to research the teachers' perceptions and practice of multigrade teaching and to enable them to further improve the multi-grade teaching model. The research team included the university researcher (first author), teachers, and field education officers from PES–P. The adoption of an action research approach was taken in the belief that classroom teachers can be the most appropriate persons to identify problems, and to find solutions, provided they are engaged in the research process. Hence, the teachers' role in the study was that of reflective practitioners, who would evaluate their own practice and so make a contribution to the development of a theory of effective practices in multi-grade teaching. The teachers maintained regular diaries, in which they wrote about what was going well and what was not working. They wrote about the plans, as they were practised and experienced, rather than sharing the envisioned plan. The diaries provided them with a safe place to record lessons learnt, as they tried out novel approaches. Risk-taking was scaffolded by the university researcher, and was a shift away from the usual practice of teachers being expected to teach flawlessly with little or no room provided for calculated risk-taking.

In addition, efforts were made, during the course of the action research, to break teacher isolation by creating structures for collaborative work among teachers so that they could learn from, and with, each other. The management of PES–P supported this effort by providing resources for joint workshops—for the teachers to develop materials suitable for multi-grade practice, and to share their successes with each other. There was evidence to demonstrate that the teachers had learnt from their peers and incorporated those lessons in their practice. Furthermore, there was an increasing sense of community among the multi-grade teachers who were otherwise quite isolated. However, in a resource-strapped environment, such face-to-face meetings and workshops could only be conducted during the vacations when schools were closed. Also, the terrain and weather conditions were not conducive to regular meetings between teachers who were spread out over a distance.

Initial findings revealed that the perceptions of the teachers and members of the community, about multi-grade teaching, were very negative. Multi-grade teaching was considered a last resort, to be replaced by mono-grade teaching as soon as possible. It was a common belief that children taught in a multi-grade classroom would not get enough attention from the teacher, and that they would spend their time waiting for the teacher's attention rather than being meaningfully engaged in learning. Indeed, the multigrade practices observed during the initial phase substantiated these views. Teaching was a combination of teaching the whole class, as if it were a mono-grade class, and 'split' teaching, when teachers divided the class into two or more grades, spending time teaching one grade while students in the other grades worked on their own. It was observed that many unattended children were either sitting idle or were making a lot of noise, forcing the teacher to discipline them. In some classes, teachers had involved students of a higher grade in working with the students from lower grades, but they had not been given any specific tasks to enable them to do so.

Some of these perceptions of multi-grade teaching were, no doubt, influenced by the perception of education as the receiving of academic knowledge from a teacher. For example, in response to a suggestion from the university researcher that parents should be given a greater role in schools, one teacher responded by asking, 'How will the parent provide the official knowledge as given in a textbook?' Another teacher's immediate response was, 'They cannot become teachers, how will they teach?' A third commented, 'Parents pay us fees to teach their children. How can we pass our responsibilities on to them?' There were interesting arguments about whether it was important that parents teach what is in a textbook, or whether they should impart knowledge as they knew it or had experienced, it. As a result of the initial phase of the action research, several potential areas of action emerged: one was to challenge the prevailing notions among teachers and the community that mono-grade was always a better option for schooling—multi-grade was seen as a transitionary phase; another was to work alongside teachers, in order to help them develop contextually appropriate multi-grade teaching practices.

One way of challenging individual assumptions is to undertake a critical analysis of existing propositional knowledge. To this end, the university researcher led seminars in which she encouraged the teachers to review the historical development of schools, and helped them understand that mono-grade teaching had become a learning space of convenience and graded textbooks a matter of simplifying learning for learners. Through this process, the teachers became aware of the evolution of mono-grade and multi-grade schools, as options to be taken based on the context. One of the strategies for appropriate multi-grade teaching practices was to invite members of the community to support education as part of the schooling. However, there was resistance and disagreement among the teachers vis-à-vis the concept of the community support being more than the providers of material resources. Their view was that the parents, in the unschooled and poor community, were hard pressed and had nothing to offer inside classrooms. For example, the expectation that all parents would be expected to supervise homework: this would be difficult for parents who were unschooled and could not read or write. However, they agreed, as a test case, to identify topics in which they thought the parents would be able to make a contribution; the teachers, collectively, planned tasks for the parents who came to work with the teachers. These plans included inviting parents and village elders to talk about local history, their own professions, health and hygiene, and engaging parents in the creation of low-cost aids.

In summary, it was found to improve multi-grade teaching, the teachers required the support of their peers or adults from the community who had a wide base of experiential knowledge. This, in turn, required the problematizing of the perceptions of education quality—as being synonymous with scholastic knowledge and achievement. Engagement in the process of action research demonstrated that teachers had formed complex perceptions of multi-grade teaching.

Discussion: Politics and Practice of Action Research

The essence of action research is to build on the developmental gains made during the cyclical process of action and reflection. This cyclical process enables participants to gain deeper, more nuanced, and complex insights into their social reality, and to develop responses accordingly (Kemmis, McTaggart and Retallick, 2004; Kemmis and McTaggart, 2005; Kerkale and Pittila, 2006). However, this perspective of research and development assumes continuity of participation and regular engagement in collaborative inquiry. These assumptions need to be critiqued and questioned. For example, generally speaking the Northern Areas of Pakistan are politically more stable and therefore disruptions in data collection, of the kind noted by Valero and Pais (this volume), were not an issue, but distances are vast, terrains difficult to travel, and means of communication are not well developed. These geographical conditions, and the under-developed communications infrastructure, posed a challenge in establishing norms of inquiry via regular face-to-face meetings, especially at the initial stage when collegial relationships are being initiated. Maintaining regular contact posed significant challenges, with a considerable dilution of effort. Hence, although face-to-face meetings appear to be important, if not essential, in building support for project participation, they represent a substantial investment of staff time and other resources. The advent of technology, such as mobile phones and other means of communication, have started to provide alternatives to face-to-face communication. An implication of considering these alternatives is that the potential for creating a community of inquirers would need to be carefully thought through and worked into the warp and weft of the action research project.

In Pakistan, and many other low-income countries, teaching does not enjoy the status of a full-fledged profession with the associated expectation that teachers will engage in continuing professional development (Halai, 2007). However, action research is increasingly seen as a form of professional development for teachers, with a concomitant expectation of sustained engagement and commitment on a long-term basis. Many academics in universities are willing to make this commitment because it yields professional and career benefits to them. Moreover, the time and energy they invest is seen as an unavoidable element of their role. In the action research project reported here, the university researcher negotiated access through the relevant gatekeepers; consent was also sought from the teacher participants. However, in the absence of a culture of teaching as a profession, practitioners in the field do not necessarily see any advantages in investing considerable time and effort. In the relatively professional culture within the PES–P, the teachers participated in the action research project. To what extent their participation was voluntary, and to what extent it was due to 'felt pressure' from the senior management, is a moot point because the practice of action research, as empowering is a highly political process.

Philosophically and practically, the issue of benefits accruing from a long-term action research project needs careful scrutiny. For example, in the context of rural Pakistan (possibly also in other developing world contexts), there is an influx of externally funded 'development projects' creating expectations of a modest honorarium being paid for participation in the projects.

However, accepting payment for contribution and participation in action research is contrary to the spirit of ownership and critical consciousness for change—which characterizes action research. Moreover, traditional procedures for entry negotiations in a research sites, and ethics review policies and procedures in academic institutions, are concerned about the 'voluntary consent' of participants, and *assume* commitment without necessarily examining the assumption. Given the issues raised above, and the politics inherent in action research, a reasonable stance would be to work towards the ideal of 'voluntary consent'. One approach is to recognize that consent is not a one-off event to be undertaken before the start of a project; rather, it is a process and needs to be negotiated throughout the course of the project (Halai, 2008; Hemmings, 2006). Consent could be sought through formal procedures, such as consent forms, and through informal conversations. More significant to this case is the recognition that there are degrees of participation; therefore, the consent to participate should take the extent to which different participants would be involved into account.

What constitutes valid knowledge, for inclusion in the school curriculum, is an ideological and political decision (Clandinin and Connelly, 1995). Likewise, notions of what counts as effective schooling are based on personal theories of effective schools, often derived from people's own experiences of schooling, or based on the largely Western normative accounts of schools. In the multi-grade teaching study, assumptions about multi-grade teaching—as a deficit model—were challenged through sustained intellectual input from the university researcher, who had considerable experience in the field. Likewise, the position of privilege accorded to academic knowledge of the textbooks, over the experience and wisdom of the community, was questioned mainly through the efforts of the university researcher. Hence, it is important to recognize that, at times, challenging deep-rooted assumptions may require intellectual endeavour from an expert. This positioning of an expert, in the context of action research—which is seen as a participatory and empowering process—raises issues of power in a number of ways. Some of these are generic issues, such as the position of the university researchers as having a 'high status' and the teacher–researcher a relatively 'low status'. However, for the purpose of this chapter, there were issues of power that were specific to the context of the South. For example, against the backdrop of communities that were largely unschooled, power was constituted by traditional assumptions about the role of teachers being knowledgeable and of education being a process of acquiring academic knowledge. Moreover, the action research project described here aimed to build a critical mass in the community, to sustain the change process beyond the life of the formal project. In the multi-grade teaching project, it involved teachers working with the community members to support the process of a more realistic and relevant education, and also to support the management of a multi-grade group of learners through the contributions of the community members. However, this process was resisted by the very teachers whom it was supposed to support. The teachers felt that the parents, and other community members, were unschooled and therefore not fit to be educators. Their perception of education was limited to that of academic knowledge accrued from books.

Concluding Remarks

Action research projects aimed at reform in education often assume a normative, largely academic, perspective on education. This perpetuates a view of the school as an institution for, and of, academic education, creating a potentially large gap between the school and the community, especially in poor and otherwise disadvantaged situations. The unschooled community is seen as unsuitable to work within the school, for an improvement in the quality of education provided. The critical questioning of assumptions that underpin a social situation is key to realizing the transformative potential of action research. It often leads to a breakdown in traditional barriers and hierarchies. However, in the context of the developing world, relationships are often authoritarian and feudal in nature, so that the breaking down of barriers within the education setting would be neither meaningful nor possible, if not seen as a process that engages with the wider social setting. In the particular case of education, this means actively reaching out to the wider community—beyond the confines of the schools and classrooms (Halai, 2011).

To conclude, action research provides a way forward for change and improvement in social situations by bridging the gap between knowledge and action. The essence of action research is to enable the questioning of key assumptions underpinning the social situation. However, in the context of the low income, conflict-ridden, and often unschooled settings of the developing world, the politics of an 'empowering and participatory' process need to be questioned and the assumptions underpinning the methodology need to be problematized.

References

Clandinin, D.J., and Connelly, F.M. (Eds.). (1995). *Teachers' professional knowledge landscapes.* New York, NY: Teachers College Press.

Eikeland, O. (2006). 'Condescending ethics and action research.' *Action Research,* 4(1), 37–47.

Grundy, S. (1987).*Curriculum: product or praxis?* Lewes, UK: Falmer Press.

Haggarty, L., and Postlethwaite, K. (2003). 'Action research as a strategy for teacher change and school development?'. *Oxford Review of Education,* 29(4), 423–448.

Halai, A. (2004). 'Action research to study classroom impact: is it possible?'. *Educational Action Research,* 12(4), 515–534.

Halai, A. (2007). 'Status of teachers and teaching: conclusions, implications and recommendations.' In A. Halai (Ed.). *Teacher status: a symposium* (pp. 100–110). Karachi, Pakistan: Aga Khan University Institute for Educational Development.

Halai, A. (2008). 'Initiating change in mathematics classrooms: Lessons from Pakistan.' In F. Shamim and R. Qureshi (Eds.). *Schools and schooling practices in Pakistan* (pp. 27–45). Karachi: Oxford University Press.

Halai, A. (2011 forthcoming). 'Teachers as participants in classroom reform: Promise and perils of action research.' In S. Rizvi (Ed) *Multidisciplinary approaches to educational research: Case-studies from Europe and the Developing World.* London, UK: Routledge

Halai, A. (2011). Equality or equity: gender awareness issues in secondary schools in Pakistan. *International Journal of Educational Development* 3(1), 44–49.

Halai, A., Rodrigues, S., and Akhlaq, T. (2008). *Teacher empowerment through collaborative action research: concepts, possibilities and challenges* (EdQual Working Paper Curriculum No. 1). Bristol, UK: EdQual Research Programme Consortium.

Hemmings, A. (2006). 'Great ethical divides: bridging the gap between institutional review boards and researchers.' *Educational Researcher,* 35(4), 12–18.

Kemmis, S., and McTaggart, R. (2005). 'Participatory action research: communicative action and the public sphere'. In N.K. Denzin and Y.S.

Lincoln (Eds.). *Sage handbook of qualitative research* (3 ed., pp. 559–603). Thousand Oaks, CA.

Kemmis, S., McTaggart, R., and Retallick, J. (2004). *The action research planner* (2 ed.). Karachi: Aga Khan University Institute for Educational Development.

Kerkale, J., and Pittila, I. (2006). 'Participatory action research as a method for developing leadership and quality.' *International Journal of Leadership in Education*, 9(3), 251–268.

Little, A.W. (2001). 'Multigrade teaching: towards an international research and policy agenda.' *International Journal of Education Development*, 21(6), 481–497.

Miller, B. (1989). *The multigrade classroom: a resource handbook for small, rural schools*. Portland, OR: Northwest Regional Educational Laboratory.

Ministry of Education (2006). *National curriculum for mathematics grades I–XII, 2006*. Government of Pakistan Ministry of Education, Islamabad.

Ministry of Education (2009). *New education policy*. Government of Pakistan Ministry of Education, Islamabad www.moe.gov.pk.

Nolen A., and Putten J. (2007). 'Action research in education: addressing gaps in ethical principles and practices.' *Educational Researcher*, 36(7) 401–407.

Pridmore, P., and Vu, S. (2006). 'Adapting the curriculum for teaching health in multigrade classes in Vietnam.' In A.W. Little (Ed.). *Education for all and multigrade teaching: challenges and opportunities* (pp. 169–191). Amsterdam, Northlands: Springer.

Notes

1. According to the new education policy, the primary and middle schools are being merged as 'elementary schools', and the age limit at all levels of schooling is increased by one year (MoE 2009).

2. Pakistan is a federation with four provinces, i.e. Punjab, Sindh, Balochistan, and Khyber Pakhtunkhwa (previously North West Frontier Province; NWFP); the federally administered areas; and the federal capital Islamabad.

11

Undertaking Research on Early Childhood in KwaZulu-Natal, South Africa

Hasina Banu Ebrahim and Helen Penn

Introduction

This chapter is an attempt by two researchers, from very different backgrounds and with different experiences, to understand and analyse data from a research project on early childhood undertaken by one of us in KwaZulu-Natal. There are two issues involved. Firstly, did the original project brief rely unduly on conventional expectations of childhood, imported from the global North, which were then exposed by the research? Secondly, did the interpretations of the authors differ according to their North–South perspectives?

A brief note about the authors is relevant. Hasina Banu Ebrahim is a researcher in the Faculty of Education at the University of KwaZulu-Natal. She has studied and worked in South Africa exclusively, but is extremely keen to take advantage of the recent discussions and discourses about early childhood—current in Europe and America—which challenge some of the conventional understandings about early childhood. Helen Penn is an English Professor who has worked in a number of countries in the global South, including South Africa, and has published widely on the relevance and application of ideas of childhood from the global North to the global South (see, for example, Penn, 2001, 2008a, 2008b, 2010). The two authors have collaborated on several projects. In this case, Hasina Banu Ebrahim, together with two other researchers, was awarded a UNICEF research grant to investigate the concept of early childhood development programmes in South Africa, as resources for the care and support of poor and vulnerable young children at a practice level to inform policy. Helen Penn suggested that it would be useful to discuss the understanding and application of the research for a wider audience outside South Africa.

This chapter describes the research that was undertaken and what each of the authors made of it. In doing so, it contributes to the wider debate considered in this book about the research interests and priorities across the North–South divide.

The Background to Early Childhood Development in South Africa

Post-apartheid South Africa has national plans for the realization of the UN Convention on the Rights of the Children (CRC) (Porteus, 2004). Because of financial constraints, the South African government relies on partnerships with international non-governmental donor organizations (INGOs) to detail and implement various aspects of CRC. Recently, the UNESCO Education for All Global Monitoring Report stressed the importance of CRC in relation to early education and care (UNESCO, 2007a). South Africa accepts that early childhood education and care (called early child development or ECD in South Africa) is an important area for intervention, and is working with UNICEF to reshape ECD as a public provision for children from 0 to 4 years.

A national audit revealed that only 16 per cent of children aged 0–4 years were able to access centre-based provision, funded directly or indirectly through the government (Williams et al., 2001). However, more children appeared to be participating in informal or local ECD programmes run by non-governmental organizations. UNICEF has funded research to explore and document such ECD programmes (Biersteker, 2007). In particular, UNICEF has funded research into programmes that seemed to be innovative in meeting the needs of poor children aged from 0 to 4 years. The aim is to identify and upscale *effective* ECD programmes that would be supported by the South African government.

The Dominant Model of Early Childhood

INGOs traditionally use a model of early childhood intervention premised on what is said to be 'scientific' understandings of children, childhood, care, and family. These understandings, about early childhood interventions—originally derived from Euro–American ideas of child development—have been augmented by recent rhetoric about human capital theory and neuroscience (Heckman, 2000; Garcia, Pence and Evans, 2008). Early intervention is seen to be particularly cost-effective in promoting long-term changes in children, making them more able and self-sufficient adults. The economic analysis of the profitable rate of return of investment in early education relies heavily on longitudinal evidence from early childhood interventions in the USA—evidence which is freely lifted out of its original and parochial context (Penn and Lloyd, 2007).

There have been attempts to underpin these economic arguments with ideas extrapolated, often wrongly, from neuroscience (Thomson and Nelson, 2001). The brains of young children are seen to be very malleable and susceptible to particular kinds of intervention offered in early childhood programming—lots of individual adult carer–child talk, a child-orientated play environment, familiarity with consumer goods such as toys and books etc. These ideas about economics and neuroscience, and their application to early childhood, have been taken so seriously by the World Bank and other major donors that the rhetoric of early childhood interventions has been crudely taken up in many large scale international programmes—without any consideration of what it means to lift and transpose ideas and practices about early childhood from one context to another (Penn 2008b; 2010). The 'evidence' about young children, from the USA, is axiomatically taken as universal and scientific, and therefore applicable anywhere in the world. Briefly summarized, the argument runs that all children can succeed given the right kind of push at the beginning, and that societies will be richer as a consequence because more children will be successful. This broad approach underpins UNICEF's belief, as an INGO, in supporting early childhood services (Penn, 2010).

This claim, for scientific universalism for a specific approach that is deeply rooted in a specific North American context, serves to minimize the difficulties about the resourcing and delivery of early childhood programmes. For instance, the model of a patchwork of small entrepreneurs, church-based community enterprises, and a few highly targeted government services, along with a high reliance on parental participation, characterizes North American early childhood, education, and care (ECEC) provision, and is assumed to be the norm by many INGOs. In fact, many European and Asian services are provided more systematically. Jones and Villar (2008), for example, as a basis of their work in Peru, claim that *only* government intervention in ECEC is likely to be effective in the long run. The approach adopted by the INGOs also fails to understand the deep inequalities and hardships that characterize life for so many children in the South.

Importantly, such an approach also ignores cultural context; in particular, it relies on an individualized notion of human progress and development that is deeply at odds with the collective notions still inherent in many societies. Attention to how the community, as a collective, shapes childhood experiences runs the risk of being masked. *Ubuntu*—the notion of mutual obligation and respect—has been an important concept in South Africa, and used in the context of early childhood, although there is a range of views about its current application and relevance in a rapidly changing society like South Africa (Penn and Maynard, 2010). Nsamenang (2008) argues that, in Africa, an expert frame of reference of Eurocentric values detaches programming from valuing the indigenous worldview, values, and practices that shape children's daily lives. For example, the middle class concept of child-centeredness positions children as external to the adult world. Rogoff (2003) argues that this concept creates the idea of segregation based on age, with children in segregated spaces where they are removed from daily realities. In Bangladesh, Blanchet (1996) contends that child development is an organic process that is unrelated to age. The author notes that the naming of a person as *a child* or *not a child* is dependent on the concrete situations in which one is involved. It is more common to speak of being *old enough* or *being too young.* In South Africa, it is not uncommon to see young children involved in activities, such as fetching water, doing household chores, and tending to the sick (Muthukrishna, 2006).

Another important aspect to consider is the notion of family and care. Along with many other INGOs, UNICEF (2007a, 2007b) argues for a family-centred focus to ECD. But, in a society where cultural concepts are very different from those in the North, and where there is extreme poverty and dislocation, what are the norms for good parenting? Bray and Brandt (2007) draw attention to the limitations of dominant child care models used by international organizations. In an analysis of a UNICEF child care manual, Engle, Menon, Garrett, and Slack (1997) note how a decontextualized model of care is posited. Six major types of care behaviours—namely, feeding and breastfeeding, food preparation and handling, psychosocial care, care for women, and home-health practices—are presented; each category features as an essential component of good quality care. The authors argue that this is a narrow understanding of child care.

The emphasis, then, in many texts on early childhood has been on individual striving and success of individual children empowered by the pedagogic techniques of the adults working with them. The children, in turn, are nested within caring—and mainly nuclear—families. The research reported here aimed to move beyond the narrow notions of early childhood and to make salient a contextual account which privileges local interpretations and experiences. On the basis of a more accurate and appropriate picture of children's lives, it would then be possible to assess, more acutely, the relevance of the services being provided.

The Research Brief, Approach, and Process: Hasina's Account

As noted above, UNICEF commissioned research on the concept of ECD programmes, as resources for the care and support of poor and vulnerable young children at a practice level, to inform policy. UNICEF also required the researchers to undertake a stakeholder analysis and identify the range of people, including children, who were potentially affected by/involved in the ECD programmes. Two projects of a local NGO, which used a community-based approach to ECD, were chosen by UNICEF for its innovations in rural KwaZulu-Natal. At the grassroots level, these projects were said to be driven by community members and family facilitators (FFs). Three researchers from the University of KwaZulu-Natal undertook the study. All three had some experience in researching communities in KwaZulu-Natal.

In order to make sense of the concept of a community-based ECD programme, the research team chose not to use a macro-level survey approach—which attempts to predefine and measure features of the experiences of a large sample of people. We wished, instead, to access people's viewpoints, interpretations, experiences, and actions in a particular context. We considered that open-ended, qualitative methods would be more sensitive to the contextual realities, experiences, and actions of people on the ground. We hoped that this, in turn, would lead to a wider understanding of practice.

The research team identified the children attending the programmes, primary caregivers, FFs, project coordinators, and community leaders as the primary stakeholders. The officials in the government departments, and volunteers in the municipality, were identified as secondary stakeholders. Both these social groups had the potential to contribute to the understanding of the complex realties and processes associated with a community-based ECD programme.

The context was poverty-stricken, and in dire need of social and economic upliftment. The project areas were governed by traditional leaders, and therefore required particular protocols for access. There was poor infrastructure. Water and electricity was provided to few homes. Few early childhood centres received subsidies from the Department of Social Development; the centres had to supplement their income through parent fees. Those children, within close proximity, who did not attend the centres were unable to afford the fees because their parents/caregivers were unemployed. Most children were in home-based care with family members and other caregivers. These children were targeted for intervention by the FFs.

The context information assisted in developing the data production techniques. The Director of the NGO, whose project we were investigating, stated the need to be flexible and take into account the low levels of literacy in the community. With this in mind, a multi-method approach was designed. The research team thought it best to work with broad categories and design questions around them. For example, in the category 'children in the community', we asked questions about the difficulties the children experienced. Focus group interviews were designed to stimulate discussion by primary caregivers, FFs, and community members. Individual interviews were undertaken with secondary stakeholders. Site visits and observations at play groups were used to secure data on practice in action. Informal conversations with primary stakeholders, such as the FFs, caregivers, and grandmothers, were viewed as important given the need to be flexible in the data production process.

Since none of the researchers was fluent in IsiZulu, facilitators from the NGO acted as research assistants. The research assistants were briefed on how to facilitate the translation process. The researchers explained that respondents would be given the opportunity to talk in whichever language they felt most comfortable. If this was in IsiZulu, given the differences in the languages, the research assistants would record the words of the participants and then translate them as accurately as possible.

Consent letters were prepared in both English and IsiZulu. The research activities began with an explanation of the nature, and aims, of the research. Where necessary, this was conducted in IsiZulu. The researchers were aware that, in poor communities, the presence of representatives from INGOs and government departments might create the expectation of tangible benefits. Hence, it was made clear—at the outset—that we were involved in research, that all participation was voluntary, and that anyone could withdraw if they so chose.

Researchers greeted and thanked respondents in their mother tongue, with relevant gestures. Respondents were given opportunities to ask the researchers questions. In relating to the caregivers, especially the grandmothers, the discussions had a personal focus, in particular relating to their well-being. During site observations and playgroup sessions, researchers held conversations with children, about their performance, and joined in some activities—such as skipping, and throwing and catching a ball.

The Research Brief: Helen's Comments

Many reports of research projects in the South belong to the category of 'grey literature'. The projects are conceived of as attempts to inform INGOs about local situations, often with hastily devised briefs, and then hurriedly carried out. International research for academic institutions, funded by research bodies, on the other hand, is usually time-consuming, expensive, more long-term, and addresses more general issues. The question is whether grey literature can be used in an international academic context.

I agreed with Hasina, that it was important to obtain a locally contextualized account of an informal ECD project. But, although I have visited South Africa many times, I could not understand, from this account, what was going on or who did what. I returned Hasina's initial draft with many queries and comments. Hasina patiently answered the queries, but I still found the project hard to grasp. What did a family facilitator do? And with whom? How was she selected? Was she paid? How was the NGO run? What is a community-based approach and what is community development in a fractured community? Whose voices were being represented in the research and whose were being left out? I had assumed that, as well as having a particular local function, the research might also be an independent contribution to debates about how young children might be perceived, and what sort of care seemed to be appropriate for them. But, this research project was commissioned by an INGO and, from the start, locked into a situation that took many aspects of context for granted. In that sense, the report to the INGO was 'grey literature'. In fact, I subsequently realized that it is not only grey literature that is so parochial; much research, in the field of early childhood, takes context for granted. The difference is that the research context is usually Anglo–American/European, and the authors do not feel it necessary to explain it. Even within a European context, it is striking how much practices differ between countries and how parochial the reporting of those practices is (Penn, 2010).

I also agree that qualitative methods were appropriate to the aims of this research project. But, I viewed questions about the standards of empirical evidence, and the burden of proof, differently. The research was intended to give a more in-depth view of an existing situation; but, from my point of view, it did not test out some key concepts and ideas or investigate critically enough. I was concerned about sampling, and data collection and analysis. The main conduit to informants was the Director of the NGO. Because of the difficulties of access in research projects in poor communities, the Director of the NGO was used as a key informant who could gain access, for the researchers, to those participating in the project. This posed a possible conflict of interest since the Director suggested who the researchers might talk to in order to evaluate her project. The researchers judged that knowledge of the context outweighed any more independent form of sampling of respondents and, in any case, to do anything else would be very difficult and might threaten the NGO. At any rate, sampling was not posed as a contentious issue. Similarly, I was unclear about how extracts from the data had been compiled. The power and impact of certain statements, in illustrating the difficulties recipients encountered and their responses to those difficulties, had been prioritized. Again, I underestimated the need, in the researchers' eyes, for very marginalized people to be seen and heard.

Community Involvement and the Care Environment for Children: Hasina's Account

The research project data identified two themes that were underestimated in conventional reckonings of ECD: community involvement and the nature of the care environment for children.

The community-based approach to ECD was developed, in partnership with other NGOs, in a rural locality in KwaZulu-Natal. This joint project helped the NGO to develop a model for intervening in the lives of young children in rural and deep rural areas. The NGO wanted to replicate the model in another community. The Director stated that she had approached a rural community, near her organization, for permission to initiate a community-based approach to ECD. The first project began after the leadership understood how the community would be involved in, and benefit from, the project. People from a neighbouring community heard about the project, from a retired health worker from the community who had links with the NGO. Supported by the senior traditional councillor, she approached the NGO for the expansion of the project into her locality. The Director noted that both these individuals became the driving force for the second project.

In commenting on community involvement in the projects, the Director explained that her organization took a developmental approach. She noted that, in this approach, the community was enabled to participate actively and take ownership of their affairs. Both of the NGO's projects, under consideration, had set up local forums or community support structures which consisted of members from the traditional and political leadership—well respected members from the community—a representative from the NGO, and from the FFs. A focus group interview, with the community support structure in the second project, was held. Members described their role as selecting and monitoring the FFs, problem solving, and making decisions regarding issues related to the project. Members were asked why they served on the committee:

> Chairperson: We are very concerned about the children's safety and well-being.
>
> Treasurer: For the love of the community. We must work for something for the children.
>
> Secretary: I felt I had to be part of it. A lot of children are given alcohol. The young ones are growing up and they are learning. The only way to help the community is by working with the children.

The researchers noted that, as insiders, the members had a deep knowledge of the problems facing young children and their caregivers. They spoke about how poverty, unemployment, violence against children, disease, alcoholic caregivers, and a growing population of orphans—due to HIV and AIDS—were affecting young children's lives and community cohesion. The FFs, who had been chosen by the committee, should 'love children, love the community, be trustworthy and not expect much in return.'

But, there were also tensions of a gendered nature. Traditionally, the African notion of fatherhood is when a man shows the responsibility of caring for, and protecting a child. Richter and Morrell (2008), however, contend that migrant labour during the colonial period, and disruptions due to war and famine, have made it difficult for men in Africa to fulfil the social expectations of fatherhood. An interview, with the senior traditional councillor, revealed the difficulty in mediating the role of a social father:

> When I talk about kids they (the community) does not take me seriously. I am the wrong person. The male does not look after kids. It is new for the community. They say we will try and we will see. They don't have any hope. They need an attitude change.

In an interview, the ward councillor explained that the police and the traditional leadership were part of a system to deal with the perpetrators of sex crimes—elderly men and women were voted, by the community, to deal with crimes. The ward councillor noted that there were tensions in the reporting process, especially in the case of 'hidden' crimes. The researchers noted that meting out justice, according to the traditional laws, was in tension with children's right to protection. An interview with a volunteer worker at the trauma unit for sexually abused children drew attention to this:

> When a child is sexually abused and the case reaches the traditional leader for action then a traditional way of dealing with it is used. The person is asked to pay a cow for the crime because of the loss of virginity. The abuse goes on and on. This disturbs the child.

Households headed by females were a strong feature of the local communities we investigated. In South Africa, 43 per cent of African children live with their mothers, usually in crowded households (Statistics South Africa, 2008). In this project, multi-generational households consisted of grandparents, and biological mothers and aunts, but few teenage mothers and fathers. Grandmothers featured as the main caregivers, even in cases where grandfathers were present. Swift and Maher (2008), in their research on poverty and HIV/AIDS in early childhood in South Africa, noted that grandmothers played a key role in childcare, even in cases where mothers and fathers were alive. In the communities investigated, children were left with grandmothers for several reasons: death of parents, mothers and fathers employed in the urban areas, mothers and fathers finding new partners and abandoning their children, and alcoholic parents neglecting their children.

In such a situation, the economics of caring for the children was a struggle. The incomes of the grandmothers was mainly from pensions and child support grants. In South Africa, child support grant is an unconditional cash grant paid to parents and caregivers who are poor. It is considered to be the largest programme in South Africa for alleviating poverty (Hall, 2009). Yet, grandmothers said that the child support grant was inadequate to take care of the children. Also, it could be hard to obtain—because of missing documentation and the stigma attached to HIV/AIDS. FFs spoke about their role in linking families with government services, like the Departments of Social Development and Health, in order to facilitate benefit claims.

Grandmothers who participated in the project spoke about the difficulties they experienced. They spoke about the battle to bathe, clothe, and feed the children, and to send the older ones to school. One grandmother noted how the mother of the child she was taking care of withheld the child support grant and used it for her own benefit. Edin and Lein (1997) argue that poverty and its correlates can sap energy, undermine competence, and reduce a sense of control in a parenting environment. In order to cope with the demands of taking care of young children, the senior traditional councillor noted, in an interview, that some grandmothers were feeding their grandchildren alcohol. He also spoke about the ways in which the project was bringing about change:

> Grandmothers sometimes feed the kids with African beer. They don't have time to look after the kids. No one takes care of them. Now, slowly, there are changes. Kids stay with the FFs and then go home.

Community members from the support structure spoke about how some young children had nowhere to go when their parents died. In an FF's account on the difficulties facing young children, she commented on how fathers' girlfriends were quick to claim custody of children once they were aware that the children were receiving child support grants. The Director noted that some children lived in homes with very sick adults. In the focus group interview with the FFs, they noted their role as one of identifying children at risk and reporting these to structures set up by the projects.

The caregivers spoke about the FFs as critical support structures in the intimate care environment. The Director explained that, in the absence of money and in cases of illness, caregivers, especially grandmothers, were virtually housebound with small children and no one to talk to. During site visit conversations, two grandmothers had the following to say about the FFs:

> Grandmother 1: I speak to her about my problems. She knows where to get help. She tells us that children must be clean. She gives advice in a nice way. She tells us how she teaches the children and why she teaches them games.

> Grandmother 2: She talks about things happening in the community like when the minister was coming to talk.

Caregivers in the focus group interviews said the following:

> Caregiver 1: Whenever we have any problems, we are free to talk to them because they are like part of the family.
>
> Caregiver 2: They have taught us how to be careful when handling someone that is sick. We know now that at least if we don't have gloves we can use plastic bags to tie the wounds until we get to the clinic.
>
> Caregiver 3: I as a parent cannot talk to my children about all their problems. They are free to talk to the FF about their problems at different stages because she can understand and give advice. She is not old and does not live with them.

FFs, in turn, spoke about people in the community lacking in the hope to be able to change their life circumstances. They, therefore, distanced themselves from their children. One FF noted that, due to daily stresses and beliefs, people in the community did not play with children, particularly babies. During her interview, the Director spoke about disabled children being marginalized in the communities. At the community support meeting, a member noted the plight of disabled children: 'Children that are physically challenged are locked up for the whole day. They don't even get fresh air. The parents are embarrassed about having disabled children.'

The care environment is hard, for all concerned, in a disrupted community, and people may act harshly when under pressure. The FFs were able to listen to some of the concerns about the care of young children in the community and act upon them.

The researchers observed group activities conducted by the FFs. The FFs invested in a play approach mediated through the IsiZulu language. The children participated in discussions. They did finger counting, painting, repeated rhymes/alphabets, and sang songs. The children demonstrated their physical prowess by clapping, stamping, and thumping in traditional dances. They played with toys that the FF carried to the sites. During a site visit, a three-year-old noted, '*I like it when M comes to play. She brings toys and cars.*' She also spoke about enjoying ball games.

The researchers noted that, in the context of poverty, the children took an active part in the daily activities of family life. They fetched water, tended to sick adults, and informed neighbours about the lack of food. The FFs and the Director spoke about how older children were trained as buddies, to provide an additional link to support caregivers. They described the role of the buddies as playing with younger children and tending to them when caregivers were unable to do so.

Community Involvement and the Care Environment for Children: Helen's Comments

It is clear, from this account, that the community described is, in many ways, very dislocated and fractured. On the other hand, the Director of the NGO who directs the project appears to have a theory about community viability and community self-help—a slightly rosy view of it as a self-healing entity that can draw on older traditions to reconstitute itself. This model assumes that a self-help approach is not only a practical way forward, in the absence of other services, but that the autonomy of marginalized local communities should be respected as much as possible. The community support structures and the FFs seem to be the way of putting this theory, of community development, into practice. Yet, because the main access to the community, for the researchers, has been through the Director of the NGO—who holds these views—there is no critical discussion or consideration of an alternative point of view. The research project, as it is reported, gives examples of the Director's approach to community development but does not challenge it in any way. Community may be an important concept, but how important?

Children in this community lead very hard lives. In this sense, the conventional INGO notion of individual self-realization and development through early childhood intervention—raised initially in this chapter—is fairly meaningless. This is no small point. But, if this is an inadequate conceptualization of childhood, what other models are being put forward—implicitly or explicitly—by the project? Are the support structures being described viable for young children leading difficult lives? These questions were not raised.

This project was conceived, not as an international research project but as a local evaluation for UNICEF. Extrapolating from it, for an international academic audience, may be more than the data warrants. On the other hand, academics from the North also need to understand the very real difficulties and challenges of carrying out research in marginalized communities, and in interpreting the data obtained.

Overall Comments: Hasina

My accounts, and Helen's comments, highlight the insider–outsider perspectives and tensions that characterize dialogue in a research space. Helen's Northern academic grounding, experiences in the global South, and her distance from this particular project allowed her to use a particular outsider frame of reference for evaluating my Southern accounts. She was able to identify the shortcomings of research producing grey literature. This being the case, it is natural that Helen would comment on the need for a more critical stance and testing of concepts and ideas.

As an insider to the South African ECD context, I am an integral part of the ongoing developments and debates around policies and programmes for young children. By participating in advocacy work for ECD, I have also taken an activist position that is not divorced from my role as a researcher. In undertaking the research project described in this chapter, my immediate concern, which was shared by the other team members, was to gain a deep understanding of how an alternative to centre-based provision worked so that it could be considered as part of public service for ECD. Given the need to present the practice components of alternative programmes to centre-based provisioning, the focus fell on investigating 'what works' within a short timeframe. So, as Helen would say, the team was locked in a situation from the beginning.

There are, however, procedural sensibilities that Helen grappled with from her frame of reference. Helen's concern with the sampling procedures and dominant role of the Director is legitimate. While independent sampling is usually a requirement in any research project, in the rural context of KwaZulu-Natal the team was aware of the fact that the people from the Zulu ethnic background—with a low socio-economic status—may be less willing to participate in research. Heavy responsibilities and scepticism about the value of research is always a threat in the situation described above. The Director had an intimate knowledge of the members of the community, by virtue of living close to the research sites and working with the community over a long period. Trust and relationships were already in place. This outweighed the concern about a conflict of interest. With regard to data analysis and representation, Helen's concerns about the compilation of the extracts and the development of the themes excluded the possibility of creating visibility and space for marginalized voices. Another aspect that Helen drew attention to was how the theory of community development, as presented by the Director, shut off possibilities for a discussion on alternatives. At face value, it would seem that the researchers were short-sighted and lacked a critical edge. However, in the context of experts imposing their ideas of development on poor communities in South Africa, and in the need to recognize the community as a resource for sustainable early childhood development, the insider perspective left the theory of the Director unchallenged.

Continuation of Methods from the North or New Methods for the South: A Joint Statement

The dialogue in this chapter tells an important story. The novice researcher from the South gives the account, and the experienced English professor from the North gives the critical comments. The 'enlightened' Northern research voice uses particular standards to question research activities. Researching in the South, and in particular in poor and vulnerable communities, however, has its own sensibilities which may resonate, contradict, and have the potential to produce new ways in which we do research.

This dialogue is especially pertinent in the field of early childhood, which is relatively new as an academic discipline and relatively poorly researched outside the global North. The argument is less about North–South relationships, and more about their application in this field. First class research, by South Africans, is already taking place in South Africa. In the field of medicine, for example, studies of maternal health or of male violence—carried out by research institutes and universities within South Africa—have earned international renown. In anthropology, too, there are world-class South African researchers. However, in a relatively new disciplinary area, like early childhood, there is less certainty and more controversy. Even more than in other academic disciplines, there are arguments about research paradigms and research language; journals are devoted to exploring these controversies in approach (see, for example, the widely read and cited journal *Contemporary Issues in Early Childhood*). It is probably the case that, as researchers, we fall on slightly different sides of the paradigmatic divide between empiricism and postmodernism, which gives an additional edge to our comments, both singly and jointly.

These controversies, in the literature on early childhood, have not really registered in the world of INGOs and charities. A recent review by one of us—of the work of INGOs and charities in the ECEC—suggested that most of them, uncritically, accept the North American standardized discourse based on human capital theory, and draw on so-called universal norms of childhood (Penn, 2010). Both of us take issue with such an approach. The question that drew us, to try to work together in the first place, is what alternatives are possible. Hasina considers that finding ways of understanding the needs and views of very poor people in highly marginalized communities should be prioritized. Helen agrees, but considers that it is important not to lose sight of empirical rigour in the process, in order for the work to have a sharper focus and impact outside the immediate community in which the research takes place. For both of us, the primary task is to rework relations between the North and South in a way that makes a shared learning process for research possible. This would go some way towards working from a broader knowledge base, with perhaps new recognition of concepts emerging from the South. The South then can take on the status of producing research theory for global knowledge.

Acknowledgement

We would like to thank Peter Rule and Bev Killian for their participation, as team members, in the local study, and Loveday Penn-Kekana for her helpful comments on the text.

References

Biersteker, L. (2007). *Early childhood development—rapid assessment and analysis of innovative community and home based childminding and ECD programmes in support of poor and vulnerable babies and young children in South Africa 2007.* Pretoria, South Africa: UNICEF.

Blanchet, T. (1996). *Lost innocence, stolen childhoods.* Dhaka, Bangladesh: The University Press.

Bray, R., and Brandt, R. (2007). 'Child care and poverty in South Africa: An ethnographic challenge to conventional interpretations.' *Journal of Children and Poverty.* 13(1), 1–19.

Department of Social Development and UNICEF. (2008). *Parental/primary caregiver capacity building training package (Low literacy level version).* Pretoria, South Africa: Department of Social Development.

Edin, K., and Lein, L. (1997). *Making ends meet: how single mothers survive welfare and low-wage work.* New York: Russell Sage Foundation.

Engle, P.L., Menon, P., Garrett, J. L., and Slack, A. (1997). 'Urbanization and caregiving: a framework for analysis and examples from southern and eastern Africa.' *Environment and Urbanization,* 9(2), 253–270.

Garcia, M., Pence, A., and Evans, J.L. (Eds.). (2008). *Africa's future, Africa's challenge: early childhood care and development in sub-Saharan Africa.* Washington, DC: World Bank.

Hall, K. (2009). 'Children's access to social assistance.' In S. Pendlebury, L. Lake and C. Smith (Eds.), *South African Child Gauge 2008/2009* (pp. 79–81). Cape Town, South Africa: University of Cape Town Children's Institute.

Heckman, J.J. (2000). *Invest in the very young.* Chicago, IL: University of Chicago Irving B. Harris Graduate School of Public Policy Studies.

James, W. (Ed.). (2000). *Values, education and democracy: report of the working group on values in education.* Pretoria, South Africa: Department of Education.

Jones, N., and Villar, E. (2008). 'Situating children in international development policy: challenges involved in successful evidence-informed policy influencing.' *Evidence and Policy,* 4(1), 31–51.

Muthukrishna, N. (Ed.). (2006). *Mapping barriers to basic education in the context of HIV and AIDS: a report on research conducted in the Richmond District, KwaZulu-Natal.* Pietermaritzburg, South Africa: University of KwaZulu-Natal School of Education and Development.

Nsamenang, A.B. (2008). '(Mis)Understanding ECD in Africa: the force of local and global motive.' In M. Garcia, A. Pence and J. L. Evans (Eds.), *Africa's future, Africa's challenge: early childhood care and development in sub-Saharan Africa* (pp. 135–149). Washington, DC: World Bank.

Penn, H. (2001). *Early childhood education and care: key lessons from research for policy makers.* Brussels, Belgium: European Commission Directorate-General for Education and Culture.

Penn, H. (2005). *Unequal childhoods: young children's lives in poor countries.* London. Routledge/Falmer.

Penn, H. (2008a, July). *Early education and care in Southern Africa; think-piece for CfBT Educational Trust.* Reading, UK: CfBT.

Penn, H. (2008b). 'Working on the impossible: early childhood policies in Namibia.' *Childhood,* 15(3), 378–398.

Penn, H. (2010). 'Travelling policies and global buzzwords: how INGOs and charities spread the word about early childhood in the Global South.' *Childhood,* 17.

Penn, H., and Lloyd, E. (2007). 'Richness or rigour? A discussion of systematic reviews and evidence based policy in early childhood.' *Contemporary Issues in Early Childhood*. 8(1), 3–18.

Penn, H., and Maynard, T. (2010). *Siyabonana: we all see each other: building better childhoods in South Africa*. Edinburgh, UK: Children in Scotland.

Porteus, K. (2004). 'The state of play in early childhood development.' In Chisholm, L. (Ed.). *Changing class. Education and social change in post apartheid South Africa* (pp. 339–366). Cape Town, South Africa: Human Science Research Council.

Richter, L., and Morrell, R. (2008). 'Fathering: the role of men in raising children in Africa—holding up the other half of the sky.' In M. Garcia, A. Pence, and J. Evans (Eds.), *Africa's future, Africa's challenge* (pp. 151–163). Washington, DC: World Bank.

Rogoff, B. (2003). *The cultural nature of human development*. Oxford, UK. Oxford University Press.

Statistics South Africa. (2008). *General Household Survey 2007 Metadata*. Cape Town, Pretoria: Statistics South Africa.

Swift, A., and Maher, A. 2008. *Growing pains. How poverty and AIDS are challenging childhood*. London: Panos.

Thompson, R.A. and Nelson, C.A. (2001). 'Developmental science and the media: early brain development.' *American Psychologist*, 56(1), 5–15.

UNESCO. (2007a). EFA Global Monitoring Report 2007: *Strong foundations, early childhood care and education*. Paris: UNESCO.

UNICEF. (2007b). *The early childhood resource pack: young child survival, growth and development* (2 ed.). New York, NY: UNICEF.

Williams, T., Samuels, M.L., Mouton, J., Ratele, K., Shabalala, N., Shefer, T., and Strebel, A. (2001). *The nationwide audit of ECD provisioning in South Africa*. Pretoria, South Africa: Department of Education.

12

The Power and Politics of Studying the Impact of Educational Reforms in the South

Roshni Kumari, Razia Fakir Mohammad, and Nilofar Vazir

Introduction

This chapter presents an analysis of the issues and challenges related to the implementation of a methodological framework conceptualized for a large-scale study in the South. The methodology was designed on the basis of relevance and appropriateness to the nature and context of the research, taking into consideration the ethical dimensions as well. However, field experiences and later analysis suggest that it was crucial to respond to the unfolding contextual realities while collecting data in the public sector situated within the rural context of Pakistan. In addition, an important unfolding reality had been the power and politics involved in conducting research in general, and studying the 'impact' of educational reform projects in such contexts in particular.

Although there have been a growing number of studies that have looked at power and politics in educational research, the need for more published accounts, of the process of doing this kind of research, has been emphasized (e.g. Cookson, 1994; Walford, 1994). This chapter, therefore, makes a contribution in relation to highlighting the political dimension of studying impact in the context of the South. The findings present an intriguing and complex interplay, between the nature and purposes of the study, the contextual realities, and the methodological and ethical choices made during the course of the study.

The findings discussed in this chapter emerge from a large-scale study conducted in a rural setting in the province of Sindh, Pakistan. Attainment, access, and quality of teaching and learning have been major issues in rural Pakistan. Consequently, various national and donor-funded initiatives have been undertaken to achieve reform at the level of classroom teaching and learning. This research was designed to examine the impact of donor funded in-service teacher education projects: or, specifically, whether or not the interventions in teacher education have made any difference in the quality of teaching and learning in rural Sindh.

The chapter begins by providing a brief background to the research, including a description of the research context, so as to situate the findings and discussion. A description of the background is then followed by the conceptual framework for the study. The issues and challenges of implementation are discussed in detail, followed by insights offered for research in the context of the South.

Background to the Research

Since the 1980s, some foreign-funded teacher education interventions have been undertaken in order to improve the overall quality of teaching and learning in classrooms in the context of rural Pakistan. A number of improved learning outcomes were anticipated: increased enrolment and retention in schools for all students in general, and for females in particular; reduced number of failures and repetitions; increased achievement rate; and increased participation by students in their learning. A brief review of some of the documents related to donor-funded projects, such as project planning and evaluation reports and summary documents, indicated that reasons for children's low participation and retention included a poor quality of teaching (and in particular, lack of variety in teaching methods), limited resources or teaching aids for teaching and learning, outdated textbooks, and assessment based on factual recall which encouraged rote-learning. Inadequate structures and mechanisms for monitoring and evaluating exacerbated existing problems; examples include the inefficiency of school-based support, and poor coordination between the school management, educational system, and community. Therefore, in order to improve learning outcomes, the projects focused mainly on four areas: (a) access and equity; (b) teacher training and development; (c) curriculum enhancement; and (d) academic coordination.

Several initiatives have been undertaken to improve the quality of teaching and learning, including establishing more schools, recruiting local teachers, free access to textbooks and uniforms for students, financial rewards for student attendance and retention, and establishing teacher training colleges able to offer pre-service training, supported by a variety of forms of in-service training, including short and long training courses for teachers by national and international teacher educators and other teacher education institutes.

However, at various levels, it has been suspected that the quality of teaching and learning, in general, has not improved much. In spite of the huge level of input and investment, there is little evidence of impact at the classroom level. For example, the current document on the National Education Policy 1998–2010 (Government of Pakistan, 1998) states that 'the existing teacher education program is considered [as] not being adequately responsive to the demands for quality education in the school system' (p. 47). The report on Policy Dialogue on Key Issues in Education (AKU–IED 2003) has also indicated a strong need for reform in teacher education, and identified a lack of comprehensive and clearly stated aims for teacher education. Moreover, a National Conference on Teacher Education,[1] held in Islamabad on 20–22 December 2004, raised similar concerns—that teacher education was resulting in a poor quality of teaching and learning in Pakistani schools. At the conference, one of the major concerns raised in relation to the donor-funded projects had been the observation that the impact of these projects is short-lived, i.e. it ends with the end of the project. This clearly raised questions regarding the impact of the initiatives—whether or not the initiatives had had any impact on the quality of teaching and learning, and to what extent. Why educational innovations come and go without generating any sustainable outcomes and how the situation can be improved have been growing concerns in Pakistan.

Hence, this study was initiated in order to study issues related to the impact and sustainability of teacher education projects in the province of Sindh, Pakistan. The impact of teacher education on teachers was assessed in terms of the change in their knowledge, skills, and attitude, and how this change was reflected in their practice.

Conceptualization of Research: Methodological Framework

The research was conducted in two phases. The first phase of data collection involved entry negotiations, initial conversations, and seeking permission from senior officials in the ministry for access to project-related documents. This phase of the study also involved understanding the conceptualization, anticipated outcomes, and planning process of the donor-funded projects. The second phase, on the other hand, looked at the impact of the projects in terms of changes in teaching and learning practices at the classroom level.

Data was collected through a combination of qualitative and quantitative approaches, including document analysis and follow-up interviews with relevant stakeholders, large-scale questionnaire administration, classroom observations, and semi-structured interviews.

During Phase I, we gathered, in both print and electronic forms, official project-related documents about the history and implementation of the various foreign-funded in-service teacher education initiatives, including evaluation and research reports, and other official documents of the Ministry of Education and its projects (e.g. appraisal reports, Planning Commission Reports, project completion reports, evaluation reports, etc.). However, important information was missing from many documents, including details of the key persons involved in conceptualizing, planning, and implementing the projects, and of the teachers who participated in these teacher education projects and other stakeholders. This information was essential for the conduct of

Phase II of the research. In addition to document analysis, we also conducted in-depth interviews with all government officials and project representatives who were involved in the various stages of the projects, including project conceptualization, design, planning, implementation, and evaluation (or writing completion reports). This included interviews with government officials from the provincial and federal ministries, representatives from the donor agencies, project directors, project team members, and some 'master trainers'.

Phase II was conducted in three districts of the province of Sindh—selected to provide maximum representation of the various forms of training offered in the districts while, at the same time, minimising, the physical distances that the researchers would need to travel. Since this phase involved studying the impact at the classroom level, the participants at this phase were mainly the beneficiaries of the various forms of training, including teachers, master trainers, and supervisors. Within each participating district, two *talukas* (an administrative sub-division of a district) were selected. The survey sample included all the relevant teachers and teacher trainers from the six *talukas*.

As mentioned earlier, one of the methods used for data collection was a survey. As the teacher education interventions (project input) were made on a large scale, for a larger population, the survey was used to provide an initial baseline of information. The questionnaire was developed, and designed, in light of the available standard guidelines, provided in the literature on questionnaire development (e.g. Silverman, 2000; Cohen and Mannion, 1994; Oppenheim, 1992). As a result, the questionnaire was printed in three languages (provincial, national, and official), the language was kept simple, and technical jargon was avoided.

The use of specific examples to facilitate understanding, and the avoidance of over-loading any question with multiple concepts/ information were other important considerations for the design of the questionnaire. Moreover, the questionnaire was piloted with a large group of teachers in one district, which resulted in changes to the questionnaire (particularly related to language and content) before ts actual administration.

Initially, we planned a postal survey, in order to minimize the cost (i.e., in terms of time and resources), as our population was geographically spread and the number was very large. However, there were possible risks that the participants might not respond to us or might not have access to the questionnaire because of the unreliable postal services. Therefore, we decided to carry out face-to-face administration, with the support of the district education offices in the respective districts. Several meetings with the government and district education officers were organized, to identify and implement the most effective strategy for questionnaire administration. It was decided to use 'cluster formation' as a strategy for survey administration—one school would become the cluster school for the teachers from the nearby schools in the *taluka* to gather at. Despite the physical presence of the researchers the help provided with completion, and clear written instructions as well as verbal explanations in Urdu, Sindhi, and English, many participants did not fill the questionnaires out completely, or they filled them with irrelevant details.

An initial analysis of the survey findings revealed that, though the questionnaire was supposed to be filled only by trained teachers, many untrained teachers had done so as well. Questionnaires from untrained teachers were removed, leaving

1712 questionnaires from trained teachers. Out of these, 12 teachers from each district were selected for classroom observation and interviews, in order to understand the contexts in which the participants worked, their own learning, and its impact on their teaching and learning practices. The selection of teachers, for observation and interview, was carried out on the basis of the information provided in the questionnaire, focusing specifically on the nature and level of their participation in the projects, their indication of learning or impact of projects on their teaching and learning, their accessibility, and their willingness to participate. Details of the selected teachers were sent to government officials to facilitate access to the teachers and their classrooms.

From Conceptualization to Implementation: Issues and Challenges

The previous section described the overall conceptualization of the research, the methodological choices, and related decision-making. The journey from conceptualization to implementation, however, posed many challenges. This section, therefore, presents some of the issues and challenges faced during the implementation phase. Our analysis suggests that various issues emerged due to the bureaucratic set-up in the public sector, political influence of authorities within the schools and districts, and a lack of professional commitment and clarity regarding participation in the research and training. We used on-going strategies to address the various issues faced during the fieldwork; for example, strategies such as detailed negotiations with different stakeholders at different levels and at different points in time; facilitation of the research participants; involving education officers to facilitate data collection; 'clustering', as a strategy, for survey administration; and, the presence of the research team to facilitate survey administration. All these strategies were particularly relevant and significant for our study purposes, since this was an impact study conducted after a decade of teacher education interventions. Based on our awareness of the contextual realities, as well as past experiences of conducting research in such contexts, we had anticipated that participants might face difficulties in recalling information for a variety of reasons, including the elapsed length of time between the project initiatives and the current impact study. Therefore, we were prepared to use a variety of memory recall strategies to assist the participants in recollecting their project-related learning experiences. For example, through initial document analysis, we had extracted relevant historical and factual data regarding the various projects that we used while framing questions during the development of the questionnaire and interview guides. We used specific examples, collected through different levels of data collection and analysis (e.g., from document analysis to survey analysis to interview data analysis), to aid participants in recollection of their experiences.

However, in spite of having planned for the study in the ways discussed above, we faced various challenges and issues in gathering transparent, relevant, and objective data. This left us with incomplete information that is identified in our findings and analysis below.

Issues of Limited Access

As already discussed, in order to gather information regarding project-planning processes (conceptualization, implementation, and evaluation) and their purposes and outcomes, we analysed relevant documents and planned follow-up conversations with relevant stakeholders in the Ministry of Education, both at the provincial and federal levels. Also, their consent was sought, to access the documents, through initial informal meetings. Although we had done detailed strategic planning for our visits— getting prior permission, informing them about the study and visit plan, negotiating times, venues, and focus—the process took much longer than anticipated because of the overall culture and work dynamics of the public sector. For example, meetings at a higher or ministry level, called on an *ad hoc* basis during our conversations/meetings, would often become a competing priority for them.

We were granted permission to access documents from the relevant departments. However, accessing the material, even with official consent, proved to be very difficult; the documents were under the supervision of various other units or departmental sections; in many cases, they gave differing reasons for why the documents we needed could not be shared with us. Even in cases where we succeeded, this represented a significant investment in terms of our time and energy. On many occasions, we spent hours sitting in public offices waiting for the relevant documents to be provided. In addition, the documents we received mostly provided quantitative information about the project design, implementation, and evaluation issues. Frequently, therefore, the materials and documents provided were not as relevant or useful for our understanding of project-related implementation and achieved outcomes.

The government officials had been very cooperative and facilitative in providing information through interviews;

however, very often, the information shared would be at a generic level rather than specific to the projects under discussion. For example, the discussions with key stakeholders suggest that most of the projects did not achieve their full measurable targets and, therefore, the project's impact in the documents was reported as minimal. However, they did not analyse issues related to limited outcomes of the teacher education projects, and their role in the planning and implementation of these reform processes. They would, for example, talk generally about the existing situation, the issues related to poor quality, policy implementation, or government structure, and its negative impact. High-ranking officials involved in planning or implementation, such as project directors or key decision makers, gave responses such as:

In my view, they [the government] do not give power to the education officials. Why do they not empower [the] education sector? Hierarchy for [the] education sector is important in this country. [For the government] [the] Custom and Excise and Taxation Department is important, but Education is not important!

. . . People [involved in the projects] find these [projects] lucrative, as for instance, [position withheld] keeps four vehicles of the project under his personal use. One is driven by his daughter, one by his son, one by his wife, and one by himself. Thus, they produce fraudulent bills for petrol. To justify this, they tamper [with] the speedometers of the vehicles artificially and show the vehicles are used for official purposes. If this practice is monitored, no action is taken on such monitoring reports.

. . . Frankly speaking, the foreign training component is to some extent political. We [the government] try our best to observe merit, but sometimes, it does not work. . . . some people get retired soon after they complete their foreign training. [Authors' translation from Urdu]

Although the quotations above reveal many important issues regarding the improper use of resources or lack of empowerment, these remarks tended to be opinions or views about projects in general, rather than providing specific details about the projects that these high ranking officials had been responsible for. In fact, they ignored specific questions related to their involvement in project planning and/or implementation. Due to the generic nature of the responses, in spite of cross-questioning and further probing, many issues remained unanswered for us, for example: what specific outcomes were anticipated and how were they achieved; what were the various layers of authority and hierarchy that influenced their decision-making. Therefore, access to meaningful and specific data remained a major issue, despite all our efforts and the time expended.

In the field, we discovered that, in many cases, the information provided by the teachers was incorrect, inaccurate, or incomplete. Teachers were not found in the schools indicated by their questionnaires. We also found that although the teachers had written the name of a particular training programme, further probing revealed that they had not really undertaken the training they specified (discussed below in detail) and, in cases where they had, their experiences were not particularly relevant for us since they were not teaching the subject in which they had received the training. For example, one Social Studies teacher was sent for training in the subject area of Science; however, on her return, she was asked to teach English and Home Economics. Another teacher said that she prepared Social Studies teaching materials during her subject-specific training; however, on her return, she did not teach this subject:

> Since my return, I was not given Social Studies by [name of headteacher withheld] as there was an old/senior teacher already present. I was only able to share what I had learnt with the headteacher [instead of implementing the learning at the classroom level].

Similarly, some teachers informed us that although they were not interested in attending the training sessions, they were forced to attend the sessions. Hence, their responses during interviews were at a generic level and quite brief. Mostly, opinions were expressed which highlighted the general significance of training rather than specific details regarding the training that they had attended. The situation described above has implications for teacher education. Learning is linked with its context and takes place within the context. Teachers learn with a purpose and clarity; they also require facilitative conditions to implement, in the real context, the theories/ ideas learnt during the training in order to further develop their practice. Therefore, in the absence of a clear purpose for training, the teacher training experiences remained at a theoretical level.

In many cases, the teacher data could not yield specific examples of the attributes of their learning—that occurred during the teacher training programme—and/or discuss its impact, though the questionnaire data gives evidence of specific responses. This raises an issue of contradiction in their verbal and written responses, some reasons for which are mentioned below. Moreover, very few teachers allowed us to observe their classes; the majority of them said it would not be useful, for us, to observe their teaching for various reasons: examinations, revision, students' limited attendance, and so on.

Moreover, the supervisors (responsible for in-service teacher training) were not, as such, involved in any academic supervisory role at the practical level. They were mostly involved in providing administrative assistance at the district offices. Also, in many cases, the people who underwent international and national level training either retired or were transferred to other departments not particularly relevant to the focus of the training. This, again, reflects the similar situation discussed above in relation to the teachers' training and its limited application.

Though conducting an impact study after a decade-long gap was never going to be an easy task, the various contextual realities discussed above further contributed enormously to the difficulties of collecting specific data in relation to the impact of the projects under study.

Unfamiliarity with the Culture, Norms, and Ethics of Research

Cultural Interpretation of 'Voluntary and Informed Participation'

As discussed above, detailed negotiations were planned with the government officials at various levels, to ensure that they facilitated data collection and developed a shared understanding regarding the nature, purpose, and processes of research. They promised their full cooperation; however, during the field visits, we found that the required database or profile of the teachers (as beneficiaries of training) was not available at some district offices. Also, in some districts, the relevant district officers had not undertaken any prior communication with the participants, despite our mutual planning and negotiations. This resulted in confusion as the teachers came, but were not aware of why they had been called there. Consequently, some who came had not received the relevant training, others came thinking it was a selection for a training programme, and yet others came thinking it was a training session. This 'forced' participation influenced the nature of participation and the quality of the data collected. The teachers informed us that this was a common practice in the public sector, where they would either be called at very short notice, or without any prior communication about the purpose or any expectations of them.

Another issue was that since there was no record of the trainee teachers, and almost all the teachers available had been invited to participate in the activity by the officials, much of the data found was irrelevant and/or incomplete.

Threat of Information Sharing/Influence on Data

In some cases, we ended up conducting the interviews in the headteacher's office. At times, this was due to lack of space but, at others, it appeared to be a deliberate attempt, by the authorities, to 'manage' the process. As a result, the teachers tended to give general comments, rather than specific examples, regarding their learning and implementation. Also, even in cases where we managed to conduct interviews in separate rooms, we realized that the overall culture was such that it did not allow us space for individual interaction with the selected participants; they would be surrounded by a crowd of teachers who would keep interjecting during the participants' responses, in spite of the researchers' polite requests for exclusive interviews. As their interference, in many cases, influenced the participants' responses, we were unable to access the individual's experiences related to specific training/projects. In some cases, we used this as an opportunity to identify some other potential participants (based on their training experiences), whereas, in others, we ended up conducting more interviews with some irrelevant groups as a strategy to prevent their constant interference in our relevant interviews with their colleagues. Obviously, not only did this have implications on the nature of data collected but it also had implications in terms of the time spent on the process.

Although the questionnaires were written in three languages— English, Urdu, and Sindhi—it was clear that many participants had difficulty in filling the questionnaires themselves. This may have been partly due to the teachers' limited experience of, and engagement in, reading official documents or academic materials. It is also probably due, in part, to the fact that in rural schools, due to limitations of supply, teacher selection criteria does not require adequate academic and/or professional qualification; the teachers, despite their extended experience of teaching, do not develop sufficient reading and writing skills in what is still regarded as an 'oral culture'. Also, some stated that they could not complete the questionnaire because they were unable to recall their training or the related experiences. Despite the research team's facilitation (including translation, explanation, and memory recall cues), they appeared uncomfortable filling the form out independently and, on many occasions, we saw a clerk completing the questionnaire for the teacher. The headteachers/ government officials present were found to be giving cues for recall, using the allowances received during the workshop as a reference point; for example, we overheard them saying, '*the workshop in which you all were given 1200 rupees*'. Observations also indicated that some teachers copied responses from other colleagues, whereas others were filling forms for their colleagues thereby generating issues of authenticity in the data. Further probes revealed that, in addition to other reasons, this was also due to the teachers' inability to fill out the questionnaires since (as discussed above) all writing work was generally carried out by the administrative staff of the school. Some teachers also approached their master trainers and/or senior teachers, to fill out the forms, due to their perception that advice should be sought from an expert or experienced person before submission. In some cases, teachers appeared quite reluctant and bluntly refused to fill out the questionnaire, saying that they had not received any training at all which was quite contradictory to what the headteacher had told us about them.

The government officials had asked all the teachers to participate in the questionnaire activity. It proved very challenging, for a small research team, to monitor the large numbers of teachers. There was insufficient space to arrange all the teachers in two or three groups which could be facilitated by the two or three researchers available in the field. Therefore, different clusters were formed, at a time, to accommodate the teachers for the exercise. Consequently, in some cases, the researchers had to accept offers of assistance from government officials in administering the questionnaire. However, we realized later that during the data collection process, the supervisors were reading the completed questionnaires, so raising ethical concerns. Their presence also posed a threat to many teachers. Many of the male teachers were reluctant to provide complete information, and approached the researchers towards the end to ask for their cell phone numbers so that they could provide more information—expressing concern that they were not very comfortable providing all the required details in the presence of the government officials—although none of them actually called. Moreover, the supervisors/government officials also influenced their memory and responses by sharing and imposing their own experiences and perspectives regarding teacher training in Sindh.

Throughout these examples, it is quite evident that the overall culture posed various threats that hindered the participants from sharing information. Also, the political–cultural context was such that the data was influenced in different ways, and at many points, during the data collection.

Perceptions about 'Research' and 'Researchers'

Data collection was also influenced by the various perceptions that the participants had regarding research and researchers. As mentioned above, the participants came in (for the survey administration) assuming that this was some kind of performance evaluation, a selection test for training, or some other kind of test. In some cases, they feared that this was a performance appraisal that might have implications for the security of their job or for promotion. This perception was reflected not only in the various comments and queries made by the participants but also in their attempts to consult some of their seniors, officials, or colleagues while filling out the forms. Similar perceptions were evident in the teachers' initial interest and motivation to participate in the interviews, assuming it to be a selection process for training. In many cases, they lost interest in the activity once the purpose had been clarified. Detailed negotiation and counselling, on the part of the researchers, was required for participants to understand the purpose and nature of their participation in the questionnaire administration.

Some teachers were not motivated enough to recall the information, as they were looking for remuneration in cash and/ or kind. When they were informed about the purpose of the exercise, some teachers seemed reluctant to fill the questionnaire. In this connection, one important finding was that the participants had linked the training with the training allowances that they had received; they were unable to recall or discuss the purpose of the training and related learning outcomes, but remembered the amount they received. For example, one participant shared that her motivation for the training came from the amount (10,000 rupees) that she was informed she would receive in this training; she was particularly interested as then she would be able to pay for an impending surgical operation. Despite having received the training, she was unable to link teaching with the training received; relevance of the training and its practice to the real classroom and daily situation was missing. Teacher commitment, and follow-up to the training, was a recurring issue noticed in many cases. Our data suggests that, in this culture and context, financial gains were an important motivating factor in many instances. It was difficult for teachers (in those instances) to see any value in participating in an activity (the current research) that offered no financial rewards as they had been used to such compensation in the past—by various organizations and by the public sector which provide such allowances to teachers for their participation in training. In some cases, their expectations had appeared quite justified (for example, when they had spent money travelling to the clusters where the survey was being administered). However, as the education officers had advised us that the teachers lived in the neighbourhood and data collection would occur during their official time, we did not anticipate that this would not be the case nor had we made any provisions for such expenses in the research funding available to us. Nevertheless, such issues created serious ethical dilemmas for the researchers in the field.

Moreover, some teachers refused to fill out the questionnaire because of their biases against the department of the university that the researchers belonged to, assuming that we represented that department. They had been against the philosophy behind one of the initiatives taken by that department—an issue that continued to be a matter of some debate at the point of the study and its data collection. Thus, the participants' biases, regarding the role of the researchers and their agenda, also created barriers for us in accessing relevant data.

Reflections and Insights

The findings above provide numerous insights into conducting research in the context of the South. More importantly, they highlight the power dynamics and political dimension of conducting an educational impact study in such a context. Although the dimensions of power and politics have been emphasized and discussed in studies conducted in the North as well, the context of the South, and particularly the rural public setting discussed in this chapter, poses unique challenges and requires responses of a different and creative nature. These challenges can be summarized as: (a) issues of access, (b) issues of authenticity, and (c) the gap between the culture of the context and the research culture.

The research was conducted in a context that was highly bureaucratic, centralized (despite recent attempts at decentralization), and top-down in terms of its approach and various processes. In such contexts, access to information and key stakeholders becomes quite challenging as there are various gatekeepers at various levels who control, manipulate, and direct the flow of information. The difficulties of accessing in-depth views of influential officials at the top level of hierarchy have been well-articulated and well-represented through Fitz and Halpin's (1994) comments that '. . . senior government officials are well-versed in controlling any information they provide, and present considerable difficulties in decoding the views expressed, which creates problems of access and maintaining the role of objective enquirers' (p. 5); this is manifested through, for example, the choice of topics: 'certain topics are discussed and others dismissed' (Ball, 1994). However, the issue of 'access' emerged as a much broader and constraining issue—access to relevant documents, access to relevant key stakeholders, access to relevant and meaningful data—all due to the kind of context we were dealing with in this study. The overall bureaucracy of the system was such that despite various layers of approvals and assurances of cooperation on the part of the then-involved government officials, accessing the relevant documents and information had been a challenging, time-consuming, and cumbersome process. Additionally, it seems that the overall lack of appreciation for 'informed' decision-making has generally led to unsystematic and inconsistent efforts to consolidate and make meaningful use of the data collected. Accessing participant and project related information, therefore, remained an issue in such a context. Moreover, accessing the participants was difficult because of the issues of frequent and often unjustified transfers of project staff or beneficiaries, based mostly on favouritism, political interference, or other such reasons that have character-ized the cultural context of the public sector in Pakistan for many years. An important investment, and consistent theme, in the current study, therefore, had been the on-going negotiation of access and power.

One dimension of the context is the public sector setting in which the study was conducted (as discussed above). Another important dimension, however, is the broader context of the research—educational research—concerned with educational reform projects, aiming to assess their impact and outcomes. Broadly speaking, both education and research can be viewed as intrinsically political (Simons, 2000; Randall, Cooper, and Hite, 1999). The very fact that the current research—intended to study the impact and outcomes of teacher education reform projects—turned it into a highly political and high-stakes activity in which the findings of the study could have significant implications for the different stakeholders involved at various levels in the project's conceptualization, implementation, and evaluation. The projects being studied were donor-funded projects; the findings could, for example, presumably affect future funding opportu-nities. The outcomes, and the related performance of the educational officials, could have implications for their future roles; also, there could be implications of these projects for educational policies. Simons (2000) captures the complexities involved in such processes in the following quote:

> In evaluation, there is a further complicating factor that influences the precise decision taken in any one context. The inherently

political nature of evaluation means that politics in the site often intrude upon an evaluation research process to the point where they challenge the procedural ethics that guide the conduct and reporting of the evaluation. In such circumstances, evaluators are faced with a dilemma of how to continue to act professionally and ethically while managing conflicting political pressures without being captive to anyone's particular vested interest (p. 38).

Though her comments were related to the conducting of evaluations, they have equal relevance to the current study—in the context of which, power and politics came into play more strongly and in a variety of forms. In Pakistan, training in itself has become a highly political activity. Due to the nature of the opportunities provided through training (e.g., foreign travel, monetary benefits in the form of training allowances), selection for training becomes a much sought-after activity in cases where such allowances are provided. Thus, politics plays a large role in training-related decision-making at various levels and layers of authority, frequently resulting in the selection of irrelevant or unsuitable candidates. For us, this political context added further difficulties in the accessing of meaningful data and relevant stakeholders, and in dealing with the issues of irrelevant data, incomplete information, and a limited or lack of specific examples of real learning experiences.

Moreover, the specific cultural attributes of the context under study, in many instances, raised ethical concerns of various kinds for the researchers. The above findings quote instances where standard ethical notions, such as 'informed participation', 'prior consultation, negotiation, or consent seeking', and individuals' space and privacy were not respected in accordance with the norms and principles of ethical research. These are alien notions in many such rural public settings. This is reflected, for instance, in the cultural interpretation of voluntary participation, the top-down flow of information, lack of prior information sharing, and so on. 'Research ethics versus contextual reality': while this has been a consistent theme for our on-going reflection and response to the emerging situation, the whole concept of research ethics needs to be re-examined through the lens of the context of the South—as we are conducting research in settings where research and related nuances are relatively unfamiliar concepts.

Power dynamics also came into play in the way in which the researchers were perceived. At various points, we were variously perceived as members of an influential university of repute, evaluators, performance assessors, a training selection team, representatives of donor agencies, and proponents of—or at least associated with—controversial views. All these perceptions, held by different participants at different stages of the study, reflected the nature of power that they associated with researchers *vis-à-vis* their own sense of empowerment (or lack of it). This had implications for the negotiations for access to data and for the nature of the data generated. Most of these perceptions were due to the existing culture, and to an overall unfamiliarity of the research culture and its processes: they would generally associate their experiences of filling out questionnaires, responding to questions, and classroom observations to performance appraisals and evaluations by supervisory bodies or to the selection process for training—where remuneration, in the form of training allowances, is an established and expected practice. Thus, the huge gap between the culture and norms of research, and the specific culture and context of the South where the study had been conducted, influenced data collection in the ways discussed above. In such a context, financial gain, rather than contribution to knowledge generation (as research participants), presents itself as a motivating factor. Researchers studying such contexts need to take these perceptions and influences into consideration while designing studies.

The role of power and politics is an important dimension and needs to be taken into account while planning such educational research. Our purpose in writing this chapter is to invite reflection and to develop greater insights with regard to the political dimension of studying impact in the context of the South. We tend to agree with Fitz and Halpin (1994) that, in the end, 'the factual information gathered . . . may be less important than the knowledge gained about the social and political context of policy making [educational reforms in this case] at this high level' (p. 5). We hope that the chapter will provide an insight for researchers, of the need to study the settings that reflect the power dynamics, when designing research for the context of the South.

Concluding Thoughts

The findings discussed in this chapter have highlighted the challenges posed by studying a context that is unique and different in so many ways from the contexts of the North. What is important is to recognize and acknowledge, and address, these differences while designing and conducting research in such contexts. This has implications for research training in the contexts of the South.

It is relevant and important to make an observation here that most of the training for research in the South relies heavily on research textbooks produced in other contexts. Our collective and extensive experience of research training, and supervision of novice researchers, suggests that beginning researchers tend to adopt those research concepts as 'standard practices' without realizing the contextual relevance. Therefore, through sharing our journey from conceptualization to actual implementation, this chapter has been an attempt to emphasize the contextual realities vis-à-vis the methodological choices and approaches one has to make.

What we have emphasized, here, is to realize and understand the context, and to show 'responsiveness' towards it. Despite the information gaps and biases in the data, we did not reject their information but instead tried to make sense of it by understanding the context which caused the gaps and biases. We examined our limitations in relation to what we could gather as data, and described the nature of the gaps, biases, and other similar issues in an open and transparent manner. In conclusion, we tend to agree with Vithal (2002) that, in such research contexts, the interpretative paradigm of research is the most appropriate one as it forces researchers to develop a more caring and creative research approach with a sharper concern for the ethics and politics of the research setting and research relationships.

References

AKU–IED. (2003). *Policy dialogue on key issues in education*. Karachi, Pakistan: Aga Khan University Institute for Educational Development (AKU–IED).

Ball, S.J. (1994). Political interviews and the politics of interviewing. In G. Walford (Ed.), *Researching the powerful in education* (pp. 96–115). London, UK: UCL Press.

Cohen, L., and Mannion, L. (1994). *Research methods in education* (4 ed.). London, UK: Routledge.

Cookson, P.W. (1994). 'The power discourse: elite narratives and educational policy formation.' In G. Walford (Ed.), *Researching the powerful in education* (pp. 116–131). London, UK: UCL Press.

Fitz, J., and Halpin, D. (1994). 'Ministers and mandarins: educational research in elite settings.' In G. Walford (Ed.), *Researching the powerful in education* (pp. 32–50). London, UK: UCL Press.

Government of Pakistan. (1998). *National Education Policy (1998–2010)*. Islamabad, Pakistan: Ministry of Education.

Oppenheim, A.N. (1992). *Questionnaire design, interviewing and attitude measurement*. London, UK: Pinter Publishers.

Randall, E.V., Cooper, B.S., and Hite, S.J. (1999). 'Understanding the politics of research in education.' *Educational Policy*, 13(1), 7–22.

Silverman, D. (2000). *Doing qualitative research: a practical handbook*. London, UK: Sage.

Simons, H. (2000). 'Damned if you do, damned if you don't: ethical and political dilemmas in evaluation.' In H. Simons and R. Usher (Eds.), *Situated ethics in educational research* (pp. 39–55). London, UK: Routledge.

Vithal, R. (2002). 'Crucial descriptions: talking back to theory and practice in mathematics education through research.' In P. Valero and O. Skovsmose (Eds.), *Proceedings of the Third International Mathematics Education and Society Conference* (pp. 501–511). Copenhagen, Denmark: Danish University of Education Centre for Research in Learning Mathematics.

Walford, G. (Ed.). (1994). *Researching the powerful in education*. London: UCL Press.

Note

1. In December 2004, a major Conference on Teacher Education was held in Islamabad as part of the USAID Pakistan Teacher Education and Professional Development Programme.

13

Logic, Observation, Representation, Dialectic and Ethical Values: What Counts as Evidence in Educational Research?[1]

Dylan Wiliam

What is the purpose of educational research? Stokes (1997) proposes that there are two important dimensions to the conduct of research in any field: the extent to which the research is conducted with a view of how it will be applied (i.e. the pure-applied distinction), and the extent to which the research is motivated by a concern for fundamental understanding (see Table 1). For Stokes, the Danish astronomer Tycho Brahe exemplifies research that is motivated neither by a quest for fundamental understanding nor by considerations of use.

Where considerations of use are important, but fundamental understanding is not, the result is pure applied research—exemplified by the work of Thomas Edison. Pure basic research, where fundamental understanding is a concern but considerations of use are not, can be exemplified by the work of the Danish physicist, Niels Bohr. Finally, where both considerations of use and fundamental understanding are important, we have 'Pasteur's quadrant'—use-inspired basic research.

Table 1: Types of research as classified by Stokes (1997)			
		Considerations of use?	
		No	Yes
Quest for fundamental understanding?	No	Applied research unmotivated by applications (Brahe)	Pure applied research (Edison)
	Yes	Pure basic research (Bohr)	Use-inspired basic research (Pasteur)

G.H. Hardy, a mathematician, argued forcefully that considerations of use were irrelevant to his research: 'I have never done anything "useful". No discovery of mine has made, or is likely to make, directly or indirectly, for good or ill, the least difference to the amenity of the world.'(Hardy, 1940 p. 150). Interestingly, much of Hardy's 'pure' research has, in recent years, found application in nuclear physics, but Hardy certainly undertook his work unmotivated by considerations of use. However, there appears to be a widespread acceptance that while there is a place for 'pure' research in education, most educational research should be concerned with the improvement of educational processes and outcomes. Indeed, for over fifty years, one of the major criticisms of educational research has been that too much educational research has been motivated more by a quest for fundamental understanding than by considerations of use. In 1945, J. Cayce Morrison, Assistant Commissioner for Research at the State Education Department in New York, lamented that there was 'too wide a gap between research at its best and much of its practice in education' (Morrison, 1945, p. 243).

At times, the concern with considerations of use has led to a simplistic focus on 'what works'—most notably resulting in the establishment of the 'What Works Clearinghouse', which provides a 'trusted source of scientific evidence for what works in education' (What Works Clearinghouse, 2010). The idea that educational research should provide simple answers to simple questions was also memorably encapsulated in the questions asked by Senator Robert F. Kennedy, to the Commissioner of the United States Office of Education (Harold Howe), at the hearings of the Senate sub-committee on Education in 1966: 'What happened to the children? Do you mean you spent a billion dollars and you don't know whether they can read or not?' (Wickline, 1971, pp. 7–8).

In this chapter, I suggest that if we wish to undertake and promote research in 'Pasteur's quadrant'—research that is motivated both by considerations of use *and* by a quest for fundamental understanding—then we need to think more deeply about simplistic notions of 'what works'. As writers in this volume have noted, this simplistic notion of 'what works' has come to dominate the funding of development aid. So, whether or not research methods in education are universal is an increasingly important issue. Some writers, such as Valero and Vithal (1999), have argued that differences in context and culture require the development of different methods, and even definitions, of research. Others (e.g. Pring, this volume) argue that these differences can be accommodated within the standard 'Western' view of educational research. Below, I use the classification of inquiry systems developed by C. West Churchman to attempt a synthesis of these apparently conflicting perspectives.

Churchman (1971) proposed a classification of inquiry systems based on what was the primary, or most salient, form of evidence, and he labelled each category of inquiry systems with the name of a philosopher whose own stance, according to Churchman, typified the category: Leibniz, Locke, Kant, Hegel, and Singer.

In a *Leibnizian* inquiry system, certain fundamental assumptions are made and, by the use of formal reasoning, deductions are drawn. Within a Leibnizian inquiry system, such as pure mathematics, the most important form of evidence is rationality—do the conclusions follow logically from the assumptions? Leibnizian inquiry systems, therefore, take no account of data from the 'real world' and are, therefore, of little use in educational research.

In the 'naive inductivist' paradigm (Chalmers, 1978), we collect empirical data and then attempt to build coherent accounts of the data or, conversely, we might validate theoretical accounts by finding out whether the predictions arising from those theoretical accounts accord with our observations. This interplay of observation and theory is the hallmark of *Lockean* inquiry systems, which are the standard method of inquiry for the physical, life, and earth sciences. The key requirement for a Lockean approach is that it is necessary for all observers to agree on what they have observed. Even in the social sciences, there are many situations where considerable progress can be made because the relevant data are sufficiently widely agreed upon to provide a fruitful starting point for the Lockean inquirer. On the other hand, if observers disagree on what they have observed, then the Lockean inquirer cannot begin. To the Lockean inquirer, incompatible observations mean that at least one of the observations is wrong.

However, philosophers of science have long recognized that there can be no such thing as 'scientific detachment'; all observations are theory-dependent. As Werner von Heisenberg observed, 'What we learn about is not nature itself, but nature exposed to our methods of questioning' (quoted in Johnson, 1996, p. 147). The idea that observational data is not neutral, but rather a consequence of the assumptions made by the inquirer about which kinds of data are worth collecting, is embraced within a *Kantian* inquiry system. Kantian inquiry subsumes both Leibnizian and Lockean systems by deliberately framing multiple alternative perspectives on both theory and data.

One way to do this would be by building different theories on the basis of the same data. Alternatively, two (or more) theories related to the problem could be generated, with appropriate data for each theory then being collected. The result might be that it may not be immediately apparent where the two theories overlap and where they conflict; this forms the essence of the distinction between Lockean and Kantian systems. Within a Lockean approach, where two theories are not identical they must make different predictions about something; it is then possible to perform what Robert Hooke termed a 'crucial experiment' (Lohne, 1968) to determine which was correct. For the Kantian inquirer, the two theories may simply be different ways of looking at the same phenomenon, where it is not possible to put one theory beside another and compare them; in other words, they are *incommensurable* (Kuhn, 1962). However, it may be possible to begin a process of theory-building that incorporates the different representations of the situation under study.

This idea of reconciling alternative theories is more fully developed in a *Hegelian* inquiry system, where antithetical and mutually inconsistent theories are developed. Not content with building plausible theories, the Hegelian inquirer takes a plausible theory, and then investigates what would have to be different about the world for the *exact opposite* of the most plausible theory itself to be plausible. A crucial question for the Hegelian inquirer is, 'What would have to be different about the world for the exact opposite of my conclusion to be plausible?' If the answer is, 'not very much', then this suggests that the available data underdetermines, to a significant degree, the interpretations that are made of them.

The tension produced by confrontation between conflicting theories forces the assumptions of each theory to be questioned, which might then result in sufficient clarification of the issues to make a co-ordination possible, or even a synthesis, of the different perspectives at a higher level of abstraction. The differences between Lockean, Kantian, and Hegelian inquiry systems were summed up by Churchman as follows:

> The Lockean inquirer displays the 'fundamental' data that all experts agree are accurate and relevant, and then builds a consistent story out of these. The Kantian inquirer displays the same story from different points of view, emphasizing thereby that what is put into the story by the internal mode of representation is not given from the outside. But the Hegelian inquirer, using the same data, tells two stories, one supporting the most prominent policy on one side, the other supporting the most promising story on the other side (Churchman, 1971, p. 177).

It is tempting to view these four inquiry systems as a hierarchy and, in a sense, there undoubtedly is a logical order relation. The Hegelian inquiry system is a special case of a Kantian inquiry system, where the multiple representations are constrained to create a dialectic. The Lockean inquiry system (which clearly subsumes the Leibnizian inquiry system) is also a special kind of Kantian inquiry where one representation is singled out as privileged. However, this does not mean that Kantian inquiry systems are always to be preferred, since they may produce such complexity that progress is impossible—the most complex representation of a problem is not necessarily the most useful. There is a trade-off between parsimony and completeness, and therefore there is a choice to be made. In other words, we can inquire about inquiry systems, questioning the values and ethical assumptions that these inquiry systems embody.

This inquiry into inquiry systems is itself, of course, an inquiry system which is termed *Singerian* by Churchman, after the philosopher E.A. Singer (see Singer, 1959). Such an approach requires a constant questioning of the assumptions of inquiry systems. Tenets, no matter how fundamental they appear to be, are themselves open to challenge in order to cast a new light on the situation under investigation. This leads directly, and naturally, to an examination of the values and ethical considerations inherent in theory building.

In a Singerian inquiry, there is no solid foundation. Instead of asking what 'is', we ask what are the implications and consequences of different assumptions about what 'is taken to be':

The 'is taken to be' is a self-imposed imperative of the community. Taken in the context of the whole Singerian theory of inquiry and progress, the imperative has the status of an ethical judgment. That is, the community judges that to accept its instruction is to bring about a suitable tactic or strategy. . . . The acceptance may lead to social actions outside of inquiry, or to new kinds of inquiry, or whatever. Part of the community's judgement is concerned with the appropriateness of these actions from an ethical point of view. Hence the linguistic puzzle which bothered some empiricists—how the inquiring system can pass linguistically from 'is' statements to 'ought' statements—is no puzzle at all in the Singerian inquirer: the inquiring system speaks exclusively in the 'ought,' the 'is' being only a convenient *façon de parler* when one wants to block out the uncertainty in the discourse. (Churchman, 1971, p. 202).

Within a Singerian inquiry system, one can never separate the meanings of a piece of research from its consequences. Educational research is a process of *representing* educational processes; the representations are never right nor wrong—merely more or less appropriate for a particular purpose—and it is perfectly fair to expect the researcher to defend the appropriateness of the representations. Greeno (1997) suggests that educational researchers should assess the relative worth of competing perspectives by determining which perspective will contribute most to the improvement of educational practice' of course, this evaluation must take into account the constraints of the available resources (both human and financial), the political and social contexts in which education takes place, and the likelihood of success. While the Lockean, Kantian, or Hegelian inquirer can claim to be producing knowledge for its own sake, Singerian inquirers are required to defend—to the community—not just their methods of research, but also which research they choose to undertake.

Churchman's classification of enquiry systems provides interesting perspectives on the chapters in this volume. Many of the authors have drawn attention to the fact that, as Valero and Vithal pointed out in their original 1999 paper, contextual effects are more important in some contexts than in others. More precisely, in some settings, aspects of context that are 'bracketed out' (in other words, are ignored) in the design and conduct of the research do not materially affect the inferences drawn from the data collected or the actions that follow on from those inferences. In other settings, however, ignoring aspects of the context renders inferences so limited, or so hedged around with cautions, as to be effectively worthless. The Lockean inquirer's approach to context is to try to tame it through measurement. Within this perspective, context represents a stimulus to further building. If one cannot explain the observed outcomes because of the effects of context, then operationalizing details of the context will provide a better explanation. For example, in many countries in the South, teacher absenteeism is a significant problem; it is not uncommon to find up to a quarter of the teachers employed at a school to be absent on any given day, for reasons apparently unconnected to illness or disability. The Lockean inquirer incorporates teacher absence, as a variable in the analysis, to improve the scope of the theory.

The Kantian inquirer, on the other hand, would tend to see the effects of context, not as variables to be controlled through measurement, but as opportunities for building new theories on the phenomena under study. While these theories may be related to the previous theories, they may be incommensurable. For example, rather than trying to incorporate teacher absenteeism as a variable within the existing theory, a Kantian inquirer might look at teacher absenteeism as a new line of inquiry which may, or may not, intersect with the original issue under study.

The debate, addressed in the chapters in this book, can be seen as a debate between Lockean and Kantian approaches to inquiry. Those who, while acknowledging that context has more impact in some settings than others (e.g. Khamis, Pring), nevertheless advocate that the universality of research methods can be seen as Lockean inquirers. In contrast, those who argue that research in the South requires different methods can be thought of as Kantian inquirers, building alternative representations of the phenomena under study. Indeed, the whole project of this book can then be seen as a Hegelian approach to inquiry. We have sought to tell the strongest possible story regarding the universality of research methods, and the strongest possible story about the impossibility of universal research methods. Of course, the Lockean inquirer wants to know which of these two stories is correct, while the Kantian inquirer accepts that they are simply different, and the Hegelian inquirer wants to see how the engagement between these two positions advances the debate.

Churchman's inquiry systems provide a useful perspective on the increasing preoccupation of many donor agencies with 'what works' in education and development. To the Lockean inquirer, an emphasis on what works is unobjectionable. Donor funds are limited, and therefore it makes sense to ensure that whatever funds are available are spent in the best possible way. Where some evaluations show promising results, but others fail to do so, this is a spur to the Lockean inquirer to collect better data, or to build better theories, so that the ambiguities can be resolved.

The Kantian inquirer, on the other hand, might ask 'What is lost by focusing only on what works?' and may even reject that what works is an appropriate question. To the Lockean inquirer, the rejection of what works as an evaluative criterion might well appear incomprehensible, but to the Kantian inquirer it is completely acceptable (and perhaps, to the Hegelian inquirer, necessary).

Within a Singerian frame of reference, however, we can integrate these different perspectives by focusing not simply on what is, but also on what ought to be. The Singerian inquirer accepts that a simplistic emphasis on 'what works' may lead to undesirable outcomes, but also accepts that donor agencies may nevertheless insist on evaluating the success of different kinds of interventions in these simple terms. The question is then no longer about which is right, but about what the ethical implications of the different courses of action are. Accepting the simplistic 'what works' mentality of a donor may distort one's research, but it may also create possibilities for moving people to action that the Singerian inquirer judges are worth the risk. Of course, the Singerian inquirer also accepts that this is not simply a personal decision; one should also be prepared to defend the choices, not just about how research is done but also what research is done, to the research community. For Leibnizian, Lockean, Kantian, and Hegelian inquirers, what matters is the generation of new knowledge. For the Singerian inquirer, new knowledge is not enough; it is also essential to be able to justify that the knowledge brings about effective action. Echoing the distinction that Aristotle drew in the Nicomachean Ethics (Aristotle, 2000) between science (*episteme*) and practical wisdom (*phronesis*), the Leibnizian, Kantian, and Hegelian inquirers ask 'Is this right?' while the Singerian inquirer asks 'Is this good?'

Thus, for the Singerian inquirer, research in the South addresses the same question as research in the North. The context may be different and isolating relevant variables may be more difficult, or even less appropriate, but ultimately educational research, whether conducted in the South or the

North, should be driven by both a quest for fundamental understanding and by considerations of use to bring the transformative capacity of education to improve lives.

References

Aristotle. (2000). *The Nicomachean ethics* (R. Crisp, Trans.). Cambridge, UK: Cambridge University Press.

Chalmers, A.F. (1978). *What is this thing called science?* Milton Keynes, UK: Open University Press.

Churchman, C. W. (1971).*The design of inquiring systems: basic concepts of systems and organization.* New York, NY: Basic Books.

Greeno, J.G., and The Middle-School Mathematics Through Applications Project Group. (1997). 'Theories and practices of thinking and learning to think.' *American Journal of Education*, 106, 85–126.

Hardy, G.H. (1940). *A mathematician's apology.* Cambridge, UK: Cambridge University Press.

Johnson, G. (1996). *Fire in the mind: science, faith and the search for order.* London, UK: Viking.

Kuhn, T.S. (1962).*The structure of scientific revolutions.* Chicago, IL: University of Chicago Press.

Lohne, J.A. (1968). 'Experimentum crucis.' *Notes and records of the Royal Society of London*, 23(2), 169–199.

Morrison, J.C. (1945). 'The role of research in educational reconstruction.' In N.B. Henry (Ed.), *American education in the postwar period, part 2: structural reorganisation (The forty-fourth yearbook of the National Society for the Study of Education)* (Vol. 44: 2, pp. 238–265). Chicago, IL: University of Chicago Press.

Singer Jr., E.A. (1959). *Experience and reflection.* Philadelphia, PA: University of Pennsylvania Press.

Stokes, D.E. (1997). *Pasteur's quadrant: basic science and technological innovation.* Washington, DC: Brookings Institution Press.

Valero, P., and Vithal, R. (1999). 'Research methods of the 'North' revisited from the "South".' *Perspectives in Education*, 18(2), 5–12.

What Works Clearinghouse. (2010). *About us*. Retrieved 21 June 2010, from http://ies.ed.gov/ncee/wwc/aboutus/

Wickline, L.E. (1971). 'Educational accountability.' In E.W. Roberson (Ed.), *Educational accountability through evaluation* (pp. 7–18). Englewood Cliffs, NJ: Educational Technology Systems.

Wiliam, D. (2008). 'What should education research do and how should it do it?'. *Educational Researcher*, 37(7), 432–438.

Note

1. Much of the first part of this chapter is drawn from Wiliam (2008).

14

Afterword

Michael Nettles

'Aristotle was asked how much educated men were superior to those uneducated: "As much", said he, "as the living are to the dead".' (Diogenes Laërtius, 1925, p. 9)

The picture of school, that we each envision, varies with locale. Mention the Alps, and we might imagine a rosy-cheeked youth trekking on skis in a mountain setting. Allude to the African plains, and thoughts may run to group lessons and a bony-kneed youngster, among cohorts, squatting under a shade tree. Slide in a reference to a madrassa, and we conjure a boy in rote recitation and a girl, locked out, stealing a furtive glance in. What is the common thread? Whether in the most dangerous neighbourhoods, the most remote villages, or the most deprived slums, children globally demonstrate, daily, that learning is possible. Children want to know, to explore, to discover. Children want to learn.

Researchers, meanwhile, want the intellectual challenges of investigating, researching, and chronicling. In the global South, they trek difficult distances and subject themselves to treacherous circumstances to understand how communities educate their youth. These researchers are the education pioneers—adventurers who hope to capture a very un-Western view of learning.

In terms of global scope, there is much to investigate. As Vithal notes: 'The "South" is also the majority context—there are more children . . . in "South-like" contexts who do not go to school or do not attend school regularly than all the children in the North who attend school.'

In terms of topical scope, there is much to question: Which research model would be most successful for the global South? Can we point to one that is different from the North? What paradigm might be unique, and yet universally applicable?

Khamis brings a more basic approach to the task of the education researcher. He starts with the learner and asks: 'What is the purpose of the research and how is such research used, by whom, and how does it relate to the teaching and learning we construct in school?'

In a joint paper, Ebrahim and Penn raise more questions than they answer, as they set out to examine an early childhood development study in South Africa from both a Northern and Southern lens. Ebrahim focuses her concern on understanding and prioritizing the needs of the most disadvantaged, while Penn insists that researchers adopt Northern notions of empirical rigour while delving more broadly beyond the community. Each retains her own priorities.

If we accept a dichotomy of perspective between the global South and global North, we wonder if an alien researcher can even understand the context of a Southern underdeveloped region, student body, teaching staff, or community. Valero and Vithal say 'No'. Pring says 'Yes, of course'; after all, everyone is human. Is there a logical way to bring these two camps together?

Still, a similar diversity of problems exists in the USA. There are remote rural areas, urban ghettos, and isolated mountain and prairie areas. By definition, these regions share Northern values and standards, yet global problems exist. Some students fail to read or compute, do not attend school, or quit. Some mourn friends killed by gang warfare. Some schools lack sufficient texts, and others endure leaking roofs. Can a US Northerner appreciate or intelligently discuss the problems of the US South, and vice versa? Within the USA, mores and ethics vary. Problems of violence, poverty, and chaos share a similarity that is all too familiar worldwide.

It is troubling that Northern influences in development and tourism have caused Southern cultures to be eradicated, as Qureshi points out. There is no remedy for lost culture and vanished heritage. Likewise, in the North, assimilation often accounts for culture being destroyed. Progress was the theme of the twentieth century. Now, with the twenty-first century leaping into its second decade, modernization is rampant. Villagers in remote areas see cell phones inviting communication with an interconnected globe, awakening people to advances in technology. After all, it is a form of advancement that village parents complain of multi-grade schools as insufficient, demanding the very best classrooms for their children—as Hussain and Halai point out.

An anthropological approach may be the best way to study these communities. If we make good use of all ethnographic methods available, can we not figure out ways to understand different cultures without disrupting them? Maybe not. Ethnographic field methods require constant negotiating in cultural contexts. How can one be sensitive to a foreign culture—to study it, but not ruin, influence, or otherwise alter it? We cringe when we see a newspaper travel section boasting about a remote undiscovered paradise, expecting rank commercialization in a few years. Maybe the act of publishing such an article guarantees a region's transformation, just as creating a school in a remote village ensures future change. That is the tension between preservation and progress. Do we wonder if, in turn, just researching an area invites alteration? As in the sciences, it might not be possible to measure something without perturbing it.

Take, for example, Bashiruddin's research collecting reliable biographical and autobiographical data on teachers in Pakistan. Out of respect for their elders, student teachers there imitate the established methods. While a methodological challenge could produce improved teaching practices, the culture would likewise change. In America, this kind of change is considered progress—modern, even ideal. In a world where tradition is venerated and rooted, teachers have trouble revamping educational philosophy and practice.

That said, once a research project is in place, influences must be noted on a study, whether linguistic, cultural, or societal. Some subjects are bound to drop out of projects. It makes sense to account for these problems in the interpretation of the research data. Questions abound: Does the project allow for rotating subjects? Dropouts? What should the data from a project that has rotating subjects be called? Can it be called Complex Data? Shifting Data? Messy Data? Would re-labelling it even help? Any research shift involves the reality that in chaotic places, data must reflect disruptions. As Vithal writes, those are the authentic data.

It is difficult to advance research in poverty and conflict. But, does the process of doing any research at all instil Western values on the rest of the world? Pardhan points out that women in a

Pakistani village, upon meeting a PhD student, feel embarrassed about being uneducated, and would rather have their men talk for them. The suggestion here is that the researcher, trying to get useable data, must establish trust. Ideally, this can become a research opportunity to record non-Western values.

It is a Western notion to question authority. It is a thoroughly non-Western notion to squelch the questioning of authority as a way of showing respect. Yet, a village teacher shows respect for her mentors by not criticizing them, as Pardhan notes. A subject's reluctance to critique the inefficient teaching methods of her educator—or herself—will pose problems for the project design. Looking forward, perhaps the onus is on the researcher to cultivate participation by instilling an appropriate under-standing of the project with the subjects.

The idea that the researcher comes in, records information, and just departs for parts north is probably disquieting to some in a village. It may feel as if taking a snapshot relates to taking a piece of the soul. Will an effort to engage with villagers help? Conversations probably need to continue throughout the project, without jeopardizing the project by colouring the data. In the future, perhaps those conversations need to take place for continued trust, so that the work is structured confidently.

Looking forward, it would be advantageous, if possible, for the researcher to understand a subject's language, cultures, and mores. To earn the trust of the interpreter, it seems critical that a researcher understand and appreciate the culture being studied. A project where the disdain or distrust of the interpreter is visible must be a questionable one. There should be no skimping on the front-end design of the project. Researchers should know and respect the people with whom they are working, and what is culturally and ethically important to the villagers.

Many challenges and experiences mentioned in the book involved cultural vicissitudes that seemed arresting to the researchers. If a researcher wants to investigate a different educational system, it should be incumbent at the outset to have a basic understanding of the culture, the systems of power, who is respected and why, and the problems that students and teachers confront.

Not every region will accept researchers. I am reminded of a story of a Peace Corp volunteer. He was working with water placement, bringing water to remote villages in Honduras. One village elder told him, 'Do not bring us water. If we have water, the next thing the women will want is electricity, and then they will want TV sets, and then they will sit inside all day watching soap operas. No water for us! It's just as healthy for them to have to spend their days drawing water from the river—like the generations of their mothers did.'

Some argue for a different scholarship that does not legitimize itself with reference to the North. This seems problematic when we consider the universality of some subjects. We could take the example of mathematics, a topic discussed in the book. Of course, mathematics education is set by Western cultures, but mathematics—and physics—are universal languages. For example, currently, in an international collaboration, physicists from nations spanning half the world's population are engaged in a joint effort to build a device that uses seawater to solve the world's energy crisis; scientists from the European Union are collaborating with colleagues from China, India, Japan, Korea, Russia, and the USA to demonstrate the feasibility of producing energy from nuclear fusion. Given the universality of the concepts, there may not be a need for a different way to teach maths or physics. Like music and art, one language exists—albeit with multiple expressions. Still, the fundamentals need to be the same for communication to take place.

It is true that politics is dominated by donor agencies. Foreign aid providers set the agendas for these countries, and the countries resent it. But, on the ground, people want effective and culturally sensitive leaders to teach their children, no matter what the politics—that feeling is shared globally. Is there a model for education that does not centre on Western standards?

Vithal writes: 'When notions of poverty, violence, illness, social or cultural tradition and practices protrude into the research frame, the educational and learning aspects often appear to retreat and vice versa. Researchers in the global South have an agenda to document the movement of technology and education into previously backward rural and urban landscapes. It is a painstaking enterprise and thrilling in the aftermath. Research is sticky, disruptions are frequent, findings are difficult.'

In their chapter on teacher training in southern Pakistan, Kumari, Mohammad, and Vazir agree. Their research illustrates the problems of data collection in the South, detailing how minor perturbations like university disputes, pertinent information, or financial incentives colour the research data. Huge gaps between Southern culture and the norms of research influence data collection. However, rather than rejecting information, the researchers 'tried to make sense of it by understanding the context which caused the gaps and biases'.

Kumari, Mohammad, and Vazir speak of the need to accommodate and incorporate disruptions into a study. But, what can one do with disruptions to getting data, or to changing methods midstream? If disruptions are linked to conflict—either religious, social, cultural, or political—a researcher must account for them. It is part of the diversity of the projects.

Valero and Pais put the challenge of disruptions this way:

> Education [is] set in [the] midst of deep inequities and conflict that go beyond the scope of education to solve. If research intends to provide understanding and interpretation of education practice that leads to betterment, then research must address dominant ideas that circulate in study of conflict, poverty and violence.

There is no one way to create a paradigm for research that takes the social context of the place of study into account. In essence, we seem to want to explore and understand the culture of an unstudied group, or simply get into the heads of the people. If that goal is key, then perhaps it is possible to have co-learning agreements rather than data-extraction agreements, as Vithal has suggested.

As Valero and Pais note, there is a need to shift from a theory of learning to a theory of education—to incorporate a broader theoretical framework to address everyday problems. To help to educate those vast numbers of students who go unschooled and untrained in the twenty-first century, the question has been asked: whose agenda is served by what research? Perhaps an increased North–South alliance, with collaborative research, will help offer possibilities of social transformation. In a practical way, every exploration is so different that the idea of one model for research is untenable. The bottom line, from the state of the art of research discussed, is that clinicians need to become more embedded in, understanding of, and collaborative with the people and the cultures being researched.

Wiliam concludes by saying that different cultures necessitate different approaches. Every culture is unique, and each exhibits a different way of communicating, which is why studying them is interesting and gratifying. Perhaps, he posits, we are seeking a universality of research that is impossible to find. Even if we surmount the barriers in collecting data, we are unlikely to perceive the same issues or develop the same methods—even if we ask the same questions. We can, however, appreciate each culture, each contribution, and each consequence of research whether North or South.

Reference

Diogenes Laërtius. (1925). *Lives and opinions of eminent philosophers* (R.D. Hicks, Trans. Book 5: Peripatetics). Cambridge, MA: Harvard University Press.

Notes on Contributors

Ayesha Bashiruddin

Ayesha Bashiruddin is an Assistant Professor at the Aga Khan University, Institute for Educational Development, with a wide experience of teaching ESL to adult students and English Language Education to teachers and teacher educators. She obtained her PhD from the Ontario Institute for Studies in Education, of the University of Toronto, in 2003. She has a keen interest in auto/biographical research. Some of her publications include: *Learning English and learning to teach English: the case of two teachers of English in Pakistan* and *Teaching development of two teachers of English in Pakistan.* Within auto/biographical research, she has published research papers by employing self study research. Some of them are: *Seasons of my learning; Becoming a teacher educator: a female perspective; Pakistani teacher educator's self-study of teaching self-study research.* Her most recent publication is an edited monograph with John Retallick entitled 'Becoming a teacher in the developing world', published by AKU–IED. This edited monograph includes self studies of in-service teachers from the developing world.

Hasina Banu Ebrahim

Hasina Banu Ebrahim's experience in research methodologies in the South stems from her PhD study on the constructions of childhood in early childhood centres in KwaZulu-Natal, South Africa. She explored the methodologies that positioned young children as social actors. Her study resulted in a publication on the methodological processes that characterize research with young children. In a National Research

Foundation Project on the Barriers to Basic Education in the context of HIV/AIDS, she designed and implemented participatory techniques to include the voices of young children and their caregivers. Given the contextual realities and vulnerabilities in the South, she was able to develop the notion of situated ethics in a second publication. The UNICEF study reported in this book is her continued attempt to engage with methodological issues/tensions that arise while doing research in the South.

Anjum Halai

Anjum Halai is an Associate Professor at the Aga Khan University, Institute for Educational Development, in Dar es Salaam-Tanzania. Prior to her posting in Tanzania, she was at AKU–IED in Pakistan. She has a wide experience of teaching and supervision, at both the graduate and postgraduate level, on research methods and curriculum courses. Anjum has led major research and development projects in Pakistan and Africa. Her research interest is primarily in teacher education, with a focus on multilingualism and social justice issues in mathematics. She has published widely in the field of teacher education, providing substantive and methodological insights arising from her research in rural, disadvantaged schools in conflict ridden settings.

Rana Hussain

Rana Hussain was an Assistant Professor at The Aga Khan University Institute for Educational Development, in Pakistan. She has over 40 years of teaching and leadership experience in the field of education. She has worked in the capacities of classroom teacher, teacher educator, manager, academic, and consultant in the primary education sector. Her interest areas are primary education, teacher education, and educational leadership. Her research is mostly in the areas of primary school curriculum and in studying leadership roles in rural settings.

Through her research, she has raised issues of power that challenge the transformative potential of action research.

Anil Khamis

Anil Khamis is Lecturer in Education and International Development at the Institute of Education, University of London, UK. On the CREATE project, Anil is looking at access and alternatives to formal education, particularly for the Muslim communities. His research interests include education and development, with special reference to Muslim communities, school improvement, teacher education, and educational change with respect to developing countries, research methods, and education for disadvantaged/at-risk communities.

Roshni Kumari

Roshni Kumari was a Senior Instructor and Coordinator, Research and Policy Studies at the Aga Khan University's Institute for Educational Development (AKU–IED). She has worked on a number of research projects, and published both nationally and internationally. At AKU–IED, she served in an advisory capacity for research, dissemination, and advocacy, and also took a lead role in facilitating institutional collaborations in research. Her teaching and research interests are broadly rooted in overall educational improvement and development; however, specific interests currently include leadership and learning, organizational learning, strategic planning, policy studies, and educational research. She has also had diverse experience of designing and teaching leadership development programmes for a wide range of clients. Having worked in the educational contexts of Asia, and engaged in research in this context, she has developed a keen interest in deepening understanding about Asian perspectives on leadership and learning and educational research in the South.

Razia Fakir Mohammad

Razia Fakir Mohammad is a Senior Evaluation and Research Coordinator at the Institute of Ismaili Studies, UK. Prior to that, she had been working as an Assistant Professor at the Aga Khan University's Institute for Educational Development. Her academic and professional interests are in the areas of teacher education, assessment, programme evaluation, and educational research in general, and mathematics teaching and teacher education in particular. She has served in various advisory roles and capacities, including her work with the Ministry of Education, Pakistan, in relation to mathematics curriculum review and design. Throughout her professional career, she has engaged extensively in educational research in the context of the South, and her work has been published nationally and internationally.

Michael Nettles

Michael Nettles is Senior Vice-President at the Educational Testing Service, Princeton, New Jersey, where he leads the Policy Evaluation and Research Center, and holds the Edmund W. Gordon Chair for Policy Evaluation and Research. He first joined ETS in 1984, as a Research Scientist, but left in 1989 to assume the position of Vice-President for Assessment of the University of Tennessee Systems; from 1991 to 2003, he was Professor of Education at the University of Michigan. In addition to these posts, he has held several other professional positions. From 1996 to 1999, he was the first Executive Director of the Fredrick D. Patterson Research Institute of the United Negro College Fund, where he published the three-volume *African American Education Data Book* series and *Two Decades of Progress*—the most comprehensive reference books ever produced about the educational status and condition of African Americans in the United States. From 1978 to 1984, he worked as Assistant Director for Academic Affairs for the Tennessee Higher Education Commission, where his work included academic programme review and college and university performance funding. Michael is a former Trustee of the College Board, where he served on the Executive Committee, and a former member of the National Assessment Governing Board, where he served as Vice-Chairman.

Almina Pardhan

Almina is an Assistant Professor at the Aga Khan University Institute for Educational Development in Pakistan. Her doctorate, from the University of Toronto, Canada, looked at gender issues in the context of early childhood education in Pakistan. Her teaching and research interests are in the areas of early childhood education and gender issues in education. Her research, in the remote Booni Valley of Chitral in Pakistan, and doctoral work in Karachi, have produced groundbreaking insights into gender issues in education. Almina's research also raises key issues related to ethnographic field methods when undertaken in highly gender segregated, traditional, and multilingual settings.

Alexandre Pais

Alexandre Pais earned his master's degree in Mathematics from the University of Lisbon in 2000, and started work as a mathematics teacher. During the last nine years, he has taught mathematics at several Portuguese public schools, to people from 12 to 65 years old, and he has earned his Master's Degree in Mathematics Education, also from the University of Lisbon. His doctoral research is in the development of a critical analysis on how the research discourse conveys ideologies about teachers, students, and the importance of school mathematics. An aim of his study is to construct an argumentation that explicitly connects school mathematics with the current mode of living which is characterized as capitalism.

Helen Penn

Helen Penn is Professor of Early Childhood at the University of East London, UK. She has specialized in the interface between policy, theory, and practice in early education and care. She has worked in a number of countries in Southern Africa and in Central Asia, and published widely on her research. She has also worked for transnational bodies such as the EU, OECD, and Asian Development Bank. Her most recent article 'Travelling Policies and International Buzzwords, a review of INGO policy making in the field of early years' was published in the journal *Childhood* in 2010.

Richard Pring

Richard Pring has a wide experience of leadership in research and teaching in teacher education, including 14 years as Director of the Department of Education at Oxford, in the UK. He is currently Lead Director of the Nuffield Review 14–19 Educational Studies, funded by the Nuffield Foundation, UK. His research interest is primarily in the philosophy of education. He is widely published in the field. More recent works include: *Philosophy of Education: Aims, Theory, Common Sense and Research*. London: Continuum, 2004; *Philosophy of Educational Research*, 2nd Edition. London: Continuum, 2004; *Evidence Based Educational Practice*, edited with Gary Thomas. Open University Press, 2005; *John Dewey: The Philosopher of Education for the 21st Century?* London: Continuum, 2007.

Rashida Qureshi

Rashida Qureshi has extensive experience of community participation and development research. She was at the Aga Khan University Institute for Educational Development from 2003–2009 as an Assistant Professor. Her teaching and research interests include gender in education and ethical issues in research methods in education. She is the co-editor of three books entitled *Gender and Education in Pakistan*, *Schools and Schooling Practices in Pakistan*, and *Pits, Perils and Reflexivity in Qualitative Research in Education* all published by the Oxford University Press, Pakistan.

Paola Valero

Paola Valero is a Professor and Head of the Doctoral Programme 'Technology and Science' at the Aalborg University, Denmark. She did her PhD in mathematics education from the Danish University of Education, Denmark. Her primary research interests are in democracy and education, research methodologies, and mathematics education. She has published widely in the field, about the need to develop ways of conceptualizing and researching with 'context'—in such a way that it makes it possible to understand the social and political complexity of mathematics education practices in developing societies.

Renuka Vithal

Renuka Vithal is Deputy Vice-Chancellor, Teaching and Learning, University of KwaZulu-Natal. She is a highly regarded academic with an outstanding record of research and publications. She is recognized for her dynamic academic leadership in the field of teaching and learning. She served as chairperson of the Southern African Association of Research in Mathematics, Science and Technology Education (SAARMSTE), and now serves on the Executive Committee of SAARMSTE. She is a member of the South African National Committee for the International Mathematical Union, and serves as Education Expert on the South African National Commission for UNESCO. Her interests include mathematics teacher education; social, cultural, political perspectives and practices in mathematics education; and issues of educational research methodologies.

Nilofar Vazir

Nilofar Vazir is an Associate Professor at the Aga Khan University Institute for Educational Development (AKU–IED) which she joined in 1994 as an Academic Consultant. She completed her PhD in Teacher Education from the Ontario Institute for Studies in Education, University of Toronto, in 2003. She has several years of experience teaching Early Childhood Education, both at the Montessori and primary levels. At AKU–IED, she has taught Certificate, Advanced Diploma, M.Ed., and PhD Courses. She continues to teach courses, conduct research, and supervise dissertations at Master's level. Her research interest is in issues related to teacher education and, within it particularly to early childhood education.

Dylan Wiliam

Dylan Wiliam is Emeritus Professor of Educational Assessment at the Institute of Education, University of London. His principal research focus is the professional development of teachers through a focus on the use of evidence about student learning to adapt teaching to better meet the students' needs. His current interests focus on how school-based teacher learning communities can be used to create effective systems of teacher professional development at scale. He has published over 300 articles, book chapters, and books in mathematics education, education law, and educational assessment.

Index